HISTORICAL MONUMENTS OF INDIA

HISTORICAL MONUMENTS OF INDIA

Editor-in-Chief

Swami Chidatman Jee Maharaj

ANMOL PUBLICATIONS PVT. LTD.
NEW DELHI - 110 002 (INDIA)

ANMOL PUBLICATIONS PVT. LTD.
H.O.: 4374/4B, Ansari Road, Daryaganj,
New Delhi-110 002 (India)
Ph.: 23278000, 23261597
B.O.: No. 1015, Ist Main Road, BSK IIIrd Stage
IIIrd Phase, IIIrd Block,
Bangalore - 560 085 (India)
Visit us at: www.anmolpublications.com

Historical Monuments of India

First Published, 2009
ISBN 978-81-261-3603-2

PRINTED IN INDIA

Printed at Mehra Offset Press, Delhi.

Contents

Preface

India colourful and vibrant, a land as diverse as its people. A mosaic of faiths, cultures, customs and languages that blend harmoniously to form a composite whole. One of the world's oldest living civilizations—which gave to the world—the concept of zero, the primordial sound Aum..., Yoga and Buddhism.

She is old. She is young. The two diametrically opposite, different yet unique and dynamic faces of India coexist even at this turn of the millennium. With a history of heritage, learning and civilisation dating back to almost 5000 years or perhaps even more, the modern India presents itself as an ideal country. From snow clad mountains to breezy sparkling blue sea side. From arid deserts with shifting sand dunes to lush green country sides. From ancient relics and architectural ruins dating back into antiquity to modern cities, India has it all.

To the north it is bordered by the world's highest mountain chain, where foothill valleys cover the northernmost of the country's maximum states. Further south, plateaus, tropical rain forests and sandy deserts are bordered by palm fringed beaches. Its southernmost tip is the meeting point of three Oceans.

India is a land of staggering contrast with a mingling of the tradition and modernity that is an unique experience to be in India. One will forever remember the stay in this wonderful Homeland-a land truly of mystery and enchantment. Only India can offer such an astonishing variety of contrasts.

She has given birth to numerous spiritual leaders and founders of some of the popular religions of the present day world. India probably has the most religious diversity in any country. It's the birthplace of Hinduism, Buddhism, Sikhism and Jainism and is among the few places to have a resident

Zoroastrian population. India with her veritable treasure trove of culture, mysticism, philosophy, art, music and architecture to name a few. Much of India's classical music is devotional and the North Indian Hindustani and South Indian Carnatic streams are distinct and both have a complex 'raga' framework. The legacy of dance in India is tremendous. The classical dances of India are numerous such as Kathakali of Kerala, Bharatnatyam of Tamil Nadu, Kuchipudi of Andhra Pradesh, Manipuri and Odissi from Orissa are the prominent dance forms in this country that sways to an altogether novel beat. The Yakshagana, nautanki and puppetry are ancient folk forms that live on till date. The earliest specimens of Indian painting are the ones on the walls of the Ajanta Caves dating back to 2nd century BC. The Mughals had a huge impact on Indian art. The influence of Persian art brought placid garden scenes, illustrations from myths, legends and history into Indian art. Word craft, handicrafts, architecture and sculpture all contribute to this rich and varied domain. Indian literature, both in English and in the vernacular, is ever more popular around the world.

The book aims at presenting perspectives of different aspects of Indian culture. It has topics on Indian classical music and dance, painting, ayurveda and yoga which are traditional and indigenous system of physical and mental wellbeing, language, philosophy and excellence achievements by Indian in the different branches of science and social sciences. It also includes our ancient religious and classic literature.

It is hoped that this book will be welcomed by the general readers as also scholars who are interested in the Indian heritage.

—Editors

1

Introduction

When we hear the name 'India', even though it is a distant land, there is a feeling of nostalgia in our hearts. This was the land that gave birth to one of the four major civilizations in the ancient world. It is the land where, along with China, an advanced civilization prospered. It is a great Asian nation that had an impact on all the countries surrounding it. India was also the leader of the Non-Aligned Nations which was formed after the Second World War. India is the land which introduced Buddhism. India became a colony of the British Empire, was exploited and reduced to poverty. For a nation that was once so rich in wealth and spirituality, the image of India is very confused. Moreover after the Meiji era, Japan turned its back on Asian countries including India to improve ties with Europe.

The west projects India as a mystical, magical country, but any civilization will look at people different from themselves as being mystical. Moreover European civilization and Christianity also has its own claims to mysticism as does India. We need to recognise the true image and true value of the third world starting with India, without the tinted glass of discrimination based on economy, especially now, when Japan is at last freeing itself from being a devotee of the West. And if the culture and art of India is closely observed, one will find that, as with its music and dancing, Indian architecture too has reached stupendous heights. This book intends to introduce this true image of Indian architecture, aided with a large number of photographs. Bhubaneshwar Any person who has visited India even once and seen some examples of Indian architecture has come away in awe. This is because the architecture as we know in the West differs greatly from the architecture of India.

The great temples brimming over with sculptures of gods, cave temples created by digging a rocky mountain and mosques that look like they have been built only on infinitely repeated geometrical shapes, may indeed make a person feel that Indian architecture is very mystical. However, unlike pictures or literature, a building cannot exist if it is not built rationally. Any architectural culture that knows this principle, can understand that Indian architecture too has been built along rational lines. Any original expression or original thought that has been added to this rationality is the artistic form of construction.

An inexhaustible supply of this architectural expression and work of art can be seen scattered all over the Indian subcontinent. Well, India is a vast country. It is a zone of civilization that is equal to the whole of Europe geographically and historically, in its vastness and depth of culture. Although it is a great nation with an unaccounted number of architectural inheritances, there is no colossal architectural plan of India. Enormous structures equivalent to the Great Wall of China, pyramidalis of Egypt, or the city planning of Rome, cannot be found here. Cambodia and Indonesia, which came under the influence of the Indian civilization, rather has enormous constructions in the form of and Borobudor. As in Japan and Europe, India liked rich and dense constructions of a moderate scale. Even the rich world that prefers the intimate scale, has an attraction for Indian architecture.

One might also be led to think that compared with European architecture, Indian architecture lacks consistency. One of the causes for this architectural diversity is the religious diversity of this vast land. Europe has believed in Christianity as a principle from medieval times and it continues to believe in it even in the present age. The difference between the Catholic and Protestant is not so glaring, and thus did not necessarily induce distinction of style in architecture.

The difference is similar in degree to the differences in the Shaivite and Vaishnavite groups of Hinduism or the Shia and Sunni groups of Islam. However, in India, apart from Hinduism, Buddhism was dominant in ancient age, and from the medieval age Islam has been. Added to this were Jainism, Sikhism and in recent centuries, Christianity. All these religions have greatly contributed to significant buildings in every urban landscape of the country.

Hence, adding an easy explanation of these religions here may be useful, to see its relation with architecture and may lead to a better understanding while reading through the following chapters of this book. Hinduism as everyone knows is the most prominent religion in India. However, this religion differs from the Western-concept of religions. There is no founder for this religion as there is in Christianity and Buddhism. As Jesus preached Christianity and Buddha preached Buddhism, Hinduism was not preached by any one individual.

It is supposed that the fundamentals were handed down from the heavens. Hinduism is a set of codes of conduct written in the "Vedas," in the epics "Ramayana" and "Mahabharata," and in the "Manu Smriti." If Hinduism has to be summarised in one sentence it can be called an aggregated Indian way of thinking and lifestyle. It is old styled Brahmanism when the system was not highly organised, and is a ceremonial religion in which only a person born in the Brahmin upper caste could interact between man and God. As in ancient Greece, during the 5th, 6th century BC, in Indian too many philosophers and free thinkers appeared against the religion hardened to a caste regime of birth and sacrifice.

The typical monks of that revolt were Buddha who founded Buddhism and Mahavira who founded Jainism. Mahabodhi Temple of Buddhism, Bodh Gaya Both Buddha and Mahavira were born in similar circumstances. Both were born in Bihar, in eastern India as Kshatriyas (warrior caste). After getting married and begetting children both the princes renounced their family and wealth and became shramanas or monks and after a long period of penance and meditation attained nirvana.

There is no established date of the birth and death of both these persons. There are various views, but Mahavira is considered to be senior. While Buddha took the middle path of pain and pleasure, Mahavira took the hard path of the asceticism whose fundamental doctrine was Ahimsa or nonviolence. Jainas did not create a centralised church system, and since it was not keen on propagation, Jainism did not collect a large following. On the other hand, Buddhism spread on account of its moderate nature and was well received by the governing classes, and thus it was able to overshadow Brahmanism and turn into a dominant religion in India.

Above all, the person who propagated Buddhism was Emperor Ashoka of the Maurya Empire who conquered a great portion of India during the 3rd century. As an ancient architectural inheritance, Buddhism has left many ruins all over the country; the relics of Jainism are scarce. What is more amazing is that there is not a single relic left of Brahmanism. Hence stating that, the ancient architecture of India is Buddhist architecture is not a fallacy. However, Brahmanism gained over Buddhism gradually in the 5-6th century in developing highly its religious theory. This mature phase of revived Brahmanism is called Hinduism. Originally Hindu meant people living on the banks of Sindhu river (Indus river) as viewed from the west. Their religion is called Hinduism and their language is called Hindi. Tikse Gompa (monastery) of Tibetan Buddhism, Ladakh While it had achieved an advanced stage of philosophical development, Hinduism also assimilated the native faith, gods and traditions and mores of various parts of India, captured people's hearts and became a huge system consisting of myths and codes that cannot be contained in one book of scriptures.

Buddhism that enjoyed the support of the ruling classes gradually lost its foothold after entering the age of Tantric Buddhism, heavily influenced by Hinduism and disappeared from India completely by the 13th century. Instead, it spread far and wide in the Asian countries and became a world religion and as such it is still being practised in the northern most part of India in Ladakh and Sikhism. They follow Tibet Buddhism, which is also called Lamaism. Many of the Buddhist temples and monasteries in the Indian mainland were destroyed as there was nobody to maintain them. Most of them are ruins or excavated sites now. On the other hand, early Hindu architecture followed the lines of Buddhist architecture, or converted Buddhist temples to Hindu temples. In the 7th century two unique temple styles developed for the two major gods Shiva and Vishnu, that played a major role in the stone architecture that developed 1000 years later.

Mahavira Temple of Jainism, Kumbharia Jainism did not spread much outside India. Instead it continued to thrive in west India and has left a large amount of architectural heritage. As it was a small minority group it followed Buddhism and Hinduism in its architectural style, but in the 11-15th century it developed remarkably in west India. As Jainism was a religion opposing Brahmanism, it was originally atheistic religion. It is not Gods but 24 Saviours called Tirthankaras that are worshipped in the temples. It is said that the 24th and the last Tirthankara was Mahavira. Islam that came from outside India originated in Arabia in the 7th century. Prophet Muhammad brought the words of God to the people and this was written down as the sacred book Koran.

One of its most important teachings is that there is only one God and all men are equal in front of Him. With this equality concept Islam spread quickly from Spain in the west to central Asia in the east. They build Mosques as the places of worship and other buildings in every place they conquered. As there was a preceding civilization in each area; the Islamic principles were mixed with the native architecture and thus a unique Islamic architecture for each area originated. Tomb of Salim Chishti, Islam, Fatehpur Sikri. The Islamic invasion upon India started in the 11th century, and the Islamic architecture of Persia from the west was brought in. Indo-Islamic architecture reached its pinnacle during the rule of the Mughal dynasty since the 16th century, which fused the Islamic and native architecture.

In the process however, the monotheism of Islam and polytheism of Hinduism collided with each other. According to Islamic faith, God (Allah) is the Absolute and his existence cannot be seen with the eyes, and so expressing or representing him with an image is absolutely forbidden. Not only that, it was prohibited to make the image form of man or animal, not to mention Prophet Muhammad. Hence not a single idol carving or mural painting can be found in the mosques. Thus the Hindu temple filled to the brim with images was blasphemy for a believer of Islam (Muslim).

It would be rash to think that it is because of this belief that Muslims completely destroyed the buildings and culture of infidels. Islam was rather tolerant to the pagans. Islam became the religion of the rulers in India. But the public was still free to believe in Hinduism if they paid excess tax. Even Rajput states in west India served as vassals in the Mughal Empire and maintained half-independent Hindu kingdoms.

For this reason Hinduism and Jainism was also able to survive up to the present age and many structures of great temple architecture have remained intact. Christian Memorial Church of St. John, Mumbai Christianity was introduce to India very early. Tradition says that the apostle Thomas came here for the mission work, but this has not been ascertained. The Roman Catholic Church was brought to India by the Portuguese in the 16th century and many churches and monasteries of the times still stand in Goa and Cochin.

When Britain started governing India, the Church of England was introduced, and cathedrals and parish churches were built in various places including the four big cities. Christianity as a foreign culture, as compared with Islam, strictly adhered to the European style in colonial buildings as its architectural style and fusion with native architecture was not considered. Perhaps this might show that Christianity is more the religion of non-tolerance rather than Islam.

According to the national census taken in 2001, the rate of religious population in present day India is as follows. Hindu 82.6 per cent, Muslim 11.4 per cent, Christian 2.4 per cent, Sikh 2.0 per cent, Buddhist 0.7 per cent, Jain 0.5 per cent, Others (Parsi, Jew, etc.) 0.4 per cent. In present day architecture, religion does not play a main role in its development. When a new temple is built, it would be in old style on the whole.

Probably the impact of religion in changing India's architecture has replaced by European and American culture and the development of science and technology. This personification of modern architecture can be seen clashing with traditional architecture. It is slowly but steadily changing the townscape of India and this is a common enough sight in any third world country.

Be it India or be it Europe, there are various methods in introducing the architectural culture. Probably, since there are various religions in India, introducing architecture according to religion can also be a method. However, all buildings are not necessarily religion based. James Ferguson who had discussed the Indian architecture based on religion was strongly accused for this by E.B. Havell. According to Havell all buildings are a continuation of Indian architecture and classification according to religion is but marginal. His opinion is that if Buddhism had survived much longer it would have built temples in almost same style as that of Hindu temples, and that Islamic architecture in India was none other than the Indian architecture, is correct to a certain extent. A more commonly used method is that of taking up style and technology of architecture historically.

There is also another method of looking at the buildings of every place in geographical order. Geographically India has a great disparity in climate with the cold Himalayas in the north, desert area in the west, and tropical rain forest in the south and accordingly the disparity in the architectural designs are also many. In the case of European architecture there is the tendency of limiting our image to Britain, Germany, France, and Italy. In Northern Europe, there is the wooden culture and those churches have a considerably pagan appearance. In Southern Spain, Islamic architecture can be seen in the Alhambra palace and so on. Take the ancient Celtic forms, the Byzantine East European church and the synagogue of the Jews; they will all show a wide variety of architectural forms. And since they are in the European continent they have to be classified as "European architecture." High Court in Chandigarh by Le Corbusier was also to show the total image of Indian architecture by evenly picking up architecture forms from the Tibetian Buddhism in Ladakh in the extreme north to the wooden architecture in Kerala in the extreme south, and by not limiting to the typical style of Indian architecture in the narrow range.

Apart from the classical architecture, I have also introduced colonial architecture designed by the British architects during the British rule, and the modern architecture designed after India got its independence from the British. This was because; it is thought that the colonial architecture that was built with Indian involvement is Indian architecture, as is the fact that Muslim architecture introduced to India and built in India is Indian architecture. The totality of all the buildings that were built for the various dynasties, religions, races, etc., with the Indian subcontinent as the stage, through the ages till today has to be called the "Indian Architecture."

Considering the large amount of architectural inheritance that is scattered in the subcontinent, buildings from only 160 places may seem too inadequate. But I feel that I have clearly shown in great detail the typical style or characteristics of the buildings of various different ages and areas. Hence going through this whole book will be like looking with fresh wonder at the diversity of Indian architecture. The existence of wooden structures might be most unexpected. There must not be many who have travelled to Himachal Pradesh or Kerala and seen the wooden buildings thoroughly. The villages in the Himalayas surrounded by the deodar forest are a nostalgic sight, but the wooden temple there is richly different sight.

There might have been other classification of characteristics of Indian architecture. Hopefully I want to make this book a stepping stone and want more young people to come up with fresh Indian architectural theory. Capital carving of Mallikarjuna Temple, Kuruvatti Up till now, we know the characteristic of each keyword and its various aspects in this trip of 26 Chapters. What is the biggest characteristic of Indian architecture with all of them put together? Two things can be said about this. The first one is that since the people of India liked sculpture most among figurative arts, they wanted to make their construction also look like a sculpture. When you visit an temple you will be amazed at the carvings decorating the structure from end to end regardless of whether they arc freestanding temples, cave temples, stone constructions or wooden. You begin to wonder whether the building was constructed just so that one could sculpt on them. Compared with this, mural paintings are few and they have not played as important a role as sculpture.

The Indians not only decorated the inside and outside of a building with sculpture, but considered that the whole building to be a huge sculpture. It is contrary to the thought that architecture is an art and technology to enclose 'the space' inside. Admiring the wonders of sculptural expression, often there is disappointment about the poor quality of interior space of the temple. The inside is dark, small and 'cave like,' so the whole structure is exterior oriented architecture. As time passed, the sculpture decorating the walls got more and more complicated.

If it had gone on this line only, the Indian architecture must have got biased toward an architectural deviation. Upper part of Gopura at Nageshwara Temple, Kumbakonam The advent of Islamic architecture reversed this trend. In Islam idol worship is completely banned. Islam forbids image-expression of sculpture, pictures, etc. and has developed the architecture of just a plain wall enclosing space. On the other hand, compared with the architecture in other Islamic areas, the Islamic architecture of India took to the outward expression of sculpting in response to the influence of native architecture. Even Taj Mahal, a mausoleum of Persian style has as brilliant sculpture-expression that was obtained owing to the construction by Indians.

The second characteristic is that although main Indian monuments were constructed of stone, they had held principles of wooden architecture. In ancient India, since wood was more abundant than is available now, Indian architecture started with wooden origins, and even though stone construction became more popular during medieval period, it still stuck to the principles of wooden construction in its frame and expression.

Even after Islamic architecture brought with it the arch and dome, the frame work construction with posts and beams were still adhered to and stone continued to be used like wood. Mausoleum of Akbar, Sikandra near Agra Probably, an ingrained feeling of beauty was more important than structural superiority or inferiority. The Islamic architecture transplanted to India was also influenced by this concept and the frame work-based Islamic construction that cannot be seen in any other Islamic area, was developed. "Chattri," a heavy domed roof supported only with thin posts and beams, without using an arch is one such type.

It was clear that, unlike wood, the frame work construction method where stone weak in tension is used for beam or lintel is theoretically inferior compared with the arch and dome structure where stone and brick is stacked in a radial pattern and built over a big span. Nevertheless, people from India persisted in it and completed magnificent buildings. It resembles monophonic Indian music. Compared with Occidental polyphony (many voices) monophony is theoretically inferior.

However, achievement of art cannot be compared as superior or inferior based only on principle. Even if the music of India is monophonic, with exhaustive research it has acquired an extremely advanced theory and musical expression. So also, the stone architecture of India has given rise to an extremely advanced architecture rival to Islamic or European architecture, by experiments with wooden-like post-and-beam and corbelled dome structures.

Vastu Shastra: Adherence to *Vastu Shastra*, the ancient and medieval canons on city planning and architecture, has suddenly assumed tremendous significance, particularly among the well-educated and affluent in urban India. It may be difficult to predict if this is just a fad or if it will be a way of building dwellings, offices, and factories, etc. for many years to come.

Interestingly, practically none of the practitioners of *Vastu Shastra* has an academic background. So there is a lot of genuine practice as well as hearsay going around. In this brief introduction, the intention is to give a broad overall picture of the *Vastu Shastra* with some examples.

Vastu Shastras are canons dealing with the subject of *Vastu* which means the environment. Put differently, one may regard them as codification of good practices of design of buildings and cities, which will provide settings for the conduct of human life in harmony with physical as well as metaphysical forces. These canons provide guidelines for design of buildings and planning of cities such that they will bring health, wealth and peace to the inhabitants. Mythological beliefs are certainty at the root of the origins of these canonical texts and their discourse. The first of these relates to *Vastupurusha*, which appears to be the first step in ordering a part of the vast cosmic space, the *brahmand*, for human habitation. According to myth, long ago there existed an unnamed, unknown and formless being which blocked the sky and the earth. The Gods forced it down on earth and pressed it face down. To ensure that it did riot escape again, Lord Brahma, the supreme creator, along with other gods weighted it down and called it *Vastupurusha*.

Lord Brahma, of course, occupied the central portion and in a hierarchic distribution along concentric rings assigned different quarters to different major and minor gods. Thus emerged a geometric configuration, which is called *mandala*. From one basic square, the canons have listed up to 1024 divisions of a square and given each one a name. The most popular among those have 64 and 81 divisions known as *Manduka Mandala* and *Parama Sayika Mandala*, respectively, which are widely used for temple and dwelling plans.

The *mandala* is also given an orientation with *Surya*, the sun-god, occupying the central point of periphery to east; *Varuna*, the Lord of winds, to the west; *Kubera*, the Lord of Wealth, to the north; and Yam, the Lord of Death, to the south. The rest of the squares are occupied by the other minor gods. With the positions thus assigned and the beneficial or otherwise attributes of gods established through other myths, it is possible to assign the activities of living, working and support facilities over the *mandala* and therefore the layout of a city or a building.

The *mandala* is, of course, the most popular aspect of the *Vastu Shastras* as it is constantly referred to for the location of the various activities in a building. The proper texts themselves, however, deal with a wide range of topics relating to built-environment. These include site selection, soil testing, building materials and techniques, design of temples separately by number of floors, palaces, dwellings, gates, image of the deity, their vehicles and seats even including the making of image of a *linga* for Shiva temples. All these are treated in different chapters of the canonical texts. As an example, one may mention the matter of site selection, which is dealt with in both scientific and religious terms. The method of digging a pit and refilling it with excavated earth is given scientific treatment. If a lot of earth is left out, then the soil is compact with good load-bearing capacity.

A similar test checks the seepage of water in the soil. It if is quick, the soil is obviously not good. The religious prescription suggest that if the soil is white with ghee-like smell, it is good for Brahmins, if red with blood-like smell it is good for *Kshatriyas*, yellow with smell like sesamum oil, it is good for *Vaishyas* and black with the smell of rotten fish, it is good for *Shudras*. While the first two suggestions would still find the approval of a modern engineer, the third more likely betrays the caste-ridden nature of some of the *Shastra's* recommendations.

The *Shastras* also deal at length with town planning and form of towns suitable for different purposes such as administrative towns, hill towns, coastal towns or religious towns built at a sacred place. Among the most famous examples of a town planned according to *Shastra* is the example of old Jaipur which is based on a *Prastar* type town described in several texts. Built in 1727 AD, the final form and structure of the town shows a skilful manipulation, according to the *Shastra's* prescriptions, of the square *mandala* right from the whole to the smallest of the plots, the location of activities, and distribution of the caste groups. Based on the studies carried out by scholars it is suggested that these texts were written down largely between the 7th century AD to 13th century AD, following the Gupta period. They are found in all the major languages of medieval India. Of course, the earliest references are also found in the Vedas, which deal with carpentry among other subjects.

Vastu Shastras can be said to be companion texts to *Shilpashastras* and *Chitrashastras* dealing with sculpture, icons and painting respectively. Strangely, among all these texts, those devoted exclusively to one of the areas., *i.e. vastu*, *chitra* or *shilpa* are rare. This is because in the Indian artistic traditions, each was an important and integral part of the creative endeavour largely because all of these, including performing arts such as the dance and music, were based at the temple.

Among the *Vastu Shastra* texts are *Mansar*, *Maymata, Vishwakarma Vastu Shastra* and *Samrangana Sutradhara* which is credited to Raja Bhoja. The others are believed to have been authored by ancient saints and sages. These include Lord Vishwakarma who is architect to the gods in the Nagara or northern traditions, and Maya who is architect to the gods in the *Dravida* or Southern tradition. In the northern tradition Maya is regarded as architect to the *danavas* or demons. To give some idea about the size of the text, *Masar* comprises 5400 verses organised in a total of 70 chapters.

However, the nature, content and format of the texts have recently been published and gone through, in some cases, half a dozen reprints in a span of one year. They share very little in common. As to what are the origins of the practitioners' texts recently published, I can only suggest that these would he more ritualistic practices broadly interpreted by the various *puranic* texts such as *Agni Purana, Matsya Purana* and their *Agmic* versions in the Dravidian traditions. The parallel I can draw upon is of *Brigusamhita* used by the palmists, which by itself has no serious pretensions to astronomy. The practitioners themselves are silent and unresponsive when questioned about these aspects.

One of the more recent texts goes so far as to suggest the location of two weighing scales in different parts of the plot in a factory. One was for weighing raw materials which would in that location weigh less than actual, and the other one of weighing finished goods which would register more weight than actual. Very neat, one may say, and very tempting for the factory owner.

As to the beneficial aspects of following the *Vastu Shastri's* suggestions, the available experience is equally divided. There seems to be an equal number of success stories as well as failures. Here, I believe, the analogy of the typical palmist is best. Perhaps there are genuine *Jyotish Shastris* as well as frauds. Is it that human beings want to be able to put blame on some unknown forces for failures? Or that they would want to appease the unknown to ensure a success? These are more a matter of faith rather than belief.

Fortunately, Indians are not alone in this in recent times. Across Asia there is a resurgence of these beliefs and practices. *Feng-shui*, the Chinese version of *Vastu Shastras*, is practised all over the Far East and South-east Asia. There, too, the situation is one of either you believe and practice or you don't believe and don't practice. Does this mean that one cannot explain *Vastu Shastras* on a rational basis?

These texts (*i.e.* the genuine ancient and medieval canons) dealt with the classical manner of arts and architecture. This meant that irrespective of who was doing what and where, a certain quality, content and perfection would always be achieved just by following the texts. To paraphrase Einstein's observation for a similar work, "it makes good easy and bad difficult". This means that a temple made on the banks of *Ganga* would be as perfect as one made on *Shipra* though patronised and designed by different persons.

Even those uninitiated could learn and practice the entire range of activities connected with vastu right from the selection of a site to the execution of all the elemental details. Then there is some reason to believe that some of the suggestions may indeed reflect more real concerns such as climatic suitability of locating the human activities in a building. An entrance front north ensures that it will always be in cool shade in India, besides allowing the wealth to flow in as it is the direction of Lord *Kubera*. The next alternative of entrance from east certainly brightens up the morning environment with the first rays of sun to start a great new day on a cheerful note.

Then there is a metaphysical aspect to it all. This one concerns the fears of the unknown on one hand, and attempts to intellectually grasp the nature of the world on the other hand. And between these two is the human desire to do things right, in conformity and in harmony with the unknown world and its forces. This is where particularly the *mandala* diagrams become very useful. These, in abstract terms, manifest or represent the cosmological conception of the world, albeit the world as conceived or interpreted by the ancient and the medieval scholars.

It is therefore natural that buildings and cities which represent a significant alteration of the terrestrial world be based on the *mandala* to make them harmonies with the unknown world. In other words, it, is undertaking a human act in tune with the nature as well as the unknown in the belief that these will not clash but work harmoniously to bring peace and prosperity to the builder and the inhabitants.

Architecture is a human act. It requires carving out a segment of that omnipotent, universal space of the *brahmand*, the cosmic space, for the use of the human beings. It is not often that architecture truly rises to the challenges of capturing the divine character of the *brahmand* in its folds. When it does happen the architectural experience exalts generations of people to come. Is this not true of *Mahabalipuram*, *Khajuraho*, *Kailashnath*? Or the city of Jaipur, its *havelis* as well those of *Samod* and *Shekhavati* region? Let us remember that these are all based on the *Vastu Shastras*.

2

The Architectures of Ancient India

The Indus Valley Civilization

In the field of traditional knowledge systems, the Harappan civilization which flourished during the 3rd-2nd millennia BC ranks amongst the four widely known civilizations of the Old World and covers appreciably larger area than in the early Dynastic Egypt-or Sumer. Like the other Old World Civilizations, the Harappan civilization seems to have grown from the skilful utilisation of the fertile river systems and their valleys in the north-western region of Indo-Pakistan subcontinent.

The Harappans have given systematic town planning, fortification of citadel, elaborate drainage system the idea of establishing of granaries and surplus economy, standardization of brick sizes, weights and measures, geometric instruments *e.g.* right angles, linear scale and plumb bob are the principal gifts of the Harappans to the succeeding cultures through the ages. It was the Harappans who gave the idea of welfare of the workers for the first time by establishing workmen's quarters and now it has become a necessity. Different types of hydraulic architecture is another legacy of the Harappans besides many other in social, economic and religious fields.

Kunal, Dholavira (Kotda), Banawali, Kalibangan, Surkotada, and Lothal are settlements unearthed between 1900 and 1500 BC. These sites provide the links between the Early Harappan and Mature Harappan phases of the civilization. Mature Harappan phase is closely associated with the use of weights and measures, seals and sealings and a system of writing, all facets associated with trade and commerce. Sealings were used to seal traded packages. ca. 2600 BC when the Mature Harappan phase blossomed there was evidence of trade with several sites in Western Asia (Tell Asmar, Tell Agrab, Kish, Nippur, Ur, Susa, Failaka, Tell Abraq, Umm An-Nar, Hili, Ras Al-Junayz, Tepe Yahya, Shahdad, Sutkagen Dor) and some sites in Central Asia (Shortughai, Namazga-depe, Altyn-depe, Tepe Hissar).

All these six settlements are on the banks of rivers/tributaries along the course of the Saraswati river. In these Early Harappan sites, there is evidence of town-planning (*i.e.* laying-out of streets and houses along cardinal directions), fortification of settlements and the concept of dividing the settlement into two parts: the citadel and the Lower Town. These characteristics anticipate the Mature Harappan characteristics. In Banawali, there is evidence of the use of fired-bricks even during the Early Harappan phase. It should, however, be noted that many houses at Banawali, Kalibangan and Lothal were made of sun-dried bricks.

Kunal: A small area of 1.2 hectares with a vertical deposit of over 3 m. The radiocarbon dates place the site between ca. 3016 and 2577 BC. Copper arrowheads and fish-hooks; micro-beads of chalcedony, Red ware bearing painted designs in two colours (black outline filled in with white) are characteristic of a number of sites along the Saraswati valley. Potsherds of Hakra ware (Cholistan) were also found at the site.

In the next period, painted motifs on pottery included peacock and pipal leaf, typical of the designs of the Mature Harappans. A globular jar of red ware yielded silver ornaments wrapped in a silver sheet: two tiaras (small and large), each with a large fully-opened flower having petals topped with a decoration like the Greek letter 'alpha'. Along with these tiaras was a multi-spiralled armlet which is similar to the armlet worn by the bronze statue of the 'dancing girl' from Mohenjodaro. In another house were found a large number of gold/silver-beads: cup-shaped, barrel-shaped, discular; shapes which are characteristic of the Mature Harappans. Discular beads of silver with perforation along the diameter found in Kunal (Hissar, Haryana) have occurred at Mature levels at Lothal, in gold. Other parts of the site yielded beads of lapis lazuli, carnelian, fiance. Copper objects were produced at the site as evidenced by the discovery of a Terracota crucible with molten metal still sticking to it.

The objects included: axes, fish-hooks, spearheads, iverted 'V-shaped' arrowheads, coiled cones and coiled finger-rings which are characteristic of Mature Harappans. Seven seals (six of steatite and one of shell) were found. They are square-shaped with a perforated knob at the back, again anticipating the Mature Harappans. The seals bear only geometric motifs and without any inscriptions.

Dholavira (Kotda): On one of the islands of the Rann of Kacch. Fortified settlement, with fortifications separately for the Middle Town and the citadel. The citadel commanded the entire scenario with a height of 15 to 18 m, above the surrounding ground level. Seasonal nullahs (Mansar and Manhar) flow past the northern and southern sides of the fortified area. The nullahs were bunded to supply water to the tanks and wells.

A well has been discovered south of the 13 m. wide street in the citadel. A horizontal slab of the trough had markings showing the passage of the rope used to draw water from the wall. Water drawn from the well was conducted through a covered channel to feed a nearby tank (4.35 m × 2.95 m.) with a depth of 3.58 m. Side walls of the tank were formed by vertically placed stone slabs; the upper part had stone-rubble masonry. The floor was paved with stone slabs. Sketch 1 illustrates the damming of the Manhar nullah to divert the water to the reservoir. Sketch 2 illustrates a pair of bullocks drawing water from the well.

The Citadel had Two Gateways: one on the northern and the other on the eastern side. Each gateway had an elaborate staircase. The landing of the staircase was at a depth of 2.3 m. After ten steps and a further descent of 2 m., the staircase led to a passage way which was 7 m. long on either side of the passage, there was a chamber which had a roof resting on stone pillars. In one of the chambers, a unique inscription was discovered. The ten letters of the inscription had a height of about 35 to 37 cm. and a width of 25 to 27 cm. The letters wee made of sliced pieces of some 'crystalline material, maybe rock, mineral or paste'. Perhaps mounted on a wooden board, the inscription might have constituted a signboard. Ring-stones were used to support the pillars.

The eastern gateway also had a staircase and passage way with a chamber on either side. Many well-polished stone pillars were found in site. Similar polished pillars were later found as belonging to the Ashokan times, the third century BC.

Banawali: Left bank of the Saraswati river. 20 km. from Kunal. Fired bricks had been used even by the Early Harappans as evidenced at this site. Settlement within a single fortified area. Within this area, the citadel had its own fortification, in a semi-ellipse, with wall-thickness varying from 5.4 to 7 m.

Kalibangan: Left bank of the Saraswati river. Citadel on the west; fortified Lower Town in the centre; ritualistic structures on the east. Fortification walls were made mostly of mud bricks, but at a few places kiln-fired bricks were also used. Early brick sizes were 40 × 20 × 10 cm. and later ones were 30 × 15 × 7.5 cm. Street-widths were: 1.8 m., 3.6 m, 5.4 m and 7.2 m. On the floors, soiling of terracota nodules intermixed with pieces of charcoal was overlaid with the clay floor. (The practice is followed even today in many villages.) Between 2600 and 1900 BC, Kalibangan witnessed about nine reconstructions, but not a single structure intruded on the street.

A Sealing of Clay: The bottom row shows the impressions of reeds and the knotted thread which were used to tie the package. A lump of clay had been placed over the knot and the clay was stamped with a seal. A black layer had been ruptured at three places. In between the ruptured parts of the layer are seen near-vertical cleavage lines. These are an indication of some tectonic disturbance. After this shake-up, there was no further occupation at the site and the site was abandoned. This evidence is substantiated in another part of the site showing faulted mud-brick walls. Two successive mud-brick walls are shown sunken and cleft, with a pronounced cleavage in the lower wall. "The most plausible explanation seems to be the occurrence of an earthquake which not only destroyed the houses but also forced the inhabitants to leave the site. This event may have taken place around 2700 BC, since, after a break, the recuperation of the site by the Mature Harappans is ascribable, on the basis of radiocarbon dates, to ca. 26th century BC."

The site yielded a large number of tools and other objects in copper and bronze: axes, bangles, besides a parasu, a tool used even today in Rajasthan to cut the shrubs. A row of seven 'fire-altars' were found in the citadel of Kalibangan. The altars were sunk into the ground, to a depth of about 25 cm. The sides were plastered with mud. A central cylindrical (sometimes faceted) stele of clay (sometimes fired) about 30 to 40 cm. high and 10 to 15 cm. dia. in the altar is a characteristic find in many sites. Around the stele lay circular-biconvex 'cakes' of clay; ash and charcoal were also attested. (Mughal had demonstrated that in Cholistan sites, the 'cakes' were used to support the pottery being burnt.)

The altars were so located that the offerer had to sit facing the east. Embedded into the ground next to the seven altars was a pot which contained ash and charcoal. A well, bathing pavement and a drain were close by, indicating the use of water to put out the burning embers after the metallurgical processes were completed. Another platform in the southern part of the citadel yielded a pit, measuring 1.5 m × 1 m and lined with kiln-fired bricks. In this pit, bovine bones and bones of antlers were found. It has been recorded that bones are used to in the process of oxidising and removing lead from galena to yield silver. To the east of the Lower Town on a small mound, only the remains of fire-altars were found.

Surkotada: 160 km. northeast of Bhuj in Rann of Kacch. A common 7 m. thick wall with an opening, separated the citadel and the Lower Town. The citadel was built over a platform. The entrance to the citadel was provided with a Rama, barbican, steps and guard rooms. "...was there any special reason for this small yet fortified establishment? Had we enough evidence about the war-equipment of the Harappans, we would have taken Surkotada as a garrison town." Four graves were excavated in Surkotada. None of them was the extended burial type evidenced in Lothal. In one grave, 'the pit yielded a red ware shed of an urn and very small charred human bone splinters or remains... The post-cremation human remains found in a burial bear a great significance. The relatives of the dead in all probability out of regard for the deceased used to take care of the burnt or charred bones after submission of the corpse to fire'.

Lothal: On the banks of a tributary of the river Bhogavo which joined Sabarmati which fell into the Gulf of Khambat (an inlet of the Arabian sea). Fortified settlement. Mud-wall of an average thickness of 12-13 m. On the eastern side, against which the dockyard was located, the wall measured 20-21 m. in width. Part of the wall had served as a wharf. Estuarine shells were found in the complex substantiating the structure as a dockyard. To the west of the wharf was a mud-brick platform 5.4 m × 40 m) called a 'warehouse'. A series of square mud-brick blocks were found on the platform with an intermediary passage of 1.2 m. width. In the passage were found: charred log, plenty of ash and charcoal and 65 burnt sealings of clay, with impressions of the wrapping fibre and knotted thread on one side and of seals on the other. This is evidence that the platforms had held stamped packages.

The citadel or acropolis was built on a raised platform, 5.4 m. high. Twelve bath-pavements with accompanying drains. To the south of these structures was a 'warehouse'. Apart from a house which yielded copper ingots, crucibles, etc., a bead-making kiln was identified.

Architecture and Town Planning: If by 'urban' we mean the tendency to form society, founding cities with all their attendant rules, then the Harappan people succeeded admirably. Excavations show a degree of urban planning which the Romans achieved only later, after a gap of 2500 years.

The twin cities of Mohenjodaro and Harappa formed the hub of the civilization. They are representative in the sense that planning principles employed here are followed practically without change at all other sites. Both cities were a mile square, with defensive outer walls. An orthogonal street layout was oriented toward the cardinal directions. The street layout shows an understanding of the basic principles of traffic, with rounded corners to allow the turning of carts easily. These streets divided the city into 12 blocks. Except for the west-central blocks, the basic unit of city planning was the individual house.

The Harappan house is an amazing example of a native people, without the benefit of technology, adapting to local conditions and intuitively producing an architecture eminently suited to the climate. The house was planned as a series of rooms opening on to a central courtyard. This courtyard served the multiple functions of lighting the rooms, acting as a heat absorber in summer and radiator in winter, as well as providing an open space inside for community activities. There were no openings toward the main street, thus ensuring privacy for the residents. In fact, the only openings in the houses are rather small-this prevented the hot summer sun heating the insides of the houses.

An advanced drainage system is also in evidence. Drains started from the bathrooms of the houses and joined the main sewer in the street, which was covered by brick slabs or corbelled brick arches, depending on its width.

Great Bath: In most of the sites, the central-western blocks were reserved for public architecture. Perhaps the most famous examples are the Great Bath and Granary at Mohenjodaro. The Great Bath has been the subject of much debate over its exact function. The prevalent view seems to be that it was used for ritualistic bathing-much as continues in the Hindu tradition even today. It is unfortunate that none of the structures of the Indus Valley civilization survive intact today. Unlike Egypt and Mesopotamia, the Harappan people left nothing monumental, like the Ramaaids or ziggurats, for posterity to marvel at. This may be the reason that among the majority of books on architecture, the Harappan Culture hardly merits a note. However, the planning principles and response of the architecture to climate are a lesson to us all.

Perhaps no branch of human culture reflects with greater exactitude the progress or decadence of man than architecture. In the progress of architecture from the most primitive types of human habitation of magnificent temples and palaces, we can discover the ceaseless effort of man to express his social and religious environment and his attitude towards life. In the development of architecture, we can also detect the aesthetic taste which actuated man to combine beauty with utility. The progress of Indian architecture from the primitive to the sophisticated was no exception to this historical process.

The earliest phase of Indian architecture may be seen from the remains of the ancient cities of the Indus Valley culture datable to c. 3000 B.C. From the excavated remains at Mohenjodaro in Sindh and Harappa in Punjab, it is evident that the Indian cities at that early period were scientifically laid out. There were broad roads and smaller lanes with shops and booths. The houses were probably of the story or more. The roofs were of stamped clay. Practically every house had a bathroom which was always placed on the street side of the building for the convenient disposal of water. There was adequate arrangement for drainage. A brick-lined channel flowed down every street and into this main drain ran smaller tributary drains from the houses on either side. An important feather of the drainage system was the provision of large brick culverts with corbelled roofs built on the outskirts of the city to carry away storm water. The houses were also provided with brick-lined wells.

Drainage System at Mohenjodaro: At Harappa, the remains of one of the structures has twelve parallel walls. We are unable to determine the exact significance of this structure but it might have been a gigantic storehouse. At Mohenjodaro, some buildings have cup-like depressions at street corners. These depressions probably served as receptacles for large jars.

One of the most important constructions at Mohenjodaro is the large bath built entirely of burnt bricks which could be entered at either end by means of a staircase. The broad walk at the top of the bath rested on cells filled with clay. There were walls with openings which provided access to a cloistered walk running round the bath. The eight bathrooms, to the north of the bath were provided with stairways probably leading to an upper story. The exact significance of this great bath and smaller baths has not yet been discovered, but it probable that bathing was a ritual with the people of Mohenjodaro.

The history of Indian architecture between the Indus Valley period, which came to an end some time in the 2nd millennium B. C., and the 4th century B.C. is very meager. We have to depend entirely on literature to fill this gap. From Vedic evidence, it seems possible that the idea of the fortified town was adopted by the Vedic Aryans from their Dasa enemies, though so far it has not been possible to connect these Dasas with the Indus Valley people.

The Vedic house was not a very elaborate affair and the people lived mostly in thatches houses with several rooms. The house was often provided with a central hall and several other rooms which were used for storing and living purposes.

In the epics and Buddhist literature, references are made to will-built cities and sumptuous palaces. These cities and palaces seem to have followed the same plan as that of the city of Pataliputra which, according to Megasthenes (4th century B.C.), occupied a narrow parallelog Rama and was provided with stupendous palisades with loopholes for archers. There was a deep moat around it. The Rampart had as many as sixty-four gates. The royal palace was a spacious building, the main part of which consisted of a series of hypostyle halls.

The Vedic Age

The End of Harappa : The nomads that streamed in from the Northwest towards the middle of the second millennium B.C. overwhelmed the indigenous people of the subcontinent with their superior military technology. The Indus Valley Civilization, weakened from generations of fighting the river floods, constantly rebuilding their cities, lacked the moral will to put up much resistance. In short order the magnificent cities were emptied of all population, and the *Dasyus*, as the Aryan invaders contemptuously called them, either were co-opted into the lowest rung of the new society, or migrated further south into peninsular India. Curiously, the Aryans did not settle into the well-planned cities of the Harappan culture, and instead preferred to clear forests around the riverbanks of the Gangetic plain and settle in small villages. This could be due to the inherent dislike of a pastoral people to settle in one place for very long, and thus their innate suspicion of any hint of permanence.

Or of course, it could be the sheer alien value of the architecture that they found, and they preferred to stick with the tried and tested. Curiously, the Aryans did not settle into the well-planned cities of the Harappan culture, and instead preferred to clear forests around the riverbanks of the Gangetic plain and settle in small villages. This could be due to the inherent dislike of a pastoral people to settle in one place for very long, and thus their innate suspicion of any hint of permanence. Or of course, it could be the sheer alien value of the architecture that they found, and they preferred to stick with the tried and tested. No architectural examples of this period are surviving.

The Aryans built no colossal monuments. So what is the importance of this period? It was early Aryan architectural forms that were translated into the architecture of India for thousands of years. The caves of Ajanta and Ellora, much of Buddhist architecture, were directly influenced by the simple village structures of the Aryan villages. But if there are no remaining specimens, what are the sources through which we glean knowledge about the architecture? Considerable information is given in the Vedas. These ancient texts were composed by the Aryan seers and handed down through generations orally. The great epics, the Mahabharata and the Ramayana, vividly picture village and town life during Aryavrata, or the Aryan age. In addition, carvings on the Stupas at Barhut and Sanchi, which depict Aryan village life vividly.

In India, the settlers gave up their totally nomadic existence and became part-agriculturalists. This provided the impetus to build villages, the basic unit of which was the hut. For building material, the abundant forest provided ample raw stock. The Aryan hut, in its most basic shape, was circular in plan, with a thatched roof over a bamboo network of ribs. This was later elongated to become rectangular in plan, with roofing of bamboo as well, only this time curved in the shape of a barrel. Clusters of these huts formed a courtyard, much like huts in Indian villages even today. The better-off citizens roofed them with planks of wood or tiles, and used unbaked bricks for the walls. To maintain the barrel shape of the roof, a thong or string, perhaps of animal hide, was stretched across the end of the bamboo.

The Buddhist Stupa: A trip through rural India reveals the countryside to be dotted with shrines of all sizes, shapes and denominations. (The more famous ones also have a certain notoriety, such that if you frequent them, people look at you a trifle askance). However, if we look at the modest examples, we will find that they need not be masonry structures-a stone, a tree, a mountain or even an animal will suffice.

A variety of natural objects have been conferred divinity because of their association-real or imagined-with a mythological event, or with the 'relics' of some historical/mythological figure. Thus it was that during Ashoka's time, the first Buddhist 'shrines' were mere piles of stone or rubble containing relics of the Buddha.

Over time it became necessary to 'upgrade' these structures, in conformity with Buddhism's rising status. As is common with ancient structures the world over-for structural reasons it was necessary to have a wide base, tapering towards the top. The form chosen for the Buddhist Stupa was that of a sphere-as much for the shape's metaphysical associations as for the fact that it was an antipode to the square/rectangular form of Hindu temples. According to Satish Grover, "The embryo of the most powerful architectural form of Buddhism, the famous Stupa, thus emerged for the first time under the architectural patronage of Ashoka".

Sanchi-the Centre of the Heavens: After Ashoka, by 200 B.C., the royal patronage enjoyed by Buddhism was on the wane. Gradually, under a succession of kings, Brahmanism regained the prestige it used to enjoy. Under the circumstances, Buddhist monks retired from urban conglomerates to secluded spots, where they built their places of worship and in general led a life of penance and meditation. However, assistance from the mercantile class, who had little interest in Brahmanism, was still available, and thus the Buddhist monks could, over the years, transform their humble centres into truly magnificent works of art. The foremost among these centres was Sanchi, near modern Bhopal.

Here craftsmen laboured for over a hundred years to make Sanchi a point of pilgrimage for devoted Buddhists and scholars from all over Asia for centuries. The magnificent ruin still attracts a large number of tourists today. The Sanchi Stupa basically is a dome, surmounted by a finial or 'harmika', with a circumambulatory path around it, delineated by a railing or 'vedika'. As mentioned earlier, the spherical shape of the Stupa was a structural culmination of rubble masonry piled up, and also had metaphysical connotations with the apparent shape of the universe. The harmika on top represented the Bodhi Tree under which the Buddha first gained enlightenment. And the path around provided a passage for monks who could circle the Stupa, chanting endlessly.

A structure as large as Sanchi Stupa attracted large numbers of monks for penance and meditation. In addition, there were a large number of visitors who made a pilgrimage to this, the most holy site of the Buddhists. A natural consequence was the gradual development of a large complex of buildings around the Stupa. These were typified by the vihara and the chaitya.

The vihara evolved from the humble cave dwellings of the monks. In plan, it essentially consisted of a large number of cubicles around a large central courtyard. In stark contrast to the Stupa, the viharas were models of austerity, with drab exteriors and bare interiors. This is actually not surprising-monks are not supposed to enjoy the pleasures and comforts of urban life!

The vihara was basically an extension of the urban dwelling with its open-to-sky courtyard and rooms around. The courtyard served as a community space, while the cells provided sufficient privacy for effective meditation. It has been observed (Satish Grover, 1980) that the chaitya hall evolved due to the fact that the Sanchi Stupa was an outdoor structure-not permitting use in inclement weather. Hence the evolution of the chaitya as a sort of indoor Stupa.

However, this reason seems to be a trifle strange-totally against the ethos of the monks of a life of penance and hardship. The author surmises that the chaitya served the purpose of a 'minor deity', so often found in large Hindu temples, where niches hold images of 'lesser' gods. The Buddhist monks, still a part of predominantly Hindu society, expressed this subconscious desire by building a number of chaitya halls around the main Stupa. An examination of the chaitya hall architecture reveals the same determinants as in Vedic village architecture-the barrel vaulted roof, the horseshoe-shaped entrance, railings echoing the palisade walls outside Aryan villages.

It was almost as if the craftsman, unfamiliar with the structural properties of stone, reverted to tried and tested forms with which he was comfortable-never mind that reproducing them in stone instead of wood involved far greater effort. This is a recurring feature throughout the history of Indian architecture-the lead time required before a new material is finally put to the best use possible, given its natural properties.

Buddhist Architecture in India

Indian art is an expression of Indian life and thought attuned to its vast natural background and its socio-religious traditions. It is not exclusive or sectarian in the narrow sense of the term. Its style, technique or general tenor has nothing to do with any particular religious outlook. It is fed and fostered upon a vast store-house of Indian traditions, symbols and designs. The term Hindu, Jain or Buddhist art is but a popular nomenclature to distinguish one group of monuments, including painting, cave-temples and architecture, etc., from another stand point of the predominance of one or the other religious theme. Hence, by Buddhist art is meant popularly those monuments and paintings which have for the main purpose the edification or popularisation of Buddhism. Fortunately enough in India and outside where Buddhism did exist, or still exists, there are innumerable monuments representing different phases of Buddhism and these help us to visualise the trend of Buddhist art through the ages. In Buddhist legends and Mythology, Gautama Buddha has been represented as superior not only to the popular cult divinities of the soil, such as the Yakshas, Nagas, etc. but also to Indra, Brahma and others of the earlier Brahmanical pantheon. Everything with him has been described as transcendental. This is amply represented in Buddhist art.

The Early Symbols and their Evolution: Buddhist art reflects very faithfully all the important aspects of Buddhism. In primitive Buddhism, Gautama Sakyamuni has been regarded as an ideal human being and quite naturally we find that the early Buddhist art of Bharhut, Sanchi, Bodh-Gaya and Amaravati and other places shows no anthropomorphic representation of the Master. His presence is indicated by means of an empty throne, or a Bodhi tree or a pair of footprints, or a dharma-chakra, symbolising one or the other event of his life. As the time passed, Buddhism acquired greater popularity and drew adherents from all sections of the people. The discipline and austerities of the early Buddhism were beyond the comprehension of the ordinary followers of the religion. A religion without a personal god in whom one can repose faith had but little appeal to them.

The demand of the popular mind as met by the Mahayanists who defied Buddha and introduced the concept of divine Bodhisattvas and several other deities. With the progress of time, the Buddhist pantheon was enlarged to include several hundred deities. Among the male deities, the Bodhisattva Avalokitesvara became the most popular because of his great compassion for the living creatures. He is an emanation of the Dhyani Buddha Amitabha and his Shakti Pandara (the Sukhavati-Vyuha or the Amitayus Sutra, translated into Chinese between A.D. 148-170, seems to refer for the first time to the name of Amitabha or Amitayus), Avalokitesvara is the personification of universal compassion. As described in the Karanda-vyuha he refused or renounced Nirvana in favour of affected humanity. He is supposed to impart spiritual knowledge to fellow creatures so that all, by a gradual process, may advance on the path of salvation. Different forms of the Avalokitesvara have been mentioned in the Sadhana-mala, of these the important ones are Shadakshari Lokeshvara, Simhanada, Khasharpana. Lokanatha, Halahala, Nilakantha and few others.

Buddhist Architecture: The beginnings of the Buddhist school of architecture can be traced back to BC 255 when the Mauryan emperor Ashoka established Buddhism as the state religion of his large empire. Buddhism spread rapidly throughout India and other parts of Asia. Buddhism was, as it were, a graphic creed, and correspondingly its expansion was accompanied by a distinctive style of architecture that expressed the teachings of the Buddha. In India this early Buddhist art was influenced to a large extent by Ashoka. He was responsible for the construction of several *stupas*, which are sacred mounds of brick commemorative of the Buddha. Ashoka also constructed stone pillars symbolising his creed. These were lofty freestanding monolithic columns erected on sacred sites. The most famous of these is at Saranath.

The Mauryan dynasty crumbled after Ashoka's death in 232 BC; in its wake came the Sungas, who in turn were succeeded by the Andhras. Both these Brahmanical dynasties treated the Buddhists with toleration. The initial steps of the new architectural movement involved enlarging Ashoka's *stupas*. For instance, the *stupa* at Sanchi was enlarged to nearly twice its size and elaborate gateways were added.

At about the same time that the Buddhist communities were elaborating Ashoka's *stupas*, an entirely different form of architecture was developing in western India. These structures were not, however, built of stone or wood, but carved out of living rock. It is therefore unfortunate that these structures are now referred to as "caves", as though they were natural grottoes in the mountain side, since they are actually large and well planned temples. Some of the finest specimens of this rock cut architecture are to be seen at Ajanta.

Under the reign of the 8th century ruler Lalitaditya, the central Kashmir valley became an important artistic site. A magnificent Surya temple was constructed at Martand. Though now ruined, this remains the masterpiece of Kashmiri architecture. Mahayana Buddhism flourished in the arid valleys of Ladakh, beyond the first high range of the Himalayas.

The monasteries at Alchi, dating from the 11th century, have beautiful paintings depicting the Mahayana pantheon. Cave temples were constructed in the 13th to 15th centuries at Saspol and Karsha. The monasteries at Leh and Phiyang continue to be renovated even today, and the recent resurgence of Indian Buddhism, associated not only with the conversion of lower-caste Hindus to Buddhism under the influence of Ambedkar but with the establishment of Tibetan Buddhist communities, particularly in north India, has introduced a fresh chapter in the history of Buddhist architecture in India.

Buddhist religious architecture developed in the South Asia in the third century BC.

Two types of structures are associated with early Buddhism: viharas and stupas. Viharas initially was only temporary shelters used by wandering monks during the rainy season, but later were developed to accommodate the growing and increasingly formalised Buddhist monasticism. An existing example is at Nalanda (Bihar). A distinctive type of fortress architecture found in the former and present Buddhist kingdoms of the Himalayas are dozens

The initial function of a stupa was the veneration and safeguarding of the relics of the Buddha. The earliest existing example of a stupa is in Sanchi (Madhya Pradesh). In accordance with changes in religious practice, stupas were gradually incorporated into chaitya-grihas (stupa halls). These reached their highpoint in the first century BC, exemplified by the cave complexes of Ajanta and Ellora (Maharashtra).

Pagoda is an evolution of the Indian stupa. They are found in the Ajanta and Ellora caves.

Buddhist temples were developed rather later and outside the South Asia, where Buddhism gradually declined from the early centuries AD onwards, though an early example is that of the Mahabodhi temple at Bodh Gaya in Bihar

Buddhist Architecture has its roots deeply planted in Indian 'soil'—both physically, in relation to existing construction styles, and philosophically, in relation to various cosmic theories that influenced the layout of sacred sites. The following is a brief consideration of those influences.

- This history of India opens about 2500 BC with an advanced civilisation centred in several settlements along the Indus valley. The tradition of this native agrarian people focused on fertility and included the worship of the *Mother Goddess and devotion to water or tree spirits*. About 1500 BC they were overwhelmed by 'Indo-Aryans', nomadic herdsmen from Central Asia whose tradition centred on *sacrifice at a fire altar*. The result was that Varuna, through whose navel grew the Tree of Life, was 'overlaid' by the storm god Indra who separated ocean, earth and heaven and released the sun to generate the Cosmic Cycle.
- The merging of the Aryan and native traditions was of prime importance in the *evolution of India's religious architecture* and much of the embellishment of Indian buildings involves fertility symbolism relating to Varuna's tree and the creative and regenerative power of water. The Aryans identified the *Essence of Existence* as the Purusha (later to be identified as Brahman). In defining the structure or embodiment of the Purusha, their literature (the Vedas) provides *the substance of Indian architectural theory* based on the macrocosm centred around the Palace (abode of the king) and *Mount Meru* (abode of the Gods). Post-Vedic commentary provided geometrical formulae to bind Brahma to a specific place for the purpose of worship, supplying the details for any architectural structure intended to accommodate that worship.
- There has been a tradition of religious architecture since Vedic times (1500 –700 BC) but construction was on a small and localised scale using perishable materials like timber, mud and clay and there is scant archaeological evidence available. Suggestions are that

construction centred around the sacrificial arena with the evolving form becoming a simple square cell with a conical or pyramid roof. This became the *most characteristic temple structure* gaining increasing detail and refinement during the Gupta period (4th-6th century AD) heavily decorated with architectural and figural ornament. This form was brought to its stylistic height during the 7th to 11th centuries AD.

The development of various symbols representing aspects of the Buddha's life (563-483 BC) was the beginning of a *specifically Buddhist architecture.* Traditional building styles would have been used but it was the mode of decoration which began to set these buildings apart. As support for the new religion increased so too did the need for buildings to accommodate the requirements of the expanding monastic order. Although stonework was quite common wood was still the main medium and the skill to erect stone structures enclosing appreciable space had yet to be developed.

- The *earliest Buddhist construction* of significance was the stupa, but these were sculpture not structure. Probably the most significant site is at *Sanchi* where as well as having one of the best preserved Indian stupas, the full range of Buddhist art and architecture from the third century BC to the twelfth AD can be studied here.
- The other form of specifically Buddhist construction that evolved quite early was the *rock-cut monastery.* For about six centuries, beginning around 100 BC, several monasteries were found from the cliffs and rock walls of valleys. Probably the most famous of these is at Ajanta. Their development is looked at under CAVES.
- *Line drawings* giving a good overview of different types of construction from various Buddhist countries.
- A slightly esoteric aspect of monastery construction is the *creation of a sima* (boundary). In the early years the Sangha were principally wanderers. As the order grew and more monasteries were established so came the need to define certain areas for various functions.

These boundaries can be quite general or very clearly defined for specific monastic business-the most regular being the fortnightly recitation of the rules and ordinations.

It is clear that the Buddha received gifts of land for the use of the Sangha and there are several scriptural references to dwellings being constructed for their use. One of the most famous stories is of *Anathapindika* who was so inspired on meeting the Buddha that he bought a property from Prince Jeta (the price being the gold needed to cover the whole area of land). He then built Jetavana monastery where the Buddha eventually spent much of his remaining life-over 19 years-and delivered a great many discourses. Very little remains of Jetavana as timber was still the main medium for construction-the techniques for enclosing large spaces using stone not yet being fully developed.

One early response to the need for *'permanent' monasteries* was the excavation of *rock-cut monasteries*. With timber still predominant what we commonly see in these is a duplication of the workers' skill in carpentry executed in stone with latticed windows, moulded door frames and beamed framework. This superb modelling provides valuable insights into the freestanding wooden architecture now lost. One notable exception is the cave at Karle where the facade screen is made of teak wood.

- The term 'caves' is convenient but is far from accurate. These monasteries were not housed in existing indentations but *carved from the living rock*-usually into the cliff face of a valley wall-and spaces were created, not by adding various structural members but by removing existing material. So, like the early stupas, these works are *not technically architectural* and can be viewed as sculpture rather than structure. Nevertheless the skill required to both visualise and then execute this 'inside-out' style of building, to the level of detail that we find, indicates a highly developed society.

- Excavation *began on a large scale* in the early 2nd century BC in west India and continued significantly for about six centuries with the last known excavation in Rajasthan about 800 CE. Although the principle idea was to create spaces for monks to meditate undisturbed most of these monasteries are found quite close to main trade routes.
- The *general layout* of a monastery included a pillared frontage, often with latticed windows, opening into a quadrangular hall with a verandah on all four sides. Cut into the rock on three sides were small cells and across the hall, opposite the main entrance, was an image chamber. Each monastery ideally contained these *three functional features:* the main hall for religious ceremonies and meetings of the Sangha, a series of small rooms (cells) for the use of monks and, a sanctuary-usually containing a rock-cut stupa. While much of the architectural detailing was 'wooden' the decorative artwork tended to illustrate the various life stories of the Buddha (jataka tales), including subjects drawn from folk mythology.
- One of the *most well known* of these Indian cave complexes is at Ajanta where there a great wealth of not only architectural information but a series of frescoes unparalleled in the history of Indian art, both for the wide range of subjects and the medium used.
- As the *development of iconography* proceeded so the appearance of a Buddha image became more common and the plain stupa in the sanctuary gave way to greater ornamentation and representations of the Buddha. This was true of monastic decoration generally.
- India may have laid down the basic 'architectural' principles but the development of caves was far from limited to India alone. China particularly has a long and varied history of cave monasteries starting from around 400 AD. Some of the oldest Buddhist manuscripts and Indian objects have been found here, largely due the Silk Road. One of the largest complexes,

Lung-men-near the city of Lo-yang-has 1300 caves set into the banks of the Yi river.

Mahabodhi

- One of the largest monastic settlements of India was Saranath, just outside Varanasi on the Ganga river. Ruins of numerous large and small monasteries can still be seen there. Two of the first monasteries were built here in the time of the Buddha. King Ashoka had monasteries and stupas built here-perhaps his most well known addition being the installation of a monolithic pillar with the lion capital that has come to be India's national symbol. Most of the monks and monasteries were destroyed by Muhammad Ghori in 1194. A superb example of classic Buddhist temple architecture is found at Bodh Gaya, the scene of the Buddha's enlightenment. Records vary as to construction on the site but it is clear that it has been a place of continuous pilgrimage and worship. The V&A museum has a broken upright from the railing surrounding the early tree shrine. A large monastery was erected by King Megahavarna of Sri Lanka in the 5th century AD. There was persecution in the 7th and 12th centuries and no ancient buildings have been preserved. The Mahabodhi Temple is by far the most important monument now on the site having been extensively restored in the 19th C.
- Buddhism arrived in Tibet in the 7th century but met with some resistance however by the 10th century native elements were merging with a form of east Indian and Kashmir Buddhism. The first monastery-traditionally identified as Samye, south-east of Lhasa-was built in 770 AD. There were over 3000 monasteries with perhaps 1/4 of the population as monks or nuns. The two major stylistic influences were Nepalese and Chinese. Almost no stone carving is found but cloth and wall-painting became highly developed. What we now see is a very distinctive style of architecture with splendid use of colour and ornamentation. The use of images, paintings,

> mandalas and tankas produced an extremely rich iconography and this can be seen not only artistically but architecturally. Nepalese Buddhism has merged with Hinduism and survives in a non-monastic form. Iconography has a very hybrid character.

At the Buddhist temple sites there are buildings for the display and worship of images and also small cells for residence for the monks. Some of the images halls and lecture halls are very large and can have facilities for libraries, group study, and worship. Also, there are specialised structures for large bells and drums.

The Stupa or Pagoda: There are structures that are objects of worship, the stupa or pagoda. The stupa or pagoda is an important part of the Buddhist religious ceremonies. The design of the early stupas in India was derived from Hindu burial mounds and were a solid monolithic structure. The main form was a simple dome (the anda) on a flat platform. From the top a single pillar emerges, with circular disks (chhatraveli). The pillar and umbrella-like disks are surrounded by railings (harmika) similar to the ones surrounding the stupa. Sacred relics are buried in the central core of the stupa. These might be a tooth of the Buddha or other items. Around 100 B.C the stupa began to be carved inside caves throughout northern India. Eventually colossal images of Buddha were carved into the rock. One of these images in Afghanistan is 53 meters high. Most of these sites were near the ancient trade routes where donations would be sought from travellers. Buddhism spread to Sri Lanka, Nepal, and Tibet. In Nepal the form of the stupa began to evolve with the 'all-seeing' eye being painted on each side of the stupa. Each country has varying forms of Buddhism as they blend other cultural beliefs with Buddhism. Buddhism in Tibet is known as Lamaism which was influenced by early practices of shamanism where objects of nature were thought to have spirits.

The early stupas of China were cut from rock inside caves in a square form, yet the multilayered form had overhanging eaves which were a representation of Chinese wooden architecture. A totally different monument emerges. In Korea the stupa takes the form of what would later be the Japanese wood pagoda but their pagoda is carved from stone. Japan is the last of the Asian countries to be introduced to Buddhism.

Pagoda: Pronunciation Key, name given in the East to a variety of buildings of tower form that are usually part of a temple or monastery group and serve as shrines. Those of India are chiefly pyramidal structures of masonry, tapering to an apex and elaborately adorned with carving and sculpture. In China the pagoda, derived from India, is one of the most characteristic architectural types and in general is devoted to sacred usage.

Octagonal, hexagonal, or square in plan, they are built in superimposed stories, sometimes as many as 15; from each story projects an upward-curving tiled roof. The material most commonly used is brick, often faced with slabs of glazed and coloured tile. A few date back to the Tang dynasty (AD 618–906). In Japan the pagodas were introduced from China with Buddhism. They are usually square in plan and five stories high, each story having its projecting roof. Generally made of wood, they exhibit superb carpentry craftsmanship. The Horyu-ji tower near Nara, of the 7th cent., is a noted example.

Pagoda is one part of a temple's structure, and we can trace the origin of pagodas back to India. A pagoda has its origin in old Indian culture. The Indians made pagodas as tombs, called *stupa*, before Buddhism began, but the shape of it was completely different from a Japanese or Chinese one. "Stupa" is from a word which means "to accumulate" in Sanskrit, which is the ancient language in India. Its shape was like a dome, and most of them were made from soil or stone.

The Indians stood one pole in the centre of the dome from the land to above the top of it (like an axis), and they buried bones of the cremated dead (They were mainly saints or heroes) under the pole. They thought of the pole as a symbol of the centre of the universe, which collected the energy of the universe and controlled the birth of everything. A stupa showed completeness and the balance of the energy in the universe. It was representing the universe itself. People always worshipped it.

This idea was taken over in Buddhism. Buddha asked to have his bones put in a stupa after he died, so his pupils made stupas after his death. Then, they had made stupas as the symbol of the tomb of Buddha. For this reason, a stupa was the most significant structure in a temple.

People in Southeast Asia called a stupa *Chaitya*, which came from Indian and means the place where the holy stays and was used as a synonym with *stupa*. Meanwhile, it was pronounced with an accent and then pronounced that word in wrong way. It is said that the word "pagoda" came in this way. So, "pagoda" was used as the word meaning religious tall structure (like a tower) rather than meaning the function of it.

The Bharhut Stupa: (The Sunga-Andhra epoch (2nd-1st Century BC) was one of the most creative periods of Buddhist art. Though the Sunga rulers were followers of the Brahmanical faith and Buddhism was deprived of the State patronage which it enjoyed during the reign of the Mauryan rulers, like Ashoka and some of his successors, there was no setback in the propagation or popularity of the Buddhist faith. Buddhist establishments flourished in Bodh-Gaya, Bharhut, and Sanchi in Northern and Central India, in Amaravati and Jaggayapeta in South India, at Bhaja, Nasik, Karle and Janta and at several other places in Western India.

The art of this period consists mainly in the excavation of the rock-cut temples or viharas (some of which are embellished with paintings) and the erection of railings and toranas (gateways) to the Buddhist Stupas at different places). General Cunningham found remains of the railings and on gateway of the Stupa at Bharhut (Madhya Pradesh) during the years 1872-74 and had them deposited in the Indian Museum in the year following. The Stupa in question was built during the 2nd Century B.C. In the absence of the Stupa itself it is difficult to ascertain its shape and size.

But it was probably similar to the Stupas represented on its panels and the almost contemporary Stupas of Sanchi. All these Stupas consist of hemispherical dome with a harmika above supporting the umbrellas. One of the main interest of the Bharhut sculptures consists in the representation of the birth-stories of the Gautama Budha. These stories (or the Jatakas) are of two main classes, those relating to the previous births of Buddha as a Bodhisattva (a Buddha potentia), and those of his last appearance as Gautama Shakyamuni when he attained Enlightenment of Buddhahood. The Jatakas represented on the Bharhut panels include *Mahakapi-Jataka, Latuva-Jataka, Miga-Jataka, Sujata-gahuto-Jataka, Mahajanaka-Jataka and Vidhurapandita-Jataka, Chhadanta Jataka, etc.*

The scenes on the Bharhut sculptures, relating to the life of Gautama Shakyamuni include, among others, the dream of Maya (Illustrating the descent of a Bodhisattva in the form of an elephant into the mothers womb), the defeat of Mara, Gautama's Enlightenment under the Bodhi tree, the worship of the Bodhi tree, the worship of Gautama's hair-locks by celestial beings, the visits of king Ajatashatru of Magadha and of Prasenjit of Koshala, etc. The worship of the Bodhi tree, seems to have been widely prevalent, as there are many representation of it on the sculptured panels of Bharhut, Sanchi and Amaravati. Again, in the Divyavandana it is related that the Bodhi tree was Ashoka's favourite object of worship. The lowest architrave of the Eastern Gateway Stupa I, Sanchi (1st Century B.C.) depicts the ceremonial visits of king Ashoka and his queen, Tishyarakshita to the Bodhi Tree. In the centre of the panel are the tree and the temple of Bodh Gaya. On the left is seen a crowd of musicians and devotees carrying water vessels. On the right are the king and the queen descending from the elephant and payment homage to the Bodhi tree.

The Sanchi Stupa: In addition to Bharhut, the other important centres of Buddhist art and religion in north India during this period were Sanchi (Madhya Pradesh) and Bodh Gaya (Bihar). The main interest of the art at Sanchi centres round the Great Stupa. Originally built of brick, during the reign of Ashoka (3rd Century, B.C.), it was encased in stone and brought to its present dimension about a century later. The other additions, such as the erection of the toranas and the ground balustrade were done still later, probably about 50 B.C.

of all the four gateways, the south gateways seems to be the oldest. On one of its architraves, there is an inscription showing that it was the work of one of the artisans of king Sri Satakarni (1st Century B.C.), who was evidently the son of Simuka, the founder of the Satavahana family of the Deccan. Of all toranas or gateways, the best preserved is the northern gateway which enables the visitor to have a complete idea of the appearance of all the gateways.

Each gateway is composed of two square pillars with capitals at the top. These capitals of standing dwarfs or elephants support a superstructure of architraves. Finally, on the summit of the gateway is the dharma-chakra symbol in the middle. The pillars and superstructures are elaborately decorated with representation of Jataka legends (stories of Buddha's past lives). There are also representations of the sacred trees, stupas and other motifs to indicate the presence of Gautama Buddha symbolically. As in Bharhut art, here also, in conformity with the tradition of early Indian art, there is no anthropomorphic representation of Buddha. About 50 yards north-east of the great stupa of Sanchi is another monument of the same nature but smaller in proportions. Inside this stupa the relics of two very important disciples of Buddha, Sariputta and Maha-Moggalana, were discovered by General Cunnigham.

Jaggapetta Stupa: A stylistic equivalent of the panels of Sanchi is to be found in a carving from a Jaggayapeta stupa near Amaravati on the Krishna river. This will show how little differences existed between different regions in the field of art. A monument to be ascribed to the early Sunga period is the old Vihara at Bhaja which is situated in the hills of the Western ghats to the south of Bombay. It is a rectangular chamber with several cells. The decoration of the Bhaja monastery includes among other the representation of Yakshas, a sun god on a four-horse chariot and Indra riding his vehicle, *i.e.*, Airavat. The art of Bharhut and other early contemporaneous sites has a primitive simplicity. (It is permitted by naturalism, enlivened by humour, dance and music. From the standpoint of technique the figures are in low relief, somewhat flattened with angular limbs). Although there are innumerable references in the

Jatakas and other Buddhist literature to the pointed decorations, the earliest surviving examples of Buddhist paintings are met with at the oldest Chaitya Halls at Ajanta in the Deccan, dedicated in the 2nd Century B.C. The principal wall painting in cave 10 is devoted to the illustration of the Chaddanta Jataka.

Amaravati Stupa: The Buddhist art in South India during this period is best illustrated by the remains of the Maha-Chaitya (or stupa) of Amaravati. As the earliest Buddhist Sculptures found here are primitive in style resembling those of Bharhut, it can be presumed that the Maha-Chaitya was built during the 2nd Century B.C. to 250 A.D. Its earliest pieces as noted above, show affinities to Bharhut art. The images of Buddha were introduced here about the 1st –2nd Century A.D. The Amaravati art of this period is highly elegant and sensitive.

Gandhara Art: Buddhist art entered upon a new phase with the rise of Mahayana Buddhism during the 1st Century B.C. to 1st Century A.D. The period is remarkable in that it gave for the first time the figure art or the anthropomorphic representations of the Buddha. Under the patronage of Kushana rulers (1st-2nd Century A.D.) a new school of art flourished in the Gandhara region, *i.e.* Peshawar and its neighbouring districts. Because of its strategic geographical position the region became a meeting place of various races and cultures. As a result of this, the art of the region shows mingling of both Indian and foreign ideas and motifs. Gandhara art is a hybrid product; though Buddhist in theme it is Graeco-Roman in style or technique as is evident from the physiognomy and drapery of the images.

The artists of this region have produced a large number of Buddha and Bodhisattva images along with other Buddhist deities. Gandhara art flourished for about four to five hundred years and to a great extent it influenced the indigenous art of Mathura, Amaravati and Nagarjunakonda. It exercised a profound influence upon the art of Afghanistan and Central Asia. The Buddha and Bodhisattva images of many sites in Central Asia show an affiliations to the Gandhara style. The art of the region received a great blow at the hands of the Huna invaders. Mihirakula, a cruel king of the Huna had destroyed, as Xuanzang was told during his travel to this country, the Buddhist monasteries of the region. The main centres of Gandhara art were the cities of Peshawar and Taxila, and also Afghanistan where a large number of stupas, monasteries and sculptures have been unearthed by the archaeologists.

Mathura–A Great Centre of Art: Mathura also was a great centre of art and culture during this period. Here flourished side by side all the important religions of India, such as Brahmanism, Jainism and Buddhism. It is believed that the first Buddha images were carved at Mathura simultaneously if not earlier, with the Gandhara school. Mathura has produced Buddha images of various dimensions. The Kushana Buddha or Bodhisattva images of Mathura served as the prototypes of the more beautiful specimens of the Gupta period.

The workshop of Mathura exported several Buddhist images to various other places, such as Saranath and even as far as Rajgir in Bihar. It is well known that Friar-Bala an inhabitant of Mathura had several Bodhisattva images set up at different places. Two of them were found at Saraswati and Saranath. The Kushana art of Mathura is somewhat heavy. The style and technique which the Kushana artists were trying to evolve were brought to the Gupta period. But the art of South India during this time is more elegant and sophisticated. The sculptured panels of Amaravati and Nagarjunakonda, Goli, Ghantasals, belonging to the 2nd–3rd Century A.D., are characterised by delicacy of forms, and linear grace.

Ashokan Pillar, Saranath: The architecture of the Ashokan period (c. 273-237 B.C.) gains in magnificence, as for the first time stone was employed instead of wood. The great art of the Ashokan period is mainly represented by the monolithic pillars on which edicts were engraved. The famous capital of the Saranath pillar consists of four adorned lions which originally supported the Wheel of Law resting on the abacus bearing in relief an elephant, a horse, a bull and a lion. In other extant examples, the crowning member consisted of a bull or wheel. The pillars were highly polished. There are also excavated halls of the Ashokan period in the Barabar hills. Of these, the Sudama cave consists of a circular chamber and an ante-chamber with side entrances.

Indian architecture between 200 B.C. and 20 A.D. continued to maintain the progress made in the Ashokan period. The improvement in the cave architecture may be seen in the old *vihara* at Bhaja near Poona datable to 2nd century B.C. It is remarkable for its unique relieves, one of them being identified by Dr. Kumaraswamy as Indra riding his Airavata. Bedsa and other caves near Poona of the same period consist of a nave, apse and aisle, the apse containing a solid *stupa* and the aisle continuing round the apse, thus providing the circumambulation path.

The Chaitya hall at Karle, which may be dated to the 1st century B.C., is a magnificent example of cave architecture. Its horseshoe windows, great pillars and finely carved relieves win our admiration. The remains of the railings and gateways of the Bharhut stupa may be dated back to c. 150 B.C. The railing pillars and the gateways are decorated with the figures of the guardian Yakshas and Yakshis, Nagarajas, birth-stories of the Buddha called Jatakas, floral, animal and other motifs. The Buddha himself does not appear and the chief events in his life a represented by symbols.

There was a special type of temple connected with the Bodhi-tree at the Gaya. On the strength of certain reliefs raging from 2nd century B.C. to the 2nd century A.D., it could be said that this temple was made of a gallery with vaulted roof and Chaitya windows of the usual type supported by pillars and with the ground plan like a Maltese cross.

The Sanchi stupas are of different periods. The core of the stupa No. 1 was probably built in the Mauryan age. The stupas Nos. 2 and 3 are of Sungan origin and the gateways of the Nos. 1 and 3 belong to the Satavahana period (72-25 B.C.) The reliefs on No. 2 are related to the Bharhut style, but there are some reliefs which exhibit greater knowledge of spatial relation which is attributed to the hypothetical influence of Bactrian Hellenistic art, but its more natural explanation would be the stylistic advance of Indian art.

The reliefs of the Great Gateway are marvels of decorative storytelling. The principal themes are drawn from the life of the Buddha and from the Jatakas. The bigger compositions were attempted on torana architraves.

The excavations at Taxila and elsewhere have provided us with material relating to the development of architecture between 78 and 302 A.D. The architectural style in the monasteries is fundamentally Indian, but numerous motifs, for instance, the Corinthian capital, pediments, entablatures, moldings, etc., are of debased classical order. A typical Gandharan monastery consists mainly of two structures, the stupa and the monastery with the aggregate of other building.

Among the great monuments of the Deccan during this period may be mentioned the Great Stupa at Amaravati which, though originally built in the 2nd century B.C., was provided with sculptured casing slabs and railings in the 1st, 2nd and 3rd centuries A.D. On the drum of the stupa were four projecting offsets facing each of the entrances and each displaying five pillars called Aryaka Kahambhas. The stupa was surrounded by a rail. The subject-matter of decoration are rosettes, garland-carrying aretes, Jataka stories, walled and moated cities, palace buildings, *toranas*, *stupas*, etc. The technical proficiency of the Amaravati reliefs makes them the most fascinating and expressive of the *rasa* of Indian sculpture.

There is little doubt that Indian architecture and sculpture attained their zenith in the Gupta period and are best represented in temple architecture, of which a few examples are given here.

The famous Dhamekh stupa at Saranath near Banaras datable to the 6th century A.D. is characterised by exquisitely carved ornaments, geometrical and floral. The Ajanta monolithic Caves Nos. XVI, XVII and XIX are distinguished for the beauty of their pillars and their facade decorations. The Chaitya windows with their double row of cornices in Cave No. XIX at once attract our attention. A good example of the apsidal temples of the Gupta period is the one at Ter. Among flat-roofed shrines, a prominent place must be given to the flat-roofed temples at Sanchi and Bhumara. The Shiva temple at Bhumara consists of a flat roof and decorated windows. It was provided with a variety of richly carved sculptures. The famous Mahabodhi temple at Bodh Gaya, in spite of its restoration, probably maintains its form of the early Gupta period. It consists of a high straight-edged pyramidal tower of nine stories.

Nalanda: The art of Nalanda shows very high standard of stone carving as well as metal casting. The minute execution of the bronzes specially of the smaller ones, has excited the admiration of all art lovers of the world. Several Nalanda bronzes were exported to Nepal and Tibet and also to Java. Equally interesting are the palm leaf illustrations of the Buddhist manuscripts of the Pala period. Their miniature size, colour scheme and linear grace show the skill of the painters of these illustrations. The Pala style of painting, as Pala sculptures and bronzes, very much influenced the art of Nepal, Tibet and the further East. Bodh-Gaya and Nalanda in Magadha drew pilgrims from different parts of the Buddhist world.

The Gupta Art: The Gupta period (4th – 6th Century A.D.) marks the bright period of art in India. Gupta art is marked by restraint combined with a high aesthetic sense and discipline. The main centres of Buddhist art during this period were Mathura, Saranath and Nalanda in the north. The Buddhist images of Mathura and Saranath are some of the best specimens of Indian art, never equalled by any art creations of later period. The delicate folds of the transparent garment adorning the Gupta figures were done in a beautiful style. The profusely decorated halo is another special feature of the art of the Gupta figure.

The delicate modelling of forms with meditative repose has rendered the Buddha and Bodhisattva figures of the Gupta period most attractive. The Gupta artists showed an equal ingenuity in the carving of metal images also. The bronze Buddha image from Sultanganj and also one from Dhanesar Khera together with a number of specimens found in north-western part of India are some excellent specimens testifying to the skill and ability of the Gupta metal carvers. This period is also known for excavations of several rock-cut viharas and temples at Ajanta and Ellora, in Maharashtra, under the patronage of the Vakataka King. Caves 16,17 and 26 at Ajanta are excellent examples of pillared halls with usual cells with shrines in the back containing Budha figures. The beauty and variety of the pillars are remarkable. Caves 16 and 17 were excavated in the last quarter of the 5th Century A.D. by a Minister and feudatory of the Vakataka king Harisena. The mural paintings in the Ajanta caves of the Vakataka period contain representations of scenes from Buddha's life from the conception to enlightenment. Some of them are devoted to the illustrations of Jataka stories, including one of Prince Visvantara, hero of immeasurable bounty.

The Ajanta paintings both in composition and technique are characterised by a delicacy and depth of feelings. The artists excel not only in depicting human and animal figures but also in decorative genius. They adorned the ceilings, pedestals of columns, door and window Ramaaes, with patterns and motifs of kaleidoscopic variety. Several Buddhist caves are to be found also at Bagh (Madhya Pradesh) and Ellora (Maharashtra), containing numerous Budha and Bodhisattva figures (5th – 6th Century).

Post Gupta Developments: The Gupta art tradition was followed in later period also. The art of Nalanda, Kurkihar, Saranath, Orissa and other places during the mediaeval period is based upon the Gupta art idiom. The north Indian Buddhism of the mediaeval period (8th – 11th Century A.D). is a peculiar synthesis of the Mahayana ideals and tantric elements. The concept of the Adi-Budha, the Dhyani-Buddhas, the divine Bodhisattvas as well as the concept of Shakti or the female energy figures most prominently in the Buddhist art of the period. One anachronism of Buddhist art in mediaeval period is the introduction of the crowned Buddhas with jewelleries. Though incompatible to the idea of renunciation which Buddha followed and preached, such images were made probably to lay emphasis on the concept of Buddha as a Chakravartin, the supreme universal monarch.

Nagapattinam: A flourishing centre of Buddhism in South India during the period was Nagapattinam, near Madras on east coast. There existed here in the mediaeval period a colony of the Malaya Buddhists who, patronised by the Cholas erected here two temples in the 11th Century A.D., with the aid granted by the Sailendra kings of Java and Sumatra. One of the temples was called Rajarajaperumpalli and the Rajendrachola-perumpalli. Naga-pattinum was a place of pilgrimage for the Buddhists of different places in India as well as outside. Since 1856 about 350 bronzes have been found in these vihara sites. Some of them are of the early Chola times while the rest belong to the later Chola period. The Nagapattinam bronzes are some of the finest metal works of South India.

Caves of Ajanta and Ellora : The caves are in a wooded and rugged horseshoe-shaped ravine about 3½ km. from the village of Ajintha. It is situated in the Aurangabad district of Maharashtra State in India (106 kilometres away from the city of Aurangabad). The nearest towns are Jalgon (60 kilometres away) and Bhuswal (70 kilometres away). Along the bottom of the ravine runs the river Waghur or Waghora (from the root *vyaghra* in Sanskrit meaning the tiger), a mountain stream. There are 29 (officially numbered by the Archaeological Survey of India) caves, excavated in the south side of the precipitous scarp made by the cutting of the ravine, and vary from 35 to 110 ft. in elevation above the bed of the torrent.

The monastic complex of Ajanta consists of several vihras (monastic halls of residence) and chaitya-grihas (stupa monument halls) cut into the mountain scarp in two phases. The first phase is called the Hinayana phase (referring to the Lesser Vehicle tradition of Buddhism, when the Buddha was revered symbolically). At Ajanta, cave numbers 9, 10, 12, 13, and 15 A (the last one was rediscovered in 1956, and is still not officially numbered) were excavated during this phase. These excavations have enshrined the Buddha in the form of the stupa, or mound.

The second phase of excavation started on the site after a lull of over three centuries. This phase is popularly known as the Mahyna phase (referring to the Greater Vehicle tradition of Buddhism, which is less strict and encourages direct depiction of the Buddha through paintings and carvings). Some prefer to call this phase the Vikmaka phase after the ruling dynasty of the house of the Vakamakas of the Vatsagulma branch. The dating of the second phase has been debated among scholars. In recent years a consensus seems to be converging on fifth century dates for all the Mahayana phase caves. According to Walter M. Spink, a leading Ajantologist, all the Mahayana excavations were carried out from 462 to 480 CE. The caves created during the Mahayana phase are the ones numbered 1, 2, 3, 4, 5, 6, 7, 8, 11, 14, 15, 16, 17, 18, 19, 20, 21, 22, 23, 24, 25, 26, 27, 28, and 29. Cave 8 was long thought to be a Hinayana cave, however current research shows that it is in fact a Mahayana cave.

There were two chaitya-grihas excavated in the Hinayana phase that are caves 9 and 10. Caves 12, 13, and 15 A of this phase are viharas. There were three chaitya-grihas excavated in the Vakamaka or Mahayana phase that are caves 19, 26, and 29. The last cave was abandoned soon after its beginning. Caves 19 and 26 have a rather uncommon arrangement made to the central object of worship wherein the stupa is fronted by an image of the Buddha in standing and seated positions respectively. The rest of the excavations are viharas: caves 1, 2, 3, 5, 6, 7, 8, 11, 14, 15, 16, 17, 18, 20, 21, 22, 23, 24, 25, 27, and 28.

The viharas are of various sizes the maximum being about 52 feet. They are often square-shaped. Their excavation exhibits a great variety, some with simple facade, others ornate; some have a porch and others do not. The hall was an essential element of a viharas. In the Vakamaka phase, early viharas were not intended to have shrines because they were purely meant to be halls of residence and congregation. Later, shrines were introduced in them in the back walls, which became a norm.

The shrines were made to house the central object of reverence that is the image of the Buddha often seated in the *dharmachakra pravartana mudra* (the gesture of teaching). In the caves with latest features, we find subsidiary shrines added on the side walls, porch or the front-court. The facades of many viharas are decorated with carvings, and walls and ceilings were often covered with paintings.

Changes in Buddhist thought in the first century BC. had made it possible for the Buddha to be deified and consequently the image of the Buddha as a focus of worship became popular marking the arrival of the Mahayana (the Greater Vehicle) sect.

In the past, scholars divided the caves in three groups, but this is now discredited in light of fresh evidence and research. This theory of dating believed that the oldest group of caves dated from 200 BC to AD 200, the second group belonged, approximately, to the sixth, and the third group to the seventh century.

The expression *Cave Temples* used by Anglo-Indians for viharas without the shrine is inaccurate. Ajanta was a kind of college monastery. Hsuan Tsang informs us that Dinnaga, the celebrated Buddhist philosopher and controversialist, author of well-known books on logic, resided there. This, however, remains to be corroborated by further evidence. In their prime the viharas were intended to afford accommodation for several hundreds, teachers and pupils combined. It is tragic that none of the caves in the Vakataka phase were ever fully completed. This was because the ruling Vakataka dynasty suddenly fell out of power leaving the dominion in a likely crisis, which forced all activities to a sudden halt at the time of Ajanta's last years of activities. This idea first pronounced by Walter M. Spink is increasingly gaining acceptance based on the archaeological evidence visible on site.

Cave 1: It is first approach and has no relation to the chronological sequence of the caves. It is the first cave on the eastern end of the horseshoe shaped scarp. According to Spink, it is one of the latest caves to have begun on site and brought to near-completion in the Vakataka phase. Although there is no epigraphic evidence, it has been proposed that the Vakataka king Harisena may have been the benefactor of this better-preserved cave. A dominant reason for this is that King Harisena was not involved initially in patronising Ajanta, but could not have remained aloof for long, as the site was burgeoning with activity under his rule, and the Buddhist laity would have loved to see the Hindu king participating in the pious act of patronage. Besides, most of the themes depicted are royal. This cave has one of the most elaborate carvings on the facade with relief sculptures on entablature and fridges.

There are scenes carved from the life of the Buddha as well as a number of decorative motifs. There was once a two pillared portico visible in the 19th century photographs, which has since been perished. The cave has a front-court with cells fronted by pillared-vestibules on either side. These have high plinth level. The cave has a porch with simple cells on either end. The absence of pillared vestibules on ends suggest that the porch was not excavated in the latest phase of Ajanta when pillared vestibules had became a necessity and norm. Most areas of the porch was once covered with murals of which notably high degree of fragments remain. There are three doorways: a central doorway and two side-doorways. Between the main and the side-doorways, two square windows have been carved that lit the interiors.

Each wall of the hall inside is nearly 40 feet long and 20 feet high. Twelve pillars make a square colonnade inside supporting the ceiling, and creating spacious aisles along the walls. There is a shrine carved on the rear wall, which houses an impressive seated image of the Buddha, his hands being in the *dharmachakra pravartana mudra.* There are four cells each on the left, rear, and the right wall. The walls are covered with paintings suggesting a fair state of preservation from decay. The scenes depicted are mostly didactic, devotional, and ornamental. The themes are from the Jataka stories (the stories of the Buddha's former existences as Boddhisattva), life of the Gautama Buddha, and those of his veneration.

Cave 2: Cave 2 is next to Cave 1. It looks similar to cave 1 in many respects. Like cave 1, it is relatively in a better state of preservation. It is known specially for the paintings preserved on its walls, ceilings, and pillars.

Facade: The cave's facade has a porch visibly different from cave 1. Even the facade does not have carvings as in cave 1. What we see here is an cave supported by robust pillars that are ornamented with designs. The size and general ground plan, however, shares many things in common with cave 1.

Porch: As first suggested by Walter M. Spink, the porch has cells fronted by pillared vestibules on either ends. This architectural element is not found in the porch of cave 1. That cave has simple cells on porch-ends. The reason is, as evidences indicate, similar porch-end cells once existed not only in cave 2 but most other caves began early in the Vakataka phase and transformed later as CPVs in later years. In fact, all the porch-ends in various caves as wells as on the facade's side-walls were originally blank without even a cell in the earliest, the inaugural plans that were based on the prototype of a typical Hinayana vihara. The need of the cells on the previously "wasted areas" arose as a solution to greater housing requirements in later years. It became a norm subsequently to add porch-end cells in the planning of later Vakataka excavations. Still later, these simple single cells on porch-ends were converted into CPVs or were being planned as such in order to create accommodate more room, symmetry, and beauty.

The paintings on the ceilings and walls of this porch are widely published. They depict the Jataka tales that are stories of the Buddha's life in former existences as Bodhisattva. The porch's rear wall has a doorway in the centre, which allows entrance to the hall. On either side of the door is a square-shaped window carved to lit the interiors.

Hall: The hall has four colonnade making a square in the centre of the hall. They support the ceiling. Each arm or colonnade of the square is parallel to each of the respective wall of the hall making an aisle in between. The colonnades have rock-beams above and below them. The capitals are carved and painted with various decorative motifs that include ornamental, human, animal, vegetative, and semi-divine forms.

Paintings: Paintings are everywhere except the floor or they were intended as such. At many places they have been damaged by the process of decay or human interference. Therefore, many areas of the painted walls, ceilings, and pillars are fragmentary. The painted narratives of the Jataka tales are depicted only on the walls, which demanded special attention of the devotee. They are didactic in nature meant to inform the community about the Buddha's teachings and life through successive births. Their placement on the walls required the devotee to walk through the aisles and 'read' the narratives depicted in various episodes. The narrative episodes are depicted one after another although not in a linear order. Their identification has been a core area of research on the subject since the time of the site's rediscovery in 1819.

For long the paintings were erroneously referred to as frescoes. However, we know now that it is best to call them murals because the typically known process and technique of 'fresco' painting is not found in these murals. At Ajanta, the technique used, the medium, materials, and process is unlike the examples found in the art history of other civilizations. In fact, these murals have a certain uniqueness about them that is rarely found elsewhere, even within the history of South Asian art. The process of painting involved several stages. First of all the rock surface was chiselled rough so that it can hold the plaster. The plaster was prepared of clay, hay, dung, lime, etc. Variations are found in ingredients and their proportions from cave to cave, and in various places in the same cave. While the plaster was still wet, the drawings were done, and the colours applied.

The wet plaster has the capacity to soak the colour so that the colour becomes a part of the surface and would not peel off or decay easily. As regards the colour, they were the so called 'earth colour' or the 'vegetable colour.' Various kinds of stones, minerals, and plants were used in combinations to prepare different colours. Sculptures were often covered with stucco to give them a fine finish and lustrous polish. The stucco had the ingredients of lime and powdered sea-shell or conch. The latter afforded peculiar shine and smoothness. In cave upper six, some of it is extant. The smoothness resembles the surface of a glass, which astonishes the visitor today. The brush for painting was made of animal hairs and twigs of certain plants.

Fresco at Ajanta: In its pure form the art of painting upon damp, fresh, lime plaster. In Renaissance Italy it was called *buon fresco* to distinguish it from *fresco secco,* which was executed upon dry plaster with pigments having a glue or casein base. In true fresco the binder is provided by the lime of the plaster; in drying this forms a calcium carbonate that incorporates the pure pigments, mixed only with water, with the material of the wall. During the Renaissance it was customary to prepare a cartoon of the same dimensions as the contemplated fresco. To transfer the design to the wall, pounce, or dust, was applied through perforations in the cartoon to the wet coat of plaster (*intonaco*). The plaster was made of fine sand, lime, and marble dust that was applied in small sections daily. A large fresco therefore consists of many small sections, each painted in a day.

The sections were planned in such a way as to make the joinings inconspicuous. As not all colours are lime-proof, fresco does not permit as large a palette or as delicate a manipulation of transitional tones as the oil medium. However, its clear, luminous colour, fine surface, and permanence make it ideal for bold, monumental murals. The Minoans decorated the palace at Knossos and the Romans painted the villas at Pompeii in this fashion. The technique has not altered substantially since the 15th cent., when it was brought to perfection by the great masters of the Italian Renaissance. Only dry climates are hospitable to the medium, so fresco was used rarely in N Europe. The art of fresco painting declined until the 20th cent., when it was revived in Mexico by Diego Rivera and Jose Clemente Orozco.

Northeast of Mumbai (a.k.a. Bombay), near Aurangabad, are two astonishing series of temples carved out of living rock (rock formations still in progress) over the course of fourteen centuries. During the 4th century A. D. in a remote valley, work began on the Ajanta caves to create a complex of Buddhist monasteries and prayer halls. As centuries passed, numerous Buddhist monks and artisans dug out a set of twenty-nine caves, converting some to cells, and others to monasteries and Buddhist temples. All of these were carved from the rock cliff at Ajanta. These caves are adorned with elaborate sculptures and paintings which have withstood the ravages of time.

Budhisatva—Painting from Ajanta: The sculptures are finely brought images of animals, guards and deities while the paintings tell ancient tales of courtly life and depict hundreds of Buddhist legends. Amid the beautiful images and paintings are sculptures of Buddha, calm and serene in contemplation.

Work started on the Ellora caves in the seventh century A.D. where another set of caves was created from living rock. Buddhism, Jainism and Hinduism inspired sculptors to create elaborate rock carvings. The Buddhist and Jain caves here are ornately carved, yet seem quiet and meditative, whereas the Hindu caves are filled with a divine energy and power.

The most impressive and majestic creation at Ellora is the Kailasa Temple, a full-sized, freestanding temple flanked by elephants carved out of solid rock during the Rashtrakuta kings. Pillars, podiums, spires and towers combine to produce an awe-inspiring representation of Shiva's Himalayan abode.

The cave temples of Ajanta are situated about sixty two miles north of Aurangabad in western India. The caves are first mentioned in the writings of the Chinese pilgrim Hiuen Tsang who visited India between A.D 629 and 645. The caves were "discovered" dramatically during the course of military maneuvers being undertaken by British officers in 1819. Public attention was roused and the East India company instructed the Viceroy to procure good copies of the paintings. Publicity, however, was nearly fatal to the original paintings, as many archaeologists and officials cut out the heads to be presented to museums. Therefore, in 1903, wire screens were fixed in all the important caves.

The thirty temples at Ajanta are set into the rocky sides of a crescent shaped gorge in the Inhyadri hills of the Sahyadri ranges. At the head of the gorge is a natural pool fed by a waterfall. Though this pristine spot was chosen to enable the Buddhist monks to meditate undisturbed, it should be noted that all sites of Buddhist excavations were situated close to the main trade routes.

The excavations span a period of about six centuries. The earlier monuments include both *chaitya* halls (halls divided into a central nave and side aisles by two rows of columns) and monasteries. These date from the 2nd to 1st centuries B.C.

After a period of more than six centuries, excavations once again revived during the Vakataka ruler Harishena. The sculptures contain an impressive array of votive figures, accessory figures, narrative episodes and decorative motifs. The series of paintings is unparalleled in the history of Indian art, both for the wide range of subjects and the medium. A large number of incidents from the life of the Buddha are depicted. Tales from the Jataka legends were executed vibrantly by large scale compositions depicting life in court, town or forest. Overlapping figures suggest perspective, colours are harmoniously blended, and the linework is sinuous. However, the identities of the artists responsible for the execution of the Ajanta caves are unknown. This is not only a testimony to their extraordinary faith in the Buddha, but is characteristic of Indian traditions of anonymity and abnegation of self. Even today, these cave temples at Ajanta provide the most complete illustration of Buddhist tradition.

Technique: In painting a fresco, the surface of a plastered wall is divided into areas roughly corresponding to the contours of the figures or the landscape, generally drawn on a rough under layer of plaster, called the *arriccio.* Many artists sketched their compositions on this under layer, which would never be seen, in a red pigment called sinopia. From this pigment, the underdrawing acquired its name, the sinopia. On top of this first, rough layer of plaster, a second layer is added, called the *intonaco.* This is the final layer, and would be smoothed and perfected as the painting surface.

Buon fresco technique consists of painting in pigment mixed with water on wet, fresh, lime mortar or plaster (*intenazo*). Due to the chemical make-up of the plaster, a binder is not required, as the pigment mixed solely with the water will be enough to bind the pigment to the wall. The pigment is absorbed by the wet plaster; after a number of hours, the plaster dries, and the pigment dries as well, a part of the wall. One of the first painters to use this technique was the Isaac Master in the Upper Basilica of Saint Francis in Assisi.

A secco painting, in contrast, is done on dry plaster. The pigments thus require a binding medium, such as egg, to hold the pigment to the wall. Generally, *buon fresco* works are more durable than *a secco* works. Historically, the *a secco* technique was used more often for final touches or to touch-up mistakes made in a *buon fresco* work.

Buon frescoes are difficult to create because of the deadline associated with the drying plaster. Generally, a layer of plaster will require ten to twelve hours to dry; ideally, an artist would begin to paint after one hour and continue until two hours before the drying time.

Thus, an artist would need to know exactly how much he/she could paint in those hours, before the plaster dries: this area is called the *giornata* ("day's work"). Once a *giornata* is dried, no more *buon fresco* can be done without removing the dried plaster from the wall—a task usually requiring a crowbar or other sharp instrument—and starting over. Hence the use of *a secco* to repair minor mistakes or to add finishing touches.

In a wall-sized fresco, there may be ten to twenty *giornate,* or separate areas of plaster. After centuries, these giornate (originally, nearly invisible) have become visible, and in many large-scale frescoes, these divisions are visible from the ground. Additionally, the border between *giornate* was often covered by *a secco* frescoing, which has since fallen off. The earliest form of *fresco* was Egyptian wall paintings in tombs, usually using the *a secco* technique.

Roman wall paintings, such as those at Pompeii and Herculaneum, were completed in *buon fresco.*

One of the rare examples of Islam fresco painting can be seen in Qasr Amra, the desert palace of the Umayyads in the 8th century.

The late Medieval period and the Renaissance saw the most prominent use of fresco, particularly in Italy, where most churches and many government buildings still feature fresco decoration.

Andrea Palladio, the famous Italian architect of the 16th century, built many mansions with plain exteriors and stunning interiors filled with frescoes.

Mountain and Caves

The Satbis Deori temple, which still remains in the citadel of Chittorgarh, was built based on the same style as temples on Mt. Abu. But the exterior of sanctum (garbhagriha) vividly shows Northern Style. Indian architecture in the medieval period is divided into "Northern Style" and "Southern Style," and their difference is obvious at upper structure of sanctums. While Southern Style has a tiered structure in pyramidal outline, Northern Style has one that puts emphasis on the vertical line that stretches upward, called "shikhara."

Adinatha Temple, Khajuraho: The zenith of the "shikhara style" is the worldly famous temples at Khajuraho. Although this place is merely a rural village today, it once prospered as a capital of the Chandella kingdom. It is said to have boasted 85 temples of various scales, and 25 of them still remain. Here again Jainism and Hinduism had coexisted, and there are four Jain temples in the Eastern Group. The Ghantai temple, which used to be the largest, keeps only the trace of its porch. Thus the Parshvanatha temple, that retains its entire structure, is rather smaller than the major Hindu temples in Khajuraho. However, this temple has carvings with higher intricacy, and there are a lot of masterpieces. As the statues of Jain on the exterior walls are treated subordinately, there is scarcely any distinction from the Hindu temples both from the viewpoint of architecture and sculpture. "Mountain and cave" is the term that describes the most significant feature of these overwhelmingly powerful temples.

A range of shikharas at the exterior stands for Kailasa, the holy mountain of the Himalayas. Cross section indicates that even though the interior space is made by masonry, it has characteristics of a cave temple. Since the term "garbhagriha" literally means "womb chamber," in which principal sacred statue is placed, the image of temple architecture for Indian people had always been of "mountains and caves."

Sun Temples in India

The Vedic scriptures of the Hindu religion refer to the sun as the store house of inexhaustible power and radiance. The sun god is referred to as Surya or Aditya. The Vedas are full of hymns describing the celestial body as the source and sustainer of all life on earth. The origin of the worship of the Sun in India is thus several centuries old.

References to sun worship are found in the puranas. The Ramayana speaks of Sage Agastya initiating Rama into sun worship through the Aditya Hridaya Mantra. The astronomer and astrologer Varahamirhira makes references to the intricacies of ceremonies connected with the installation of the icon of the Sun. It is also said that Iran was once a centre of Solar worship and that some of the Magha priests of Iran had been brought to India to officiate in ceremonies.

There are several temples enshrining the Sun God as the principal deity. Several temples dedicated to Shiva, feature a small shrine for Surya the Sun God. In addition, it is believed that Surya, the Sun God has offered worship at several of the shrines in Tamil Nadu; many of these shrines have been designed in such a way that the sun's rays illuminate the sanctum (of Shiva) on certain days of the year. Several of the South Indian Temple Tanks also bear the name Surya Theertham or Surya Pushkarini.

This article takes readers on a journey through seven temples dedicated primarily to Surya, Dakshinaarka Temple in the Gangetic Plains, Suryanaar Koyil in South India, Arasavilli and Konark on the East Coast of India, Modhera in Gujarat (Western India), Surya Pahar in North Eastern India and Unao in Central India. It should be mentioned here that remains of an ancient Sun temple are found at Martanda near Srinagar in Kashmir. It is said to date back to the first century AD. Ruins of a sun temple which attracted thousands of visitors in the 7th century AD are found in Multan in Pakistan.

As with all other temples in India, legends and beliefs are associated with each of the above temples. It is interesting to note that one of the beliefs shared by worshippers at these temples situated so far apart-is that visits to these temples followed by a dip in the sacred tanks associated with them would bring relief to believers ailing from blindness, leprosy and other skin diseases.

The Dakshinaarka Temple at Gaya, Bihar: There is an ancient Sun temple at Gaya in the state of Bihar. Offerings to the ancestors are made at the Surya Kunda or the Dakshina Maanas tank in front of the temple. Sun worship apparently was very popular in the Magadha region which included Gaya. Numerous old images of the Sun God Aditya are found in the Gaya region and there are still quite a number of sun worshippers in Gaya. It is said that they may have descended from the fire worshippers of Central Asia. In fact, the granite image of Aditya (this particular image here is also referred to as Dakshinaarka) or the Sun God worshipped here is portrayed as wearing a jacket, a waist girdle and high boots in the Iranian tradition. Hundreds of people visit this temple on Sundays.

Sun worship in the Magadha region that encompassed Gaya has been mentioned in the Puranas and thus this temple is said to be of very ancient origin. The current structure dates back to the 13th century, where the South Indian emperor Prataparudra of Warangal in Andhra Pradesh is said to have built it.

The Sun Temple at Gaya faces east and is located close to the famous Vishnupaada temple where a footprint of Vishnu is said to be enshrined. To the east of the temple is the tank Surya Kunda. The temple is a simple and plain one, with a dome over it. The comparatively larger sabha mandapa stands in front of the sanctum. Massive pillars line the mandapa where there are graceful stone sculptures of Shiva, Brahma, Vishnu, Surya and Durga.

There are two other notable Sun temples at Gaya, namely the Uttaraka temple near the Uttara Maanas tank and the Gayaditya temple on the river Falgu.

The Brahmanya Dev Temple at Unao in Madhya Pradesh: The Brahmanya Dev (Baramaju) temple dedicated to the Sun is located at Unao near Jhansi in Madhya Pradesh. It is a well visited temple. Local belief is that worshippers find relief from ailments such as blindness and leprosy and other skin diseases. The stone image of the Sun God stands here on a brick platform covered with black plates. Twenty one triangles representing the 21 phases of the sun are engraved in the shrine. There is a protective brass cover for the image. Sunday is the special day of worship. This temple was patronised by the Peshwas and by the ruler of Datia, a nearby town.

Sun Temple at Surya Pahar in Assam: This relatively modern Sun temple in the vicinity of the Surya Pahar Hill near Goalpara in Assam. This temple enshrines a circular stone tablet having 12 images of Aditya in a circle with an image of Kashyapa the father of Aditya in the centre. Surya is said to be the son of Aditi and Kashyapa (Prajapati or the creator of beings). Each of the Adityas os one faced and two armed. According to the Puranas the Adityas are 12 in number. The text Kalika Purana mentions Surya mountain, the perpetual abode of the sun. Sun worship was present in early Assam. Surya Pahad is referred to as a virtual gallery of archeological remains. At the foot of the hill, covering a vast area there are found a good number of Shiva lingams cut out of stone. In addition, Surya Pahar ruins contain many rock cut figures of artistic merit.

Suryanaar Temple near Kumbhakonam in Tamil Nadu: This ancient temple dedicated to the Sun is located near Kumbhakonam in Tamil Nadu. Kumbhakonam and its surroundings abound in huge temples. This well known temple enshrines the Sun-Surya, Kasi Viswanatha and Visalakshi, and the other eight celestial bodies namely Chandran, Angarakan, Budhan, Brihaspati, Sukran, Saniswaran, Rahu and Ketu. An elaborate worship protocol is prescribed for pilgrims visiting here, starting with worship at the shrine of Ganesha, culminating in circumambulating the temple nine times. This temple built in the Dravidian style is over eight hundred years old and was patronised by the Imperial Chola Kings. This temple is located in close proximity to Kanjanur, and Tirumangalakkudi housing 1200 year old temples to Shiva. Suryanaar Koyil has acquired a lot of popularity in recent times, and is one of the pivotal points in the Navagaraha Stala Tour organised by the Tamil Nadu Tourist Development Corporation.

Suryanarayanaswamy Temple at Arasavilli in Andhra Pradesh: This is a shrine of the Sun in a well preserved state.

The temple dates back to the 7th century and a Kalinga king is said to have constructed it. The image of worship is a 5 ft. tall one of black granite holding lotus buds-flanked by Usha and Chhaya. Padmapani is the name of this Sun God-Padma stands for wisdom usha and chhaya stand for eternity. This shrine is located near Srikakulam in Andhra Pradesh.

The Sun Temple at Modhera, Gujarat: The Sun Temple at *Modhera* dates back to early 11th century CE and was built by King *Bhimdev I* in 1026 CE. It was during the same period that the Jain temples at Mount Abu were constructed by Vimal Shah. The *Rudra Mahal temple at Siddhapur* also dates back to this period. Also reconstructed at the same time was the Somnath temple at Somnath Patan. Interestingly, the grand Brihadeeswarar temple at Thanjavur in South India was constructed during the same time.

Even in its ruined state, the sun temple at *Modhera* is magnificent.. There is no worship offered here now. There is no *shikhara* either. The temple has a sanctum, a pradakshina patha and a sabha mandap in front.

The exterior of the sanctum has many carved images of the Sun God, portrayed as wearing a belt and long shoes as in the Dakshinaarka temple at Gaya.

The mandapa in front of the sanctum has beautifully carved pillars with exquisite tronas adorning the entrances. The exterior of this temple is intricately carved. This temple has been designed such that the sun's rays illuminate the sanctum at dawn, during the time of the equinoxes.

In front of the temple is a colossal tank, which was once known as *Surya Kund or Rama Kund*. The tank has a series of carved steps leading to the bottom. Several miniature shrines adorn the steps of the tank-which is an art gallery in itself.

Modhera is now the site of several dance and cultural festivals. The sun temple and the ambience here provide a majestic backdrop for the exhibition of performing arts.

The imposing Sun Temple stands in the middle of a large compound, in the small town of Modhera. This temple was constructed at a time when the cult of Sun worship held its sway in many parts of India in the early medieval period. Various Hindu rulers, in their acts of obeisance, erected magnificent structures like the huge and elegant Sun Temple at Konark in Orissa, the Suraj Kund temple near Delhi, the Sun Temple at Modhera, etc. Raja Bhimdev I built the Sun Temple at Modhera in AD 1026. The Raja belonged to the Solanki dynasty, which was considered Suryavanshi or descendents of the Sun God.

The Sun Temple at Modhera is divided into three main sections. The first is the Surya Kund (Sun tank), a fascinating massive rectangular stepped tank located in front of the toran that leads one to the temple. Though the kund now stands dry, it was believed to be full of nirmal jal (holy water) in the days gone by. Devotees on their way to offer prayers to the Sun God stopped here for ceremonial ablutions and would proceed for worship towards the temple only after cleansing themselves here. Small, miniature shrines dot the steps around this kund. There are 108 of them to coincide with the number considered auspicious by the Hindus. Besides these, there are four larger shrines dedicated to Lord Vishnu (one of the principle gods in the Hindu pantheon), Ganesha (the God of knowledge and prosperity and son of Lord Shiva), Natraja (Lord Shiva as the cosmic dancer) and Sitala Mata (the goddess of the dreaded disease-smallpox).

Leading to the temple from the tank is a huge ornamental gate or toran. From the toran one reaches the sabha mandap (hall of gathering), which is a magnificent pillared hall. This hall was meant for religious gatherings and conferences. This unique piece of architecture is open on all sides, with four doorways and 52 spectacular pillars supporting the walnut-shaped ceiling. Each of these pillars is intricately carved, with every inch of available space depicting scenes from the Ramayana (a Hindu epic), the Mahabharat (a Hindu epic) and the Krishna Lila (the story of Lord Krishna).

The architectural plan of this temple follows the tradition of the time, which was having twin halls. So, while the sabha mandap was meant for religious congregations, the main temple or the guda mandap was built to house the sanctum sanatorium.

The guda mandap forms the third section of the Sun Temple at Modhera and is not attached to the sabha mandap. The guda mandap is based on a lotus-base plinth. It has friezes of the Sun God, other gods and goddesses covering its walls. Besides the depiction of various deities, one can also see on the walls, various aspects of human life like the cycle of birth and death and some erotic scenes from the Kama Sutra or the ancient Indian treatise on love.

The sanctum sanatorium, once housed the magnificent idol of the Sun God. The guda mandap has been so designed that on solar equinoxes, *i.e.* on March 21 and September 23, the first rays of the rising sun fall directly on and light up the niche where the idol of the Surya Bhagwan (Sun God) sits. It is said that the guda mandap had a tunnel, which could be used by the members of the royal family to flee, in case of an attack. Though the roof over the Garbhagriha of this hall has collapsed, the ruined shell gives an idea of the dimensions of the structure.

The Sun Temple was built by Bhimadeva of the Solanki Rajput clan. The building work was commissioned to the Silvat stone masons who had the ability to make to make the hardest stone take on the quality of the delicate wood carvings. The Sun Temple has a rectangular step tank or Surya Kund with about 108 shrines. Larger shrines to vishnu, Ganesha and the Natraja incarnation of Shiva in tandav stand on three sides of the Surya Kund, with the Sabha Mandap of the principal temple soaring on the fourth side with 52 pillars carved in intricate detail depicting tales from Ramayana and Mahabharata.

The outer facades have a string of friezes and above that is the mandovara with excellent carvings of gods and goddesses. Between the Sabha Mandapa and the sanctum sanatorium is a hall with pillars and arches and the walls have 12 niches showing the different aspects of the Sun God in each month. The outer walls are filled with sculptures of Surya and other gods. In another part of the temple you can see a whole Kama Sutra of traditional erotic sculptures in a style that of Khajuraho and Konark. Unlike Konark which rests on 12 wheels of a chariot, Modhera has built on the petals of a lotus which runs the whole length of the temple.

As in the Sun Temple at Konark, this temple was so designed that the rays of the Sun would fall on the image of Surya at the time of the equinox. Whatever remains of this temple is grand; the shikharas are notably absent but the Tronas in the frontal halls, and the intricate carvings in the exterior speak of the splendour of this shrine, which still is home to the Modhera dance festival featuring dance celebrities in performance in a natural setting. Ruins of the sun temple at Modhera in Gujarat show a lot of Magha influence. The walls of the temple have representations of the sun god wearing a peculiar West Asian belt and boots as in the Sun temple at Gaya. Mention must also be made of the huge tank in front of the temple with its multitude of images. Destroyed by the Mahmud of Ghazni, the Modhera still retains enough of its structure to convey the grandeur of its conception. Every inch of the edifice, both inside and outside, is magnificently carved with Gods and Goddesses, birds and beasts and flowers. The inner sanctum, which housed the presiding deity, faces east and was so designed that the solar equinoxes the first rays of the rising sun lit up the image of Surya.

The Sun Temple at Konark, Orissa: The grandest and best known of all Sun temples in India is the Konark temple in Orissa. This dates back to the 13th century and it represent the highest point in Orissan temple architecture. Konark is situated 20 miles to the north east of Puri. The word Konark means corner sun.

The black pagoda at Konark is a grand and magnificent temple in the form of the suns chariot drawn by seven horses marking the 7 days of the week. The 24 huge wheels, magnificently carved and decorated, mark the hours of the day. This temple was envisioned by the Ganga ruler Narashimha Deva and it was not fully completed. The main idol of the Sun God on which the suns rays fall in the morning is said to have been removed by some Portuguese navigators. The temple now comprises only of the sabhamandap and the natamandir. The main temple crumbled down many years ago.

The Sun Temple at Konark is a World Heritage Site. Konark was once a bustling port at the time of the erstwhile kingdom of Kalinga (as the present day Orissa was known in the old days) and had good maritime trade relations with Southeast Asian countries. King Narashimhadeo (AD 1238-64) was the chief patron of the Konark Sun Temple. He wanted to build a shrine dedicated to the Sun God.

The Orissa temples consist of a sanctum, one or more front porches (Jag Mandir) with pyramidal roofs, a dance hall (Nat Mandir), and a hall of offerings (Bhog Mandir) apart from the inner shrine (Garbhagriha) where the deity resides. The Deul (main temple), Jagmandir and Nat Mandir of the Sun Temple are covered with beautiful sculptural friezes and carvings.

The grandiose Sun Temple complex conceptualised by Narasimhadeo was never finished, and the inner sanctuary had to be filled up to sustain the heavy crumbling roof in the 19th century. Konark chiefly consists of the chariot called 'the Black Pagoda' by the British, and its lofty ceremonial hall. The great cube of masonry forming the temple basement is ornamented with the amazing freestanding stone wheels. The lowest zone of this base has continuous elephant and hunting friezes (carved stone panels), among which one finds intriguing mythological beasts like the Gaja-Singha, a lion riding an elephant. A series of niches separated by widely projecting pilasters are full of superb erotic sculpture. Two carved friezes with stringcourses divide the facades of the hall. The pyramidal roof which rises above this consists of corbelled vaulting with a pleasantly wavy curvilinear effect. Three distinct terraces recede to the huge stone lotus atop the shikhara.

The monumental statues of women musicians lining the roof terraces visible from a distance draw the eye to the superbly polished green chlorite relief of the Sun god standing in a frontal pose between his twin charioteers and the dawn maidens. The horses carved on the plinth too have that vibrant sense of motion, which distinguishes the Konark sculpture.

Sun temple has been declared a world heritage site by UNESCO. The Konark temple is widely known not only for its architectural grandeur but also for the intricacy and profusion of sculptural work.

The Nata Mandir in front of the Jagamohana is also intricately carved. Around the base of the temple and up the walls and roof, are carvings in the erotic style. There are images of animals, foliage, men, warriors on horses and other interesting patterns. There are three images of the Sun God, positioned to catch the rays of the sun at dawn, noon and sunset.

Konark derives its name from Konarka, the presiding deity of the Sun Temple. Konarka is actually a combination of two words, Kona (corner) and Arka (sun), which, when combined, means the sun of the corner. Konark was one of the earliest centres of Sun worshipping in India. The place finds mention in the Puranas as Mundira or Mundirasvamin, a name that was subsequently replaced by Konaditya or Konarka. Apart from the Puranas, other religious texts also point towards the existence of a sun temple at Konark long before the present temple.

Konark was once a bustling port of Kalinga and had good maritime trade relations with Southeast Asian countries. The present Sun Temple was probably built King Narashimhadev I (AD 1238-64) of the Ganga dynasty to celebrate his victory over the Muslims. The temple fell into disuse in the early 17th century after it was desecrated by an envoy of the Mughal emperor Jahangir.

However, legend has it that the temple was constructed by Samba, the son of Lord Krishna. It is said that Samba was afflicted by leprosy, brought about by his father's curse on him. After 12 years of penance, he was cured by Surya, the Sun God, in whose honour he built this temple.

The massive structure of the temple, now in ruins, sits in solitary splendour surrounded by the drifting sands. The entire temple has been designed in the shape of a chariot carrying the Sun God across the heavens. The huge intricate wheels of the chariot, which are carved around the base of the temple, are the major attractions of the temple. The spokes of these wheels serve as sundials and the shadows formed by these can give the precise time of the day. The pyramidal roof of the temple, made of sandstone, soars over 30 m in height. Like the temples at Khajuraho, the Sun Temple at Konark is also covered with erotic sculptures.

The Temple Chariot of the Sun God: Standing imperiously in its compound of lawns and casuarina trees, 35 km north of Puri on the coast road, this majestic pile of oxidising sandstone is considered to be the apogee of Orissan architecture and one of the finest religious buildings anywhere in the world. The temple is all the more remarkable for having languished under a huge mound of sand since it fell into neglect three hundred or so years ago. A team of seven galloping horses and twenty-four exquisitely carved wheels found lining the flanks of a raised platform showed that the temple had been conceived in the form of a colossal chariot for the sun god Surya, its presiding deity.

Lady Drummer of Sun Temple: The temple is a brilliant chronicle in stone, with thousands of images including deities, the Surasundaris, heavenly damsels and human musicians, lovers, dancers and different scenes from courtly life.

Maituna-Sun Temple: Equally as sensational was the rediscovery among the ruins of some extraordinary erotic sculpture. Konark is plastered with loving couples locked in ingenious amatory postures drawn from the Kama Sutra-a feature that may well explain the comment made by one of great poet of Mughal Dynasty, Abdul Fazl, in the sixteenth century: "Even those who are difficult to please," he enthused," stand astonished at its sight."

Sacred Pond: A stone's throw away from Konark beach lies the sacred pond where Samba was cured of leprosy-the miracle that allegedly inspired the founding of the sun temple. For a couple of days every year during the full or "white" moon phase of Magha (Jan/Feb), Chandrabhaga is also the site of a big religious festival, the Magha Saptami Mela.

The Chandrabhaga Mela or Magha Saptami mela in the month of February is a grand religious festival. Thousands of pilgrims converge on the pool on this day to take a holy dip in its curative waters and then shuffle off to the beach where in accordance with an age-old custom mentioned in the puranas, they watch the sun rise over the sea. The event is followed by the puja of the Navagraha.

Konark Dance Festival: A dance festival is held in an open-air theatre built near the Sun Temple every year in the month of December. Known as the Konark dance festival the event brings together eminent classical dancers of India who perform various dance forms like Odissi, Bharatnatyam, Manipuri, Kathak and Chhow. The classical extravaganza is a journey through ecstasy and a visit to Konark during this time offers you with a combination of art, craft, fun and frolic.

Magha Saptami (Sun Festival) is held at Konark on the seventh day (saptami) of the bright half of the month of Magha (January/February). During this festival the pilgrims bathe in the sea before sunrise and then proceed to the temple to worship.

Shatrunjaya: The Temple City

Angkor Wat, Cambodia: 12th century from "Angkor Vat, Description Graphique du Temple" by Guy Nafilyan, 1969, Ecole Francaise Extreme Orient. Though this is a plan of inside of the 2nd cloisters, there is a larger 1st cloisters. As the temple is modelled on Mt. Meru, the central part is separated from the 2nd cloisters and on the height of 13 metres. So the space of central shrine is connected with the 3rd cloisters only. Although the plan is a type of "Panchayatana," it is not "Mandapa" (hall) but linear corridor that connects five shrines. That is the biggest difference from Jain Temples. PLAN 3 shows the premises inside the 2nd cloisters of Angkor Wat, and outside this plan there are the 1st cloisters. The scale of the 2nd cloisters is about 5.4 m. x 3.6 m, and the composition has so much in common with the Jain ideal plan. And we get to know the central shrine of Angkor Wat is also four-faced type. That is, in making a plan of large-scale temple spreading to its four directions, it invariably requires that the central shrine is the chaturmukha type. A piece of architecture that mediates the chaturmukha of Jain temple and Angkor Wat is Somapura Mahavihara, a Buddhist temple built during the 8th to the 9th centuries, which still remains as a ruin in Paharpur in

Bangladesh. It is a temple that soars in the centre of vast precincts with some 5.4 m. × 5.4 m. This temple is clearly a four-faced shrine. Perhaps Buddhists had started to make "Chaturmukha" images influenced by Jain customs. The oldest one that belongs to the 7th century was excavated in Bodh Gaya, a holy place for Buddhists.

In Nepal, however, it is considered to have been made much earlier. It seems that originally there used to be a Jain temple in Paharpur. Thus through the temple of Paharpur, which was the only example among Buddhist temples in India that had a plan of chaturmukha type, this planning method was introduced to South East Asia. It evolved finally into the plans of Mandala-like large temples in Khamer and Java. Samvarana Roof of western mandapa Although Hindu temples in India did not develop chaturmuka type, tomb architecture in the Mughal Dynasty of the Islamic era often employed this method. Islamic architecture in India has its origin in Persia, and for garden design too, Persian form such as "Chahar Bagh" (Quartered Garden) was introduced into India. Humayun's Tomb in Delhi is situated at the centre of a large-scale Chahar Bagh, and naturally takes Chaturumukha form.

Originally in Persian gardens, however, buildings surround a garden, not the contrary. The method of setting four-faced building in the centre of Chahar Bagh is an application of Indian chaturmukha form to Islamic architecture. That is, they changed the Persian system of four 'Iwans' (half exterior space behind a large opening of pointed arch bordered by square (Rama) that were opposite to each other around a courtyard into a structure of four 'Iwans' that were combined back to back with each other, turning it into an extroverted four faced shrine form. In this context, we realise that the chaturmuka type created by Jinas played an important role within Greater India.

There are a lot of examples of chaturmukha type, but considering the richness of space produced by the plan of four-faced shrine, the temple at Ranakpur seems second to none. For instance, although the premises of Angkor Wat (PLAN 3) spread in a wide area, it is only the 3rd cloisters and central shrine that have a connection of space, since the 1st and 2nd cloisters are separated from the central part. Even though each part of Pancha-yatana (five shrines composition) is linked together, making a continuous structure like that of the temple at Ranakpur, it lacks the concept of large mandapa covered by domical ceiling, and five shrines are merely connected with straight corridors. It is same with the Mughal tombs, which also lacked attractive interior space. (In spite of belonging to Islamic architecture, they became 'Sculptural Architecture' owing to Indianisation.)

Then, why was it especially Jainas who developed chaturmukha (four faced open) type shrines? As it is impossible to come up with a complete answer to this kind of question, there is no way but to set up a hypothesis in accordance with its religious doctrine. The hypothesis is based on Jain logic. In a word, it is "Syadvada" or relativism. Contrary to many other religions, Jainism avoids dogmatism and eliminated self-righteous statements like "This is the very truth." Everything has many aspects, and each religion, doctrine, and statement has a certain sense of truth. Therefore, unilateral or absolute judgment about a matter has to be avoided. In making a decision, one should consider that it is right "in the context of certain viewpoint" (syad). It is called "Syadvada." This concept seems quite modern when we look back on the history in which a lot of religions insisted on the validity of their own gods and views of the world, which sometimes resulted in wars. Although there had been a lot of religious conflicts in India in the past and that still continues, Jainas have never committed to military conflict.

If every religion took this viewpoint of Jainism, how peaceful the world would become. I would imagine that this relativism was a driving force to develop chaturmukha (four faced) images and chaturmukha type of Jain temples. Never assuming one absolute God (Jainism is an atheistic religion), the attitude of regarding even the 24 saviours of Tirthankaras (Jinas) as existence that can be seen from multilateral viewpoints made it possible to create chaturmukha images in which 4 statues are placed back to back with each other, and to develop an architectural style of chaturmukha shrine. Chaturmukha image of Tirthankara. Basically, I had a strange impression in that

Jainas had assumed as many as 24 Tirthankaras (Jinas). Is it not enough to have only one founder like Christianity and Buddhism? Maybe it was in order to avoid a personality cult to Mahavira and deny the absolute being that Jainas presumed 23 Tirthankaras before Mahavira and provided them with equal values. Being born and developed in India, Jainism has a custom of idol worship.

Unlike idols of Christianity, Buddhism and others, however, statues of Jain Tirthankaras do not reveal distinctive personality. As all statues have similar postures of either standing or sitting, it is difficult to find any difference among them. They would hardly become study objects of art history as sculptural works. To put it extremely, they seem to be nothing but a kind of sign. What is worshipped there is not a personified or divine God such as Christ or Shiva, but the order of the world and various truths of the universe that are expressed in the signs.

In this respect, Jainism suddenly unveils its similarity with Islam. They look quite contrary to each other in terms of style, since Islam is a religion of absolute monotheism. Still, the absolute God can be interpreted not as personified existence, but as the order of the universe itself. Likewise, although idolatry is strictly prohibited in Islam, if we regard statues of Jain Tirthankaras as only signs, the worship of these two religions seem quite the same after all. They both deny the class system; in Islam, "every man is equal" under the God whilst in Jainism, "every living being is equal" under the law of transmigration. Base of a marble pillar and Image of Parshvanatha Because of the denial of idolatry, painting and sculpture have not developed enough in Islam. Instead, their creative energy in plastic arts has concentrated on architecture.

In Jainism, since they have not provided idols with personified expression or narrative character, Jainas have exerted most power into architecture. Similar to Islamic arabesque, Jainas devoted engraving work into carving ornaments of architectural elements. Perhaps it could be the reason that art historians have not evaluated highly on Jain or Islamic arts, while an architect like me has been deeply moved by their architecture. To name another example similar to this case, it would be Cistercian monasteries in Europe.

Having an antipathy against the gorgeousness of Benedictine abbeys, Cistercians strived to eliminate ostentation in paintings and sculptures. Therefore, they dedicated themselves to the exploration of architectural composition and the beauty of space. Because of this attitude, they created such monastic architecture as Fontenay in Burgundy and Le Thoronet in Provence, which deeply touch the hearts of architects, contrary to the evaluation by art historians. Jain architecture, especially the Adinatha temple at Ranakpur, should be valued in this context.

Modern Jain Temples: After Jain architecture attained its peak in the temple of Ranakpur, the development of traditional style of Indian architecture came to an end and has continued to decline since then. The time had shifted to Islamic architecture having come from abroad. Except for South India, even architecture of Hindu dynasties that had kept independence got a strong influence from Islam. In the 18th century, much of the country became a colony of the British Empire. As the fear of temple destruction gradually disappeared, Jainas started to build temples in big cities. A temple that represents this movement was built in Ahmadabad by Sheth Hathisingh, a rich merchant in the city. This temple shows the influence of Islamic architecture by employing a lot of multifoil arches. It also revives "Solanki Style" of medieval period, and traditional techniques of stone sculpture are nicely applied.

But in terms of plan, chaturmukha form, which saw the completion at Ranakpur is abandoned and the style regressed to [garbhagriha + mandapa], which had been used before the temples at Mt. Abu. Shitalanatha temple in Calcutta In Calcutta, there is the Shitalanatha temple that was also built in the same period. This temple is conspicuous in the city that had been developed during the rule of the British Empire. However, the style of the temple which looks like a combination of modern Shikhara type temple, Mughal palace and Italian Baroque style does not have the grandeur that the Adinatha temple at Ranakpur used to have. It is uncertain how Jainism will continue to exist in the future, but I privately hold an expectation that a contemporary architect like Uttam C. Jain would create a new style of Jain temple based on chaturmukha form.

Temples of Somnath : Somnath is also known by several other names—Deo pattan, Prabhas Pattan or Pattan Somnath—which it acquired during its long and eventful history. Somnath was once the most revered shrine in the country, for it had one of the twelve pre-eminent Jyotirlingas (the glowing Lingas) which held a special significance for the Hindus. Somnath's glory and fame are legendary. It is said that people from the remotest parts of the country came to worship at the shrine; revenues collected from ten thousand villages was spent on the maintenance of the temple. Two thousand Brahmins (priests) served the idol and a golden chain attached to a huge bell plate announced the commencement of prayers.

Somnath rose and fell many a time and the amazing drama of the iconoclast's zeal for its desecration and the devout Hindu's passionate desire for its restoration continued till the 15th century, when the Hindus finally gave up in sheer despair and built a new temple nearby. The present site of Somnath is a pile of ruins and little is known of the early history of this place. It is believed to have been erected by the Vallabhi Kings in about 480-767 A.D. The temple is dedicated to Someshwara, the Lord Shiva with moon in his head.

The destruction brought upon this temple by Muhammad of Ghazni in 1025 A.D. is an important event in Indian history. In his blind fury, not only did he despoil an object of beauty but tore up the pages of history, which Somnath bore on its walls. It is said that the temple was supported by pillars which bore the names of its sculptors; this information has been lost to history forever. In its external design the Somnath temple compares well with the temple of Rudramala at Siddhapur and is more or less of the same size in length. The dome, however, is as large as any other built in this period.

The temple faces to east and once had an enormous central hall with three entrances, each protected by a lofty porch. The fragments that lie scattered at a short distance from the site give some idea of the sculpture decorating the temple. The richly carved doorways, the sculptured representations of Nandi, Shiva's bull, and the figures of goddesses and their female attendants must once have presented a grand ensemble of great beauty. In the recesses of the balconied corridor, there is a mutilated form of Nataraja, the dancing Shiva. Although essentially a Brahmanical temple, the influence of Jain architecture is clearly discernible. The Kathiawar style of temple architecture in the 11th century was so widespread that instances of it can be found in Rajasthan too. There is a group of five badly damaged temples at Kiradu in the Mallani district of Marwar, each of which displays many characteristics of the Solanki style of building. Certain Gupta influences are also apparent, obviously arising from their proximity to Gupta territory. Of these five temples, the one dedicated to Lord Vishnu is probably the oldest, but the best preserved is the elegant shrine of Someshwara. The skeleton of a magnificent pillared hall still bears testimony to the intense devotion with which these deserted structures must once have been built. The square shafts of the richly wrought pillars end in the foliage motif so characteristic of Gupta decorative art, and above this is a circular disc and capital, consisting of four brackets.

The ruins of the Rudramala temple at Siddhapur on the banks of the Saraswati river testify to the ornated grandeur that the Solanki style had achieved when it was nearing its decline in the 12th century A.D. Clearly, this temple must have been one of the biggest and most lavishly decorated structures of its time.

Soon after independence (in 1947), India's first president Rajendra Prasad commissioned the restoration of the Somnath temple remarking—"The Somnath Temple signifies that the power of reconstruction is always greater than the power of destruction." It was completed in 1995 and the then President of India rededicated the services of the great Somnath temple, restored for the seventh time on the original location to the people of India.

Today, it can be visited in the State of Gujarat by pilgrims and students of history.

Temples of Kashmir : During the reign of the great king Lalitaditya, who ascended to the throne in 724 A.D., temples constructed using stone masonry sprang up in large numbers all over Kashmir. This building activity continued with the wave of religious emotion which swept over India about the same time, and resulted in a fever of temple building – Lalitaditya's triumphs in the realm of territorial expansion created a cultural climate, of which grandeur was an important ideal. The monumental Buddhist shrine at Parihasapura, now a mass of sculptured stones, and the temple of the Sun at Martand show this quality, not only in their stupendous size but also by the bold confidence with which they were built. The Martand temple has been often called "the materialized-spirit of a transcendent vision".

Built on a plateau encircled by a range of eternal stones this temple represents an architectural expressiveness of the highest order, and forms the supreme model of a style to which a great number of later temples are subscribed. Instead of the Buddhist assembly hall, where congregational worship was held, the central structure here is a sanctuary for the divine symbol. This perhaps signifies a departure from the Buddhist influence and the acceptance of the Brahmanical creed by the people. The shrine stands within a big courtyard surrounded by a pillared arcade and a series of cells. Certain features in the surface decoration of the Martand temple are of unique interest. The regularly spaced medallions, the frequent use of pilasters (cantilevers), and the pediment motif, all recall the architecture of the antique classical west (see also: the parts of a temple). The capitals of the pillars that support cornices have something Doric about them, and their moulded bases are of attic type. The encircling colonnade is also reminiscent of the Greek style.

However, experts are of the view that these influences are not deep-rooted and that the main composition is of indigenous inspiration, the product of the genius of Kashmir. The mural sculpture on the walls displays unmistakably the influence of the art movement fostered by the Pala rulers of Bengal, which was apparently of such intensity that it made itself felt in regions far beyond its geographical boundaries. As further evidence of the source of this influence, Percy Brown points out that the copper gilt image of the Sun-God installed in the cellar of the Martand temple must have been wrought in the very same foundry where expert Pala metalworkers shaped that of the famous copper image of the Buddha discovered at Sultanganj in Bengal (presently housed in the Birmingharn Art Gallery).

Avantivarman, who ascended to the throne of Kashmir in the latter half of the 9th century ushered in another memorable era of architecture. He built a group of temples at Avantipur, a township eighteen miles from Srinagar, among which that of Avantiswami, dedicated to Vishnu, still survives in part. It has been said that whereas the Martand temple is the expression of a "sudden glory", the Avantiswami temple shows greater maturity of experience and has therefore more sophistication and elegance. Graceful colonnades of pillars form an arcaded portico around the shrine and a monolithic pillar before the entrance bears a metal figure of Garuda, the king of birds and vehicle of Lord Vishnu.

Motifs borrowed from many sources, both foreign and indigenous, appear in the decorative carving, but these have been tastefully integrated into an ordered system with a recognizable unity. Designs reminiscent of Buddhist stone carvers of the Ashokan age and of the craftsmen of the Pala school are frequent, and symbols traceable to Byzantium, ancient Persia and Syria are also found. The conspicuously angular aspect of this temple is derived from the wooden houses of the valley where accumulation of heavy snow on roofs is prevented by their sloping character.

Two Shiva temples built at Pattan in the 10th century A.D., during the reign of Shankaravarman reveal that although the traditional mode established at Martand was still being followed two centuries later, the masonry tended to become more monolithic. The precision and skill with which the moldings are chiselled out of a huge stone is truly amazing.

Built in the 12th century A.D., the small, well preserved temple at Pandrethan, near Srinagar, gives a clear idea of the general plan of the temples in Kashmir at this time. The pyramidal structure of the roof, which is still intact, is a prominent characteristic of this style. The ceiling consists of beams laid on the angles, a technique obviously derived from wooden constructions. Wherever a tank is provided for ablutions, materials such as rock, brick, or stone are used for the construction of the tank. Two temples at Kiragram or Baijnath in the Kangra valley, one dedicated to Shiva and the other to Jamadagni, are notable examples of Himalayan architecture of the early 13th century. Chamba, Kumaon and Kulu also have numerous temples of the same type. The famous Doongri temple, dedicated to Hirimba in Manali in the Kulu valley, is constructed of wood, and is a striking example.

Temples of Gujarat: The temples built in western India between Muhammad Ghana's expedition to Somnath in Kathiawar in 1025-26 A.D., and the conquest of this part of the country by the Sultans of Delhi in 1298 A.D., represent one of the richest and most prolific developments of the Indo-Aryan style of architecture. The havoc and destruction caused by Muhammad Ghazni's raid, however, did not last long, for the Solanki rulers were a stable and powerful dynasty who lost no time or energy in repairing the damage. Contrary to what one might expect Ghazni's campaign of desecration seems to have given an added impetus to temple building in the peaceful period that followed. The great prosperity of the Solanki rulers was due largely to the geographical position of Gujarat which was then the focus of commerce. This was another factor which shaped the religious architecture of this region, for there is about it a lavishness which speaks of both material and emotional wealth.

But, at last however, a number of these temples were despoiled by the Muslim conquerors who dismembered them to provide material for their mosques. To complete the damage, a devastating earthquake with its epicenter in Kathiawar occurred at the beginning of the 19th century, so that a large number of temples were reduced to crumbling ruins and shapeless masses of masonry. The architectural plan of the typical Solanki temple consists of three horizontal sections, the *peetha* or basement, the rnandovara or wall-face up to the cornice, and the shikhara or spire.

The pillar is carved with motifs which are arranged in an order fixed by convention. The *garaspati* or horned rakshasas are the lowest; then come the *gajapatis* or elephant fronts, followed by ashva-thara or horses, and narathara or human forms. The mandovara is reserved exclusively for figure sculpture. The *shikhara* is distinctive, for it consists of a group of turrets or urusringas surrounding a larger central structure. The interiors of these temples are markedly peristylar, and richly carved pillars are arranged so as to form halls and aisles. The inner walls of the halls, unlike those in the Orissan temples, are profusely carved. About fifteen miles from Patan, the ancient capital of the Solankis in Gujarat, are four small temples at Sunak, Karyoda, Delmal and Kesara, all built in the 10th century and therefore the earliest examples of the Solanki style. The Surya temple at Modhera, now in ruins, was built in the same style a century later, when it had found its supreme expression.

The architectural plan resolves itself into a suttamandapa or Pillared hall, connected by a narrow passage to the gudh-mandapa or assembly hall and the garbhagriha, both forming an enclosed rectangular building. The Modhera temple is famous for its fine display of proportions and the atmosphere of spiritual grace which it conveys. In the 11th century, similar temples were built in Rajasthan and Kathiawar also. At this time, Rajputana, like Gujarat, was the traditional home of merchant princes who spent fabulous sums to commemorate their religious faiths. Vimala Shah, the Minister of the first Solanki ruler, Bhimadeva I of Gujarat, built the first Jain temple at Dilwara.

It is one of a group of shrines, for the Jains believed high places to be sacred and generally built the temples where the holy hills could be their foundation. The temple, which is 98 feet long and 42 feet wide, is surrounded by a lofty wall door containing 52 cells, each of which contains the image of a Teerthankar. Most of these have now been replaced. These cells are screened by a double arcade of carved pillars. A pavilion facing the entrance-porch contains a procession of marble elephants, each hearing a statue of Vimala Shah and his family. Most of these figures have now disintegrated.

The temple consists of an open portico and a vestibule, both formed by a simple grouping of pillars. The octagonal dome of the shrine is formed by eleven concentric rings containing patterns of endless variety and is upheld by eight carved columns. A series of sixteen brackets, bearing images of the Goddess of knowledge, support the rings of the dome. The intricately carved reliefs illustrate incidents from Jain literature and legend, including *Satrunjaya-Mahatmya*. A notable feature of the decoration is the exuberance of detail and the effective repetition of the same motif. The temple is not so much an architectural achievement as a remarkable example of tireless inventiveness and caprice in sculptured decoration.

Vatsupala and his brother Tejpala, who belonged to the Porwad Jain community and became the Ministers of Vivadhavala, built another famous temple at Mt. Abu during their terms of office. Jain literature contains glowing accounts of their charity and military prowess, and it is believed that Anupama Devi, the wife of Tejpala, was responsible for the erection of the Abu temple. Built nearly two hundred years after the temple of Vimala Shah, the Tejpala temple at Mt. Abu follows more or less the same architectural plan as the former and is among the last monuments built in the Solanki style. In the matter of detail, however, the Tejpala temple is a natural from the Vimala Vasahi, it loses in creative vigour but it amply compensates in artistic refinement and mechanical perfection.

The striking feature of the Tejpala temple is the pendant of the dome which, according to Ferguson, "hangs from the centre more like a luster of crystal drops than a solid mass of marble." The principal cell contains a colossal image of Neminatha with his conch-shell symbol on the seat. The florid reliefs and carvings on the porticoes of the 39 cells represent episodes from the life of the presiding deity. The series of Jain and Brahmanical structures at Ashalgarh near Mt. Abu and the Jain temples at Kumbharia in the neighbourhood belong to the same architectural complex. From the ritualistic point of view, however, the most complete example of a Jain temple is the Chaumukha temple at Ranapur in Jodhpur district. This is a rare instance where the architect is not anonymous. An inscription on a pillar states that Depaka, the builder of this temple, did so at the behest of "a devout worshipper of the Arhats," names Dharanaki in 1439 A.D.

The presiding deity of this temple is Rishabhadeva or Adinatha, a quadruple (chaumukh) image of whom is installed in the inner shrine which is open on all the four sides and stands in the centre of a lofty basement. Close to the angles of the rectangular courtyard are four subsidiary shrines, and eighty domes, supported by 400 columns, which surmount the entire structure. Surveyed from across the ascent, the temple has the appearance of a forest of pillars where the play of light and shade presents a fascinating spectacle.

The massive substructure of the wall which encircles the shrines in an unbroken circuit emphasises the fact that a desire for seclusion marks the devotional ceremonies of the Jains. The Navalakha temple at Ghumli and a group of the same name at Sejakpur are typical examples of contemporary architecture in Kathiawar. Palitana, located about thirty-five miles from Bhavnagar in Kathiawar, is perched on the famous Satrunjays hill, 1077 ft. above sea level.

It has been described as the "first of all places of pilgrims, the bridal hall of those who would win everlasting rest." For centuries shrines were added to this site by pious Jains who believed in the efficacy of temple-building as a means of spiritual salvation, thus making it a city of temples. The entire hill, which has two summits with a valley about 360 yards wide in between, is covered with temples grouped in separate enclosures called *tuks*, each having a principal temple and a number of smaller ones surrounding it. There are doors to the entrance of these tuks which are closed at sunset. In all, the hill is said to have eleven tuks, more than five hundred temples, big and small, and about seven thousand separate images.

The temples of the Jainson Satrunjaya hill are elaborate in detail and exquisite in their finish, although not so remarkable in their conception or in their sculptured figures.

The temple of Adinatha or Mulanayak Sri Rishabhnath, named after the first of the twenty-four Jain Teerthankars, is situated on the southern ridge. It was originally erected in 960 A.D. But was restored in 1530. It is an imposing two storied building with a lofty spire and a number of smaller shrined clusters around the base. The temple of Chaumukh or the four-faced is the largest in the Khartarvase tuk on the northern ridge. It was erected in 1618 A.D. by a rich banker of Ahmedabad named Devaraj.

Unlike the Hindu shrine which is dark and has only one entrance door, this structure has entrances from all the four sides to the antarala. There are about ten recesses which are meant for the images of Teerthankars. The pillars supporting the verandah are richly carved with flowered patterns, while the bracket capitals support musicians and dancing figures. The *Sinhasan*, or the pedestal on which the great quadruple image of Adinatha rests, is made of pure white marble. The shrine is said to have about a hundred and twenty images.

The third temple, small but unique in its arrangement, is found in the enclosure called Nandivaradwipa. Built in 1840, this structure is a square of about 32 feet with verandahs on all the sides. The interior is divided by piers into smaller squares and the arches between them support the domes of the roof. The five inner squares form a cross crowned by shikharas and have recesses for images. The five larger spires are believed to represent the five holy peaks-Satrunjaya, Ashtapada, on which Adinath, the first of the Teerthankars, attained *Moksha*, Merusihara, Sammeta-shikhara, and Samosan or Samavasarana. The Motisah tuk, named after the builder Seth Motsah Amichand, is a square with round towers at the corners and was built in 1836. It has some fifteen smaller shrines besides the main one which is dedicated to Adinatha. After Palitana the Girnar hill in the south of Kathiawar, which is about 3500 ft. above sea level, is next in importance to the Jains and is regarded as sacred to Neminath, the twenty-second Jain Teerthankar.

This site has been known from very ancient times, for a number of Ashoka's inscriptions, the earliest of them dating from 250 B.C., have been found at the foot of the hill. There are about fifteen groups of temples in Girnar among which the largest and the oldest is one dedicated to Neminatha. Little is known of the date of its construction but an inscription records that it was repaired in 1278 A.D. Subsequent restorations have changed its face so much that it is difficult to visualise its original appearance. Close to the entrance, there is an old triple temple dedicated to Mallinath, the 19th Teerthankar, and built by the famous Tejpala and Vastupala in 1230 A.D. On the way to Neminatha, there is a small but interesting temple known as Ambamata, which is visited by the newly married to ask for the blessing of the goddess for the continuance of wedded felicity.

Marikamba Temple of Sirsi : Goddess Marikamba's temple in the town of Sirsi is a splendid example of syncretic evolution of tribal and so called *brahminical* customs and rituals, befitting Hindu ethos.

Goddess Mari or Marika at Sirsi is especially worshipped as the presiding deity of all epidemics like small pox, plague, cholera and natural disasters like floods, famines and cyclones, which take toll of thousands. Through the centuries the frightened population offered sacrifices to appease this fierce and *blood thirsty* deity. Mar in Tamil and Kannada means change or concealing (*marpadu*). The goddess of hidden power (*maya*) became Amba (*mother*, Parwati, consort of Lord Shiva) to whom buffaloes, sheep, pigs, and poultry were offered as sacrifice to propitiate her. The deity slowly transformed into Mahishasu Ramardini (killer of buffalo demon), another epithet of Durga or Parwati.

Construction of Temple in India

Before we go any further, it will be worthwhile to examine the principles that guided the Hindu Temple architect and mason. How was there a proliferation of high-quality work in throughout the country? Was it a spontaneous expression of creative energy or were there some basic rules to follow, some essential unity underlying the apparent diversity? We shall examine briefly the social, religious, metaphysical and material factors that led to the production of Indian temples. Since the decline of the Gupta dynasty to the age of the Mughals, there was no central political authority through most of India. This political vacuum was filled by the priestly class, who gradually assumed power as the sole arbiters of almost every aspect of life-birth, death, puberty, marriage, business and personal.

All these 'favours', of course, had a price and those on whose behalf they 'generously' interceded with the gods would pay the priests by cash or in kind. Obviously the serious business of construction was too important to be overlooked either. While the basic concepts of construction and decoration had already been evolved, it was the Brahmins who began erecting a complex edifice of rules and layouts for different classes of building. These were purposely couched in hideously complicated mumbo-jumbo-the better to be well beyond the ken of the common man or even an ordinary craftsman. A lifetime was required to study the rules and more, if possible.

These rules sometimes assumed ridiculous dimensions. The most basic acts of building were no longer to be based on technical considerations but rather on mythological ones. Thus the Vastu Shastra was sometimes more of a hindrance than a help to the craftsmen. It is in this situation that the genius of the Indian Craftsman came to the fore. In a situation that could easily have been stifling, the mason and stonecutters came forth and created beauty simply by the plasticity of their sculpture and the sheer brute force of their forms. A large part of this was due to the institution of Senis or guilds, about which a brief mention has been made in a previous article.

Role of Senis

As early as the 7th century B.C., Indian craftsmen had organised themselves into guilds, the better to protect their special knowledge, and to gain for themselves better working conditions, and finally to ensure a minimum standard of quality of workmanship. In the senis, heredity was the route by which traditional knowledge was passed on through the generations. As soon as a boy was old enough to hold tools, he was set to work on a rough block of stone and so commenced his long apprenticeship. This was the father's sole gift and heirloom to his sons who in turn ensured that his name and style would live on. A temple project would often be of such magnitude that more than one generation of master cutters and masons would be required to finish it.

So a clan of stonecutters would settle around the building site for years. The temple site attracted young men hoping to learn as well as find work. Thus it became the focus of activity for miles around. Over the years, regional variations introduced for the building of a particular temple led to the evolution of a new style or 'school' of temple building, much like the gharanas that exist in Indian classical music even today. Hence we find distinct schools of art and architecture even within North Indian temple construction-the Orissan, Chalukyan, Gujarati, Kashmiri, and of course, the same situation in the temples of the south, which were further divided into many regional variations and schools of construction.

In all these the Vastu Shastra was the giver of cohesiveness, which ensured overall similarity of form and function, but also, as we have seen, was responsible for fettering the imagination of the craftsmen.

Vastu Purusha Mandala : the Magic

Looking at Hindu temples, it is not very easy to discern that they are composed of one repeating unit-the square. For God's own abode, the form had to be perfect and this limited the choice of shapes to the circle-a form without beginning and end, and the square-perfect for its symmetry. The circle had already been extensively used by the Buddhists in their Stupas and moreover, was perceived to be too dynamic a form for the resting place of the gods. For the Hindus, their gods had to be installed in buildings symbolising unity, inertia and permanence. The square, thus, was chosen for these qualities.

This was the origin of the square Mandala (the best translation of this in English is 'divine chart'). The mandala was further subdivided into smaller squares in a grid, those containing 64 or 81 being the most common. Each of these smaller squares was then invested with a resident deity, each with his own special attributes and powers. The distance of the deities from the centre was according to their power and perceived importance. Thus Brahma, the creator, occupied pride of place in the centre and lesser gods were relegated to the edges. A humanistic facade was given to the square by showing it to be able to accommodate a figure in a convoluted yogic posture.

It is interesting to note that this idea, that of the human figure being the basis of a system of proportion, was also used in the European Renaissance by Leonardo de Vinci, and later by Le Corbusier, planner of Chandigarh in India, in his Modular system of measurement. Thus, having acquired magical and theological properties, the Vastu Purusha Mandala was fit to be the basis of temple construction, with many permutations and combinations being used to achieve the final form. Very simply, the central square could be used for the garba-griha, while the surrounding grid formed the pradakshina-path and outer wall, and so on and so forth.

By increasing in complexity this system of proportion could spawn the most complex of forms with their basic unit remaining the square. It was by manipulation of this basic grid that the Indian architect created the greatest temples of India. The best examples, the glorious days of Hindu architecture, shall form the basis of our next article.

Northern Hindu Temple Architecture: In several areas, the painstakingly evolved theories of construction, the craftsmen and stonecutters' skill, combined with the backing of a dynasty powerful enough to conceive and execute such a concept, all combined to produce temples of breathtaking glory, which remain unsurpassed to this day.

There were four main sites, which we shall discuss:

1. The Bundelkhand region ruled by the Chandelas, especially the town of Khajuraho.
2. Bhubaneshwar, which produced its biggest temple ever.
3. Konark, on the eastern coast of Orissa.
4. Modhera in Gujarat.

Growth in South India: In the 10th and 11th centuries, the south too witnessed the construction of massive temples, great cathedrals in their own right. With the passage of time, the Chola dynasty came to dominate politics in south India. With their progression to power, the small scale of the Pallava masterpieces-the rathas and the Shore temple at Mahabalipuram-was not sufficient as a showpiece of Chola power. The craftsmen were soon to be put to a greater test.

The Great Temple at Thanjavur: At present, Thanjavur or Tanjore is an ordinary little town in Tamil Nadu. However, as the capital city of the Cholas, nothing surpassed it in wealth and power in the 11th century. In 1000 A.D the Chola king Rajarajeshwara the Great commissioned a temple, which was revolutionary by its sheer size, dwarfing all efforts made so far in the south. So the Rajaraja temple at Tanjore was 180 feet high from the ground, with a spire of 130 feet, fully 70 feet higher than the tallest spire so far attempted. This soaring height was capped by an enormous domical monolith, weighing at least 80 tons.

In this temple, which is arranged as always around a central axis, the two mandapas in front of the Vimana are also proportionately bigger. The entire complex of the main temple and its ancillary structures and subsidiary shrines is in the middle of a rectangular, defined by a portico with a double colonnade. The Vimana, though not much shorter than the projected spire at Konark, is structurally intact even after a thousand years. In this respect, the Tamil architects proved themselves far more adept than their northern peers. This was to be seen again in a later example. It was also true, of course, that the form chosen was far more prudent, a comparatively stable pyramid rather than the complex curvilinear profile of the shikhara.

Gangaikondacholapuram Temple: Growing chola power in the south was accompanied by a corresponding increase in patronage for the arts, the building of new cities and improvement in material life of the city-states as a whole. Rajendra I, the successor to Rajaraja the Great, in a bid to assert his own kingly identity, took the bold step of shifting his capital from Tanjore to Gangaikondacholapuram. As was common, the city needed to be built around its own mighty cathedral, the seat of all spiritual power.

Now the town is in ruins, and the temple scarcely less so. Yet the temple at Gangaikondacholapuram was important because of innovations that affected South Indian temple architecture in the future. The main Vimana on a base even larger than the temple at Tanjore, rises up in a concave curve, which is in total contrast to "the rigid and geometrically perfect Vimana of Tanjore, that symbolises conscious might..." while in the example at Gangaikondacholapuram "...the fluid lines...are imbued with a subconscious grace". The second innovation is the Mandapa. The huge flat-roofed hall has processional aisles that remain at ground level. To hold up such a large area of roof, a veritable forest of columns supports the mandapa. This approach is the forerunner of the famous 'halls of thousand columns' of later efforts in temple building.

Fall of the Cholas-Victory for the Pandyas: After the death of Rajendra I in 1050 A.D., the power of the Cholas slowly waned from incessant disputes with the other powers of the south-the Chalukyas, Pandyas and Kerala. Eventually the Chola Empire was usurped by the Pandya dynasty, which inherited all of its considerable wealth and trade agreements with foreign powers. By this time, *i.e.* the 14th Century A.D., considerable political changes were taking place. The most threatening was evidence of a new, irresistible force from the north-the all-conquering hordes of Islam.

Facing the challenge the Pandya rulers hurriedly threw up makeshift battlements around their cities and the heart of their towns-the temples. Thus an ancient, venerated shrine could often find itself in the position of being reduced in appearance to a fortress, that too a most utilitarian one.

For so religious a people, this was unacceptable. To change the outer covering, *i.e.* the form of the temple itself would be nothing short of sacrilege. The Pandya rulers hit upon a novel solution: raise the gates of the fortress to the level of architecture. This was the genesis of the famous gopuram, or entrance gateways of the temple cities of the south.

3

Monuments during Delhi Sultanate

The architecture of the Delhi sultanate represents a gradual evolution from an imported Afghan style using unfamiliar materials to a developed Indo-lslamic style which formed the basis of later Mughal architecture. The first building of the Delhi sultanate was the Quwwat al-Islam Mosque complex built by Qutb al-Din Aibak out of the remains of twenty-seven destroyed Hindu temples. The arcades were supported by two tiers of Hindu temple pillars placed one on top of the other to achieve the desired height.

They were built in a trabeated construction and in 1199 an arched facade was added to the east side of the sanctuary to give it the familiar appearance of a mosque. However, the arches of the screen were built out of corbels rather than voussoirs whilst the decoration consisted of Quranic inscriptions contained within dense Hindu-style foliage. In the same year Qutb al-Din began the famous Qutb Minar which has become one of the potent symbols of Islam in India. Other work carried out at this time was the construction of the Great Mosque of Ajmer which like the Delhi Mosque employed reused Hindu columns and later had an arched screen added to the front.

Ala al-Din in particular devoted a great deal of attention to the mosque by extending the area of the sanctuary as well as beginning a new minaret on the same design as the Qutb Minar but more than twice the size. Unfortunately Ala al-Din was unable to finish his work and the only part completed is a monumental gateway. Other work carried out by Ala al-Din was the foundation of Siri, the second city of Delhi.

Several new cities were founded including Fathabad, Hissar and Jaunpaur as well as the third, fourth and fifth cities of Delhi. Also at this time the influence of Sultanate architecture was felt in the Deccan when Muhammad Tughlaq II moved his capital to Daulatabad. Characteristic features of this architecture are massive sloping fortification walls with pointed crenulations and the development of the tomb as the focus of architectural design. One of the more important tombs is that of Khan Jahan built in 1369 which incorporates Hindu features into an Islamic form. The tomb has an octagonal domed form with chhajjas, or projecting eaves, on each side and domed chhatris on the roof.

Nevertheless, many of the buildings are sophisticated structures like the tomb of Sikander Lodi which uses a double dome form so that the dome may have a significant form on the outside without disrupting the proportions of the interior (a technique later used in the Taj Mahal). The tomb is also the first Indian tomb to form part of a formal garden which became the established format under the Mughals. In addition to the centralised architectural styles developed during the Delhi sultanate several vigorous regional traditions also developed. The four most significant styles are those of Gujarat, Kashmir, the Deccan and Bengal. The style of Gujarat developed independently for over 200 years from its conquest by the Khaliji sultan Ala al-Din Shah in the early fourteenth century to its incorporation in the Mughal Empire in the late sixteenth century. Characteristic features of Gujarati architecture are the use of Hindu methods of decoration and construction for mosques long after they had ceased to be fashionable in Delhi. After the conquest of Gujarat, the Mughal emperor Akbar adopted this style for his most ambitious architectural project, Fatehpur Sikri. Less well known but equally distinctive is the architecture of Kashmir where the first Islamic conquest was in the mid-fourteenth century.

The significant features of Kashmiri architecture are the use of wood as the main building material and tall pyramid-shaped roofs on mosques. The third major regional style is the architecture of the Deccan in southern India. Decaying architecture is characterised by massive monumental stonework, bulbous onion-shaped domes and elaborate stone carving, including vegetal forms, arched niches and medallions. Far to the east, in the region of Bengal and modern Bangladesh, a distinctive architecture developed using baked brick as the main building material Other characteristic features of Bengal include the use of the curved do-chala and char-chala roofs which were later incorporated into imperial Mughal architecture under Shah Jahan.

Alai Darwaza: The Alai Darwaza is a magnificent gateway built by Ala-ud-din Khalji of the Delhi Sultanate, having exquisite inlaid marble decorations and latticed stone screens. It highlights the remarkable artisanship of Turkish and local artisans who worked on it. The Alai Darwaza was an important part of the project undertaken by Ala-ud-din Khalji in his quest to decorate the Qutab complex.

The Alai Darwaza represents a new style of architecture, popularly referred to as the Indo-Islamic style of architecture. The Indo-Islamic style is neither a local variant of Islamic art, nor a modification of Hindu art, but it is an assimilation of both the styles, though not always in an equal degree. It is so because each region in India has its own form of Indo-Islamic architecture, which varies from place to place and there is no standardisation. On the other hand, Islamic art itself was a composite style, which had various Muslims influences-Turkish, Persian, and Arabic.

Though both the Indian and Islamic styles have their own distinctive features, some common characteristics made fusion and adaptation easy. Both the styles favour ornamentation and buildings of both styles are marked by the presence of an open court encompassed by chambers or colonnades. The Qutab Minar, the Quwwat-ul-Islam mosque, and the tomb of Iltutmish, which were constructed by different rulers of the Slave dynasty (1193-1290), heralded the birth of Indo-Islamic architecture. Of these monuments, the Qutab Minar is a tower symbolising the victory of the first Muslim rulers of India over the indigenous people. This fluted tower with floral patterns and Quranic inscriptions around in a flowing calligraphic style was the first monument of the Indo-Islamic style of architecture.

The Quwwat-ul-Islam mosque was the first mosque to be built in India and is made up of the remnants of 27 Hindu and Jain temples, broken down by the Muslim rulers of the Delhi Sultanate. It is also a representation of Muslim power. The tomb of Iltutmish was the first Islamic tomb to be built in India. As the concept of a domed tomb was new to the indigenous craftsmen, the resultant structural flaws in the building let to the collapse of the dome-the first one to have been built in India. Thus, one can say that the monuments belonging to the Slave dynasty mixed two cultures.

The Alai Darwaza is a perfect specimen of architecture belonging to the period of the Delhi Sultanate. It was built in 1311, by Ala-ud-din-Khalji, of the Khalji dynasty (which ruled the Delhi Sultanate from AD 1290 to AD 1316). The Alai Darwaza was a part of Ala-ud-din-Khalji's extension of the Quwwat-ul-Islam mosque. It was one of the four grand gateways; the other three could not be completed because of the death of Ala-ud-din in AD 1316.

The main structure of the Alai Darwaza consists of a single hall 34½ feet on the inside and 56½ feet on the outside. The domed ceiling rises to a height of 47 feet. The three doorways on the east, west, and south are lofty pointed arches, in the shape of a horseshoe, which rise above the flanking side bays. The entrance to the north is of an indigenous character, as its arch is semicircular in shape. The overall outlook and proportions of the Alai Darwaza is pleasing to the eye. The recessed corner arches of the attractive horseshoe forms, supporting a simple spherical dome on top of the square chamber, are an especially happy solution to the perpetual problem of supporting a good dome. It would be well worth noting that the earlier attempts at raising the dome, particularly the tomb of Iltutmish, had been unsuccessful. The dome of the Alai Darwaza, in this respect, is a notable achievement.

The plinth on each side is beautifully carved with floral and geometric patterns in both white marble and red sandstone, creating a superb polychrome effect. Perforated latticework window screens (jali) are set in the recessed windows on both sides of the entrances. These marble screens set off the monotony of the vertical lines of calligraphic ornamentation. The most charming aspect of surface decoration is the lace-like interweaving of floral tendrils, repeated with a flawless symmetry on all the three entrances, elegantly designed and perfectly built. The northern entrance is semicircular with a shallow trefoil in its outline.

The facade is elaborately ornamented in sensuous carving and patterns, characteristic of the pre-Turkish days (the first Muslim rulers of India came from Turkey). The Alai Darwaza also shows the influence of Seljuk art. The Seljuks had started fleeing Western Asia after Mongol invasions in the 12th century AD and had reached Delhi for protection. The 'spear-headed' embellishment on the three entrances is of particular importance in this regard. In addition, the surface ornamentation has been done with an eye for lavishness and detail.

Siri Fort: Ala-ud-din Khalji was a great patron of architecture and to him goes the credit of getting the Siri Fort in Delhi constructed. The fort was mainly built by Ala-ud-din to protect the people of his capital from the frequent invasions of the Mongols, who easily penetrated the weak defences of India's borders time and again to reach all the way up to Delhi. He succeeded in his mission of protecting his subjects after building the Siri Fort. Ala-ud-din Khalji built Siri Fort not only as the imperial capital of his kingdom, but also to protect the people of his capital city from the threat of the Mongols marauders. Siri Fort was a formidable fort, having strong Ramparts and unassailable walls. The fort also served as the administrative centre of the Delhi Sultanate, under the rule of Ala-ud-din Khalji (AD 1296-1316).

The kingdom of Delhi was constantly threatened by hoards of Mongol tribesmen who had been descending in waves to loot India since the 13th century. The Slave dynasty (AD 1193-1290), which was the first dynasty of the Delhi Sultanate, also faced this threat in the later half of its reign. Balban, the last important ruler of this dynasty successfully countered the

Mongol threat. In the course of time, the reins of the Delhi Sultanate passed into the hands of the Khalji Dynasty (AD 1290-1316). Ala-ud-din Khalji ascended the throne of the Delhi Sultanate in AD 1296. He was a strong monarch, who was constantly expanding his empire. Ala-ud-din was also a great builder. He built the fort city at Siri, which served as the administrative centre of the Khalji kingdom and was the first city in Delhi to be built by the Muslim rulers of India. The rulers of the Slave dynasty, who were the first Muslim rulers of India and the first dynasty of the Delhi Sultanate before the Khiljis, used Lal Kot, the fort city of the last Hindu rulers of Delhi.

He also began to put into shape his grand plans of beautifying the Qutab Minar complex. He added the Alai Darwaza, a magnificent gateway with inlaid marble decorations and latticed stone screens, which showcases the remarkable craftsmanship of the Turkish artisans who worked on it. He also planned to build the Alai Minar, which was conceived as a greater tower than the already existing Qutab Minar but the construction of this tower was abandoned after the completion of the 24.5-meter high first story.

The Mongols under their leader Taraghai plundered Delhi in AD 1303, and almost captured it. However the marauders did not capture the city and without reason turned back and left. Meanwhile, Ala-ud-din Khalji was away from Delhi, busy in one of his military campaigns in the Deccan region in South India. Returning back to Delhi from his Deccan campaign, Ala-ud-din Khalji decided to build a defensive fortress at Siri with strong fortified Ramaparts and impregnable bastions. This was the third fort to be built within the city of Delhi. The construction of the Siri Fort and the city within it began in AD 1304. The place he chose was a plain ground around five km to the north-east of the Qutab Minar where forces attacking or defending Delhi used to camp.

Tamurlane, who invaded Delhi in AD 1398, found Siri a magnificent fortress and damaged it. Later on, Sher Shah Suri (an Afghan chieftain from eastern India who ruled Delhi from AD 1540-1555 and was a contemporary of the second Mughal

Emperor, Humayun) took construction material from Siri to build his own city. Only some portions of the Siri walls can be seen today as all else has been destroyed and stones have been removed.

Influence of Islam

A Mixed-Indo-Islamic Architecture: "Nothing could illustrate more graphically the religious and racial diversity, or emphasis more decisively the principles underlying the consciousness of each community, than the contrast between their respective places of worship, as represented by the mosque on the one hand, and the temple on the other...Compared with the clarity of the mosque, the temple is an abode of mystery; the courts of the former are open to light and air, with many doorways, inviting publicity, the latter encloses 'a phantasma of massive darkness', having somber passages leading to dim cells, jealously guarded and remote ... architecturally the mosque is wholly visible and intelligible, while the temple is not infrequently introspective, complex and indeterminate."

"On the one hand was the rhythmic mind of the Hindu, on the other, the formal mind of the Musulman."

These quotes from a venerable early architectural historian serve to highlight the utter difference between Muslim and Hindu building types. There were other variations apart from the merely formal: the presence of carving in Hindu temples which was forbidden in Islam, decorative lettering on mosques and tombs which was unknown in Hindu art and architecture, the Hindu propensity for a single stone and the Muslim penchant for inlay work.

However in spite of this wide gulf, over the years a certain symbiosis did come into being between Muslim designers and master-builders and the Hindu craftsmen who carried out their bidding. Both benefited from the other's knowledge and what slowly evolved was a distinct new style of architecture-Persian in inspiration but very Indian in execution. Long referred to as Saracenic, it is now more properly termed Indo-Islamic.

We will find the development of Indo-Islamic architecture from its crude beginnings in the early 12th century to its heyday. It is not just a story about architecture, it is a whole new civilization developing in the fertile plains of India which is permanent.

Muhammad Ghori left as his viceroy in Delhi Qutb-ud-Din Aibak, who was to become the first Sultan in the Slave Dynasty After the death of Ghori, Qutb-ud-Din lost no time in declaring himself the ruler and embarked upon a vigorous campaign to quell dissidence, both in his home cities in Afghanistan as well as in and around Delhi. Recognising the strategic value of the city, Qutb-ud-Din is credited with being the first to realise that 'he who holds Delhi rules India'.

The power could be consolidated in two ways-militarily and theocratically. Once the immediate military aims were achieved, Qutb-ud-Din set about to establish himself not just as a marauding invader, but a proselytising missionary. The first mosque in India, the Quwwatu Islam (The Might of Islam) was constructed by destroying, in Qutb-ud-Din's own words, 27 Hindu and Jain temples in the region. The mosque originally consisted of a rectangular court 43.2 m by 33 m, enclosed by colonnaded cloisters. This enclosure formed the heart of the mosque, delineating a space where the faithful could kneel to pray.

It is with a closer examination of the columns that the otherwise undistinguished mosque begins to assume significance. Dismantled from temples, the columns still betray a riot of carving-human forms, gods and goddesses, flora and fauna, jewellery and other motifs-which was characteristically Hindu, but was expressly forbidden in Islamic architectural expression. The shortage of both time and money forced the Muslim ruler to reuse inherently sacrilegious elements. A compromise was effected by knocking off the faces of the deities and other human and animal forms.

The result is a curious combination-a structure which is architectonically a mosque with apparently vandalised Hindu components. The riot of defaced carving is complemented with the difference in the columns-they came from not one, but several demolished temples. Above the cloisters rise imperfect corbelled domes-the result of Hindu craftsmen striving to erect a form of which they had no prior experience.

With the cloisters complete, it was time to define the qibla or the axis along which lay Mecca. This was done by erecting a stone screen of five arches, the central one the highest at 16 m, flanked on each side by two smaller ones. Ogee-shaped, the arches are again imperfect as they are made by corbelling stone rather than by wedge-shaped voussoirs. Carved in alternating bands of inscriptions and arabesque ornamentation, the hand of the Hindu craftsman is again evident in the sinuous carving as well as serpentine, floral motifs which sneak in every so often. This mosque was later extended and enlarged by two subsequent rulers, Iltutmish and Ala-ud-Din Khalji, who between them nearly quadrupled the size of the original enclosure.

The Qutb Minar: Significance: The mosque and its ancillaries finished, Qutb-ud-Din laid the foundation of the world-famous Qutb Minar. Intended to serve a double function-both as a minaret for the mosque as well as the most visible symbol of his growing power, the Qutb with a height of 72.5 m is the highest stone tower in the world. Repaired and added to numerous times by successive rulers, the Qutb today consists of five storeys, each distinct. The lowest has alternately circular and triangular fluting, the second circular, the third triangular, while the fourth and fifth are mostly plain.

Each storey is articulated by a balcony, projecting on a system of stalactite pendentives-this feature appearing for the first time in India and no doubt imported from classical Islamic construction. The Qutb and its associated structures today is the most visible and famous landmark of Delhi, at par with Taj Mahal. Thousands of tourists, both Indian and foreign, swarming the site each day testify to its appeal. However, perhaps more important, in the evolution of the history of Indian architecture, it holds a unique place. This was the first time that Hindu craftsmen and Muslim builders allied together. It could be asserted that the result was forms and details confused and hesitant, structurally incompetent and formally subject to a myriad of influences.

Yet at no time does the Qutb complex lose its magnificence, and we see in this first stumbling step the beginnings of a long association between the two contrary cultures of Islam and Hinduism. This was to result in an architecture which was undoubtedly Islamic but distinctly sub-continental-a true fusion between Muslim sensibilities and Hindu capabilities. And ever in the future, there was the Qutb, a lofty symbol of God's will, enclosing between itself and its counterpart the 'entire paradise of God's world'.

Indo-Islamic Culture : Starting

The Qutb was the first monumental stamp of Islamic architecture in India and was the start of a long relationship between indigenous craftsmen and their Mamluk masters. The grandiosity of its concept encouraged several rulers to continue adding to the structure and adding further stages.

The Arhai-din-ka Jhompra: Shams-ud-Din Iltutmish (A.D. 1211-1236), succeeding to the throne after Qutb-ud-Din's death in a freak polo accident, was an energetic builder. The first of his notable works was the addition of a facade to the Arhai-din ka Jhompra (literally, hut of two-and-a-half days) mosque built by his predecessor at the military encampment of Ajmer in Rajasthan. Built on the same principles as the Quwwatu Islam at Delhi, this mosque at Ajmer is larger. The facade is similar to the one at the Qutb, but here the similarity ends. The central arch at Ajmer is straighter-Tudor Gothic-and the side arches are multifoil and cusped, a common feature in other Islamic work outside India. The main stylistic difference is evident in the It was not long, however, before several other additions and alterations were made on the same site.

The first of these was by Iltutmish, who doubled the size of the original enclosure of the Quwwatu Islam mosque, and added another screen of five arches to define the qibla (the axis towards Mecca). This screen, though superficially the same as in the original mosque, has better stood the ravages of time. The main differences are in the detail, with the carving using a purer Islamic vocabulary, though here too, in the sinuous curves, the hand of the indigenous craftsman is seen. The floriform low relief at the Qutb gives way to a far more geometric, rigid style. This is by no means an advance over the Qutb mosque. The arches seem almost a regression to a purer, stricter form of Islam with their monolithic and sombre appearance. Two broken minarets over the main arch resemble the Qutb in their flutings.

Iltutmish and Sultan Ghari's Tombs

Iltutmish constructed his own tomb as well as that of his son Nasir-ud-din Mohammed-the so-called Sultan Ghari or 'Sultan of the Cave'. This is probably due to the subterranean tomb chamber. The octagonal platform above was probably intended to support a pillared pavilion, the whole of which has disappeared or was never built. This platform was surrounded by a square masonry arcade on a high plinth, and according to Percy Brown, it has "such a grim and martial appearance that one of its more remote purposes may have been to serve as some kind of advanced outwork to the main fortress of the capital".

The second main contribution of Iltutmish was his own tomb, a little to the north-west of the enlarged mosque at the Qutb, built a little before A.D. 1235. A square 42 feet in side and with a height of almost 30 feet, its plain and unadorned exteriors belie its interior-the whole of which is covered from top to bottom on all four sides by rich carvings almost rivaling Hindu temple sculpture on the sandstone-clad walls. The cenotaph and the three arches of the mehrab towards the west (marking the direction of Mecca) are both in marble, again a dispute on the Quranic inscriptions.

Architecturally speaking, Iltutmish's tomb is interesting as it reveals quite clearly the first attempt in India to solve the 'dome on a square' problem-or in other words, how do you support a circular shape on a square base? In this case, a 'squinch' was employed-a half-arch/dome spanning across the corners of the square base and making the square an octagon. This can be repeated to transform the octagon into a sixteen-sided figure on which the base of the dome may rest. That the dome, if ever fully built, subsequently collapsed was a testimony to the fact that the it was imperfectly constructed-however an important start had been made and future attempts in this direction were to grow ever more confident.

After the death of Iltutmish, there is little to be seen architecturally from the early years of the Delhi Sultanate. The main reason for this were the squabbling successors of the Sultan ruling for too short a time for any effective architectural patronage. There was thus an interregnum of 60 years-with one exception. This is the tomb of Sultan Balban of the extremely short-lived 'House of Balban' (A.D. 1266-1287).

Now a ruined and totally unremarkable structure in the extreme south of Delhi, this tomb is notable because it introduced for the first time in India the principle of the true arch with radiating voussoirs. This is not only a significant structural advance, but also a sociocultural one. For it indicated that slowly but surely the Muslim rulers were ceasing to regard North India as invaded territory. Delhi was becoming a city of repute attracting men of art and learning, craftsmen, poets and historians. The early steps of creating a distinct Indo-Islamic culture were under consideration.

The Great Alai Minar: Ala-ud-Din, true to form, felt compelled to increase even further the size of the Quwwatul Islam mosque. His scheme called for increasing the size of the enclosure four times, providing ceremonial entrance gateways on each side, and a great minar, twice the size of the Qutb-the Alai Minar.

It would have been clear to anyone less megalomanic— with a vision less obscured by self-exaltation-that such a grandiose project would be impossible in the Sultan's lifetime. Indeed, the Alai Minar today is a stump (albeit a magnificent one-we can well imagine the proportions of the tower had it ever been finished), its rubble core clearly showing as it rises up to one story.

The Alai Darwaza: The only part of Ala-ud-Din's scheme which was completed was the southern ceremonial entrance-named the Alai Darwaza after its builder. It is clear from its appearance and construction that a fresh new influence was at work-this is a piece of Muslim architecture hitherto unknown in India. Historians have traced its genealogy to the architecture found in Asia Minor under the rule of the Seljuks in the early centuries of the second millennium.

The breakup of the Seljuk empire under the weight of Mongol invasions caused craftsmen and builders to be scattered far and wide, and among the places offering sanctuary was the Delhi Sultanate. Because of its revolutionary construction, the Alai Darwaza served as a model for many of its successors. The first innovation in the gateway was the system of walling, alternating between one course of stretchers-stone laid with its longer ends facing outward-and one course of headers-stone laid with its longer end going deep into the wall. The header course enabled the walling to penetrate into the rubble core and thus make the wall as a whole stronger.

This method of walling was to continue and was a typical characteristic of Mughal building. The second innovation was the true arch. This imported arcuated tradition was to play an important role as it was to provide the prototype for successive Sultanate tombs.

Alai Darwaza is a rectangular building on high plinth into which steps have been cut to access the interior. The three outer faces are very similar with a tall arch over the steps. The plinth is carved in bands, and the wall surface above is divided into two stories, each further subdivided into rectangular panels. The lower of these panels have a recessed arch while the upper ones into smaller rectangles. At each point, the articulation is marked by a mixture of sandstone and marble arabesque and decorative carving.

However, by far the most imposing feature of these facades is the central arch, rising to nearly the whole height of the structure. In shape it is rare-a horseshoe or keel arch. Around its outer rim is a band of inscribed white marble. The intrados or the inner rim of the arch shows its most distinctive feature-a fringe of lotus-bud carving.

The inner facade, facing the mosque and Qutb Minar, is different. For one, the opening is not a keel arch but a true semicircular one, and for another it is clear that in its sensual and plastic decoration the indigenous craftsman was given a much freer hand. The interior of the structure is no less remarkable for its technological innovation. First started in the tomb of Iltutmish, the weight of the dome is transferred to the square base by the same mechanism-the squinch.

In this case, the squinch consists of five recessed arches gracefully transforming the square into the octagon, and the octagon into a sixteen sided figure. Among the other architectural work of Ala-ud-Din, little remains except fragmentary and crumbling structures. And though the work of the Khiljis was not entirely confined to the capital city of Delhi, the influence of local workmen in the provinces and the eventual decline of the Khalji dynasty meant that these were never as remarkable nor of as high a standard as the Alai Darwaza at the Qutb.

Period of Tughlaq

It was a time of rediscovery and elation. From the corners of the land they came, the master builders, for a new Sultan had taken his seat. And in his old years, he had seen history. Seen empires rise and fall. And was laying the foundation of what he hoped would be an empire that would last far beyond his approaching death.

Of the three rulers of the Tughlaq dynasty, the first, Ghiyas-ud-Din Tughlaq (1320-1325 A.D.) was already aged when he became Sultan, and ruled for barely five years. The warlike conditions prevailing throughout his reign are best exemplified by his architecture, which though secular or religious, always has strong military overtones, being able to be adapted for a spirited defence if necessary. The major efforts of this man were concentrated on the building of his citadel, the city of Tughlaqabad, one of the historical seven cities of Delhi.

Today a neglected but magnificent ruin. According to Percy Brown, "all that remains of this great enterprise is a haunting scene of savage splendour... Nothing resembling this picture (of treasures and palaces) can now be seen in the huge masses of broken masonry, the unadorned nature of which suggests that the project took more the form of a stern and practical stronghold, than a work of architectural significance."

The citadel integrates outer defence with the inner city buildings, though little remains of the latter but scattered ruins. The massive outer walls were sloping, following approximately the topography of the land, sited on a high outcrop of the southern Delhi ridge. At close intervals are semicircular bastions with eyelets for archers to look down and shoot at the enemy. Little can be identified within these walls, but it is clear that there was some kind of royal palace with its accompanying residences, rooms for the women, halls of audience as well as a connecting passageway to the monument just opposite, Ghiyas-ud-Din's tomb.

The Tomb of Ghiyas-ud-Din: In stark contrast to the dilapidated condition of the fortress, the tomb of Ghiyas-ud-Din is almost perfectly preserved. This originally stood in the middle of an artificial lake, and the arched causeway which connected it to the citadel has now been replaced, with the drying up of the water body, by an offshoot of Mathura Road leading to the Qutb. The tomb itself is almost like a miniature fortress, with sloping crenulated outer walls, complete with eyelets for archery. It is almost like a rallying point for a last, hopeless defence, much in the manner of Sultan Ghari's tomb. The plan of this fortress-tomb is an irregular pentagon, with a bastion at each angle of its outer walls.

The tomb walls are clad for the most part with red sandstone and the dome with marble. The most distinctive feature, however, are its sloping walls, about which much excited scholarly discussion has taken place. The commonly accepted view is that the tomb is an offshoot, or a descendant, of a similar contemporaneous tomb at Multan (in modern Pakistan) of Shah Rukn-i-Alam.

In the latter, the use of sun-dried brick made sloping walls a structural necessity, much like Egyptian temple pylons, but this feature was transferred unchanged to the tomb of Ghiyas-ud-Din, where stone was used for the walls. The tomb continues the lotus-bud fringes found in the arch of the Alai Darwaza, and there are many other stylistic similarities. Another interesting feature is the presence of a structurally redundant lintel over the arched gateways. It is almost as if the indigenous craftsmen, still not trusting the true arch as a means of support, were being safe by introducing a lintel.

That this lintel also introduces an element of style was incidental. It is in this tomb that we first begin to get a hint of what would follow in the coming centuries. There is the same vocabulary-begun in the Alai Darwaza-of red sandstone cladding and white marble.

The massive outer walls, made for defence, could be easily toned down to graceful perimeter guards. Today, the tomb is overrun by monkeys, hundreds of them at a time, bereft of tourists unlike the nearby Qutb, yet its importance cannot be denied, the last stand of a Sultan who was destined to die at the hands of his son. The site of Tughlaqabad is desolate, ruined and magnificent-very much like the history of the Sultanate which set the base for Muslim rule in India.

The Bara-Khamba : History : Bara-khamba Road in modern Delhi is one of the major entrances to Connaught Place, and its high buildings with corporate offices and banks contributes mainly to the city's burgeoning skyline. It is also famous for Modern School (Bara-khamba Road) which has made a regular contribution to the ranks of India's rich and famous every year.

However, the name Bara-khamba or Twelve Pillars derives from the house of a nobleman originally erected there, of which little remains. The surviving evidence is of interest because this is one of the few cases when secular architecture-as opposed to religious or military-has been found in any degree of preservation this far back in time. A reconstruction of the house would show it enclosed in a high perimeter wall containing an open courtyard with rooms around, a roof terrace, an court with a chabootra or platform for sitting in the open, as well as a quirky three-story high tower, probably used for looking at the city.

Sultan Mohammed Tughlaq (1325-1351 A.D.) in whose reign this was built, was not known for much else except his wacky, ill-timed policy decisions which, visionary though they may have been, lacked the authority and persistence of the Sultan to make them really work. Among these were the shifting of the Capital to Daulatabad in the Deccan (to administer the empire from a central location). One side effect of this was the undoing of all the good work of the previous generations in Delhi, which became for a time desolate and abandoned.

A significant proportion of the population died en route to Daulatabad, and another percentage on the way back, some years later, when it was apparent that the scheme had failed. The introduction of token money instead of precious metals also had similar results, with confusion and even chaos resulting for a time. The throne of Delhi, emasculated by years of incessant warfare in the Deccan and the profligacies of Muhammad bin Tughlaq, had its coffers nearly empty by the time Firoz Shah (1351-1388 A.D.) came to power. This ruler leaves behind a wealth of architectural evidence that is a testimony both to the age in which they were built, as well as to his propensity for architecture. Today, Firoz Shah Kotla and Hauz Khas are more famous, respectively, as a cricket ground and the feeding grounds of Delhi's hoi-polloi, but they stand as mute witnesses to the dying flickers of the Sultanate. These, and more, in the next column.

After Firoz Shah

After the capricious reign of Muhammad bin Tughlaq, his cousin, the devout (and even bigoted!) Firoz Shah Tughlaq (1351-1388 A.D.) became Sultan. Firoz Shah inherited, thanks largely to the disastrous policies of his predecessor, nearly empty coffers and a disintegrating empire. This did not stop him from embarking on a vigorous campaign of building, and in the words of a contemporary historian he was eventually responsible for "1200 gardens around Delhi...200 towns, 40 mosques, 30 villages, 30 reservoirs, 50 dams, 100 hospitals, 100 public baths and 150 bridges."

These claims are no doubt exaggerated but underscore his interest in architecture. In his own words "...among the Gifts that God has bestowed on me...is a desire to erect public buildings." The architecture of Firoz Shah is stern, utilitarian, almost tragic-at times hauntingly lovely (Hauz Khas Madrasa by night), at times warningly forbidding. This is due in no small measure to its rough exposed finish (the glazed tiles having come off a long time ago) as well as the lack of skilled masons and sufficient capital. The unfortunate and appalling state of neglect of the monuments today does nothing to ameliorate this perception.

Formation of a New Capital: Firoz Shah built a new capital city on the banks of the Yamuna, called Firoz Shah Kotla, thereby abandoning the old fort-city of Tughlaqabad. Apart from the desire of the new Sultan to make his mark, this decision could also have been prompted by an increasingly irregular water supply at Tughlaqabad. The fort itself was fairly straightforward, using common-sense building principles used the world over for buildings of a similar type. The king's quarters as well as those of his wives and concubines were situated along the river-front. Within the perimeter walls of the fort were structures serving as barracks, armorers, rooms for servants, halls for audience, an imposing mosque, as well as public and private baths, a stepped well or baoli, and an Ashokan pillar removed from Ambala and mounted on top of a pyramidal three-tiered construction.

Symbolically, this was an icon of the Sultan's supremacy in North India, very much like the Gupta Iron Pillar in the Quwwat-ul-Islam mosque at the Qutb. Of Firoz Shah's numerous mosques, the chief ones are the Kali Masjid, the Begumpuri Masjid, Kalan Masjid and Khirki Masjid at Jahanpanah. This last is interesting not only for its cruciform plan, but also because it is one of the few examples of covered mosques in India. The congregational nature of worship in Islam has generally resulted in mosques having a large common open space in which to pray. But the roofing of the Khirki Masjid and dividing of the interior spaces into various small courtyards-perhaps to avoid the scorching heat of North India in the summer-effectively broke up the congregation into small groups.

Whatever the reason for this unusual Masjid, it was apparently not very successful as a building type and was not repeated. Today the Khirki Masjid has its own village-Khirki village-in Delhi, near modern Saket. Indeed, from the road, the mosque can barely be glimpsed. The narrow paths of the village twist and turn until suddenly you are face to face with an imposing structure mounted on an impressively high plinth. The village chokes the mosque, encroaches on its space-but perhaps the very unexpectedness of the building is the reason for its powerful solemnity. A failure as a building type, the Khirki Masjid today is an architectural gem tucked away in a forgotten corner of one of India's largest metropolises.

Hauz Khas Madrasa: To be forgotten is not the fate of the Madrassa-or religious school-at Hauz Khas-having for company some of the most exclusive (and expensive) restaurants and boutiques in the city. The story of modern Hauz Khas village is all too familiar-of an urban village being hijacked for its (initially) low property prices.

Today Hauz Khas sells you India-if you're a foreigner-neatly packaged, right from 'antiques' from Kerala and Tamil Nadu to fabrics to paintings, and when you're tired of it all, there are the restaurants to relax. And spend some more money. All this activity, of course, does not detract from the solemnity of the monument. Originally the site of a large water-storage tank built by Ala-ud-Din Khalji, a large school, mosque and his own tomb were added by Firoz Shah.

These buildings are laid out in an 'L' shape on a high rocky outcrop overlooking the tank. Firoz Shah's tomb is at the junction of this 'L', and is also the highest building there, surmounted by a dome with its interior finely stuccoed. Exterior surface decorations have long disappeared, of course, so what we are left with is a network of buildings, almost barrack-like in their disposition, with a mosque at one end, and teaching cells at the other, the whole composition hinging on Firoz Shah's tomb as the pivot. Jaali windows overlooking the tank (and the setting sun) make for a fine place to spend summer evenings, and the whole complex nestles in the midst of a forest-the Deer Park at Hauz Khas.

The important construction of Firoz Shah's reign would end here-except for one example. This is the tomb of Khan-i-

Jahan Telengani, an official at the court. His tomb, though otherwise decaying, marks a radical design innovation in the sense that for the first time the plan was octagonal instead of square. This may have been done to facilitate the placing of the dome at the summit, which would be far easier over an octagon than over a square. Whatever the reason, this tomb would be the forerunner and model for tombs of the next two dynasties, each of whom would refine it further, and persist even after the Mughal invasion of India.

Islamic Architecture: Regional Variations

In and around Delhi Islamic architecture retained much of the characteristics in both form and detailing of Persian Islam, with only the court at Delhi able to attract and pay the best Muslim architects and artisans from abroad. As one moves away from the main power centre, the regional Islamic satraps-whether governors of the Delhi Sultanate or newly-independent Sultan-patronised an architecture which slowly began to assume a very different identity. This identity was not constant throughout, but varied from place to place, and depended chiefly on : the distance from Delhi, which determined the level of dilution of 'pure' Islamic principles; the economic condition of the regime, responsible for the quality of finished and materials used; the local artisans available in the region and their specialisation and experience; and local Hindu architecture, which served as direct or indirect inspiration for Muslim examples.

If the Qutb Minar merely had sinuous carving which hinted at the Hindu craftsman at work, examples further away from Delhi illustrated both a riot of carving as well as formal aspects directly influenced by Hindu architecture. The main areas that produced a substantial body of architecture and can be said to have evolved a 'style' of their own are Gujarat, Punjab, Bengal, Malwa, Kashmir and some parts of south India.

The End of the Delhi Sultanate

Abdur-Rahim Khan-i-Khanan's Tomb at Delhi: Late in Jahangir's reign, Delhi witnessed an evolution from the tomb type exemplified by Humayun's tomb, which had partially continued in Jahangir's mausoleum as well. A tomb was built near Humayun's memorial for Abdur-Rahim, the khan-i-khanan during Akbar's reign. For the first time, this tomb is higher than it is wide, and the *chattris* on the terrace crowd more closely around the main dome. This composition was to be further experimented with in some more subsidiary tombs before its final refined appearance in the Taj Mahal.

Princely States and their Architecture: The confusion accompanying the decline of the Mughal empire saw an abundance of new architecture at the new seats of regional power by the Rajputs, Sikhs, Marathas and the nawabs of Oudh, Bengal and Hyderabad. Hindu rulers started to construct memorials to their dead, much after the style of the Mughals, and restarted the construction of lavish temples, neglected for long because of the lack of power and finances. The Sikhs, persecuted for long by the later Mughals, pillaged Mughal building in their turn to build their own gurudwaras or temples. The nawabs built lavish gardens, tombs, mosques and palaces. Their was no longer a dominant style, but a hybrid where Gujarati, Bengali, Deccan and Persian elements fused to produce an eclectic strain of building.

Late mediaeval Rajput architecture was noted both for its town planning and urban architecture. Rulers patronised research into ancient treatises and *shastras* of Hindu architecture and attempts were made to build accordingly. It would be fair, thus, to discuss two notable examples.

Jaisalmer : Jaisalmer is particularly noted for its havelis or private houses belonging to the noblesse. Here the court style fusing Mughal and Rajput elements was first emulated by Rawal Amar Singh (1661-1702) for the palaces and temples surrounding the lake and at Bada Bagh. His 18th and 19th century successors continued the eclectic tradition by importing the late architecture of Marwar, with its prominent oriels and balconies, many-cusped arches, half-circular roofs and luxuriant sculptural ornament. The palaces in the fort although elaborately floral, are not however Jaisalmer's most celebrated buildings.

This status belongs to the dense network of havelis in the town below the fort – the private houses of the rich and wealthy, and the noblesse, who in the dwindling of royal power became the de facto rulers, an oligarcy very much like that of late mediaeval Venice. The havelis of Jaisalmer are thus world-famous for their dense interlocking structure and their architectural devices which keep out the heat and dust. Many examples of modern Indian architecture take their inspiration from Jaisalmer's urban planning and house clustering pattern, a notable one being Raj Rewal's Asiad Games Village built for the Asian Games at Delhi in 1984.

4

Monuments of Mughals

Tomb of Humayun: The Mughal dynasty was established with the crushing victory of Babur at Panipat in 1526. During his short five-year reign, Babur took considerable interest in erecting buildings, though few have survived. Babur's son Humayun was dissolute and wayward in his early years and the Mughal empire fell to the Suris in 1540. The tomb of Sher Shah Suri is an architectural masterpiece that was to have a profound impact on the evolution of Indo-Islamic funerary architecture. Humayun re-established the Mughal empire in 1555. His tomb at Delhi represents an outstanding landmark in the development and refinement of the Mughal style. It was designed in 1564, eight years after his death, as a mark of devotion by his widow, Haji Begum. Architecture flourished during the reign of Humayun's son Akbar.

One of the first major building projects was the construction of a huge fort at Agra. The massive sandstone Ramaparts of the Red Fort are another impressive achievement. The most ambitious architectural exercise of Akbar, and one of the most glorious examples of Indo-Islamic architecture, was the creation of an entirely new capital city at Fatehpur Sikri. After the death of Akbar in 1605, his son, Prince Salim, ascended the throne and assumed the title of Jahangir, "Seizer of the World". He was assisted in his artistic attempts by his able wife, Nur Jahan.

The Mausoleum of Akbar at Sikandra, outside Agra, represents a major turning point in Mughal history, as the sandstone compositions of Akbar were adapted by his successors into opulent marble masterpieces. Jahangir is the central figure in the development of the Mughal garden. The most famous of his gardens is the Shalimar Bagh on the banks of Lake Dal in Kashmir.

In 1628 Jahangir's son Prince Khurram ascended the throne as Emperor Shah Jahan. His reign is characterised by monumental architectural achievements as much as anything else. The single most important architectural change was the use of marble instead of sandstone. He demolished the austere sandstone structures of Akbar in the Red Fort and replaced them with marble buildings such as the *Diwan-i-Am* (hall of public audience), the tomb of *Itmad-ud-Daula*, the *Diwan-i-Khas* (hall of private audience), and the *Moti Masjid* (Pearl Mosque). In 1638 he began to lay out the city of Shahjahanabad beside the Jamuna river. The Red Fort at Delhi represents the pinnacle of centuries of experience in the construction of palace-forts. Outside the fort, he built the Jama Masjid, the largest mosque in India. However, it is for the Taj Mahal, which he built as a memorial to his beloved wife, Mumtaz Mahal, that he is most often remembered. His extravagant architectural indulgence had a heavy price. The peasants had been impoverished by heavy taxes and by the time his son Aurangzeb ascended the throne, the empire was in a state of insolvency.

As a result, opportunities for grand architectural projects were severely limited. This is most easily seen at the Bibi-ki-Maqbara, the tomb of Aurangzeb's wife, built in 1678. Though the design was inspired by the Taj Mahal, it is half its size, the proportions compressed and the detail clumsily executed. After the death of Aurangzeb, the Mughal empire rapidly declined under a rapid succession of ephemeral rulers: various successor states gradually took its place. The remarkable flowering of art and architecture under the Mughals is due to several factors. The empire itself provided a secure framework within which artistic genius could flourish, and it commanded wealth and resources unparalleled in Indian history. The Mughal rulers themselves were extraordinary patrons of art, whose intellectual calibre and cultural outlook was expressed in the most refined taste

Fatehpur Sikri

Buland Darwaza: The royal city at Fatehpur Sikri, situated 26 miles west of Agra, was built at the orders of the Mughal Emperor Akbar. While Akbar himself was illiterate, he took a keen interest in literature, architecture, and the arts. He is also reputed to be a very tolerant ruler, and the buildings at Fatehpur Sikri blended both Islamic and Hindu elements in their architectural style. One of the buildings even reflects the new sycretistic faith founded by Akbar, Din-e-Ilahi, which though very short-lived remains a matter of controversy.

Popular legend has it that since Akbar was without an heir for a long time, he made a pilgrimage to the renowned Sufi saint, Sheikh Salim Chishti, to seek his blessings. When a son—later to be known as Jahangir—was born to him, Akbar named him after the saint as a mark of his gratitude and built the new capital to mark his birth. Construction of the new ceremonial capital, with its elaborate palaces, formal courtyards, reflecting pools, harems, tombs and a great mosque, commenced in 1571. A large number of masons and stone carvers worked hard on an area that was over two miles long and a mile wide; they used a brilliant red sandstone available locally, which provides the buildings with much of their lustre. Shortly after the work was completed fifteen years later, it was realised that there was a lack of an adequate water supply and the pristine complex was abandoned.

Fatehpur Sikri is now a World Heritage site. The Panch Mahal or Palace of Five Storeys, and the Buland Darwaza, a massive gate which provides entrance to the complex, number among the finest specimens of Mughal architecture, and it is even arguable that Fatehpur Sikri is the greatest accomplishment of Mughal architecture, surpassed only in reputation but not in its beauty and the awe it inspires by the Taj Mahal. The cultural politics of the site remains to be written: perhaps the mammoth chess board, where human figures were used as chess pieces and moved at the emperor's will, provides a cue.

Importance of the Taj Mahal: Shah Jahan, who commissioned the monument, was a prolific patron with effectively limitless resources. He had previously created the gardens and palaces of Shalimar in honour of his wife, Mumtaz. After her death in childbirth (she had already borne him fourteen children) Shah Jahan was reportedly inconsolable, and soon after he began construction of the Taj Mahal. His lavish aesthetic and romantic nature is apparent in every aspect of the Taj Mahal. Visiting Agra in 1663, the French traveller Francois Bernier gave the following description of the Taj Mahal and Shah Jahan's motive for building it:

> *"The Taj Mahal incorporates and expands on many design traditions, particularly Islamic, Persian, Hindu and earlier Mughal architecture."*

The overall design derived inspiration from a number of successful Timurid and Mughal buildings: these include the Gur-e Amir, Humayun's Tomb, Itmad-Ud-Daulah's Tomb (sometimes called the *Baby Taj*), and his own Jama Masjid. Under Shah Jahan's patronage, Mughal building reached new levels of refinement:, previous Mughal building had primarily been constructed of red sandstone; Shah Jahan promoted the use of white marble inlaid with semi-precious stones.

During this period Hindu craftsmen, particularly sculptors and stonecutters, plied trade throughout Asia, and their work was particularly prized by tomb builders. Whilst the rock-cut architecture which characterises much of this construction had little or no influence on the Taj Mahal, other Indian buildings such as the Man Singh palace in Gwalior were an inspiration for much Mughal palace architecture and the source for the chhatris which can be seen on the Taj Mahal. Consistent repeated design elements are employed throughout the complex. These unify the complex with a single aesthetic vocabulary.

The Taj Mahal complex is bounded by a crenulated red sandstone wall on three sides. The river-facing side is unwalled. Outside the wall are several additional mausoleums, including those of many of Shah Jahan's other wives, and a larger tomb for Mumtaz's favourite servant. These structures, composed primarily of red sandstone, are typical of smaller Mughal tombs of the era.

The wall is fronted by columned arcades, on the inner (garden) side a feature typical of Hindu temples later incorporated into Mughal mosques. The wall is interspersed with domed kiosks (*chattris*), and small buildings which may have been viewing areas or watch towers (such as the so-called *Music House*, now used as a museum). The main gateway (*darwaza*) is a monumental structure built primarily of red sandstone.

The style is reminiscent of that of Mughal architecture of earlier emperors. Its archways mirror the shape of the tomb's archways, and its *pishtaq* arches incorporate the calligraphy that decorates the tomb. It utilises bas-relief and pietra dura (inlaid) decorations with floral motifs. The vaulted ceilings and walls have elaborate geometric designs, like those found in the other sandstone buildings of the complex. At the far end of the complex, two grand red sandstone buildings open to the sides of the tomb. Their backs parallel the western and eastern walls.

The focus of the Taj Mahal is the white marble tomb. Like most Mughal tombs, the basic elements are Persian in origin: a symmetrical building with an iwan, an arch-shaped doorway, topped by a large dome. The tomb stands on a square plinth. The base structure is a large, multichambered structure. The main chamber houses the cenotaphs of Shah Jahan and Mumtaz (the actual graves are a level below). The base is essentially a cube with chamfered edges, roughly 55 metres on each side (see floor plan, right).

On the long sides, a massive *pishtaq*, or vaulted archway, frames the iwan, with a similar arch-shaped balcony above. These main arches extend above the roof of the building by use of an integrated facade. To either side of the main arch, additional pishtaqs are stacked above and below. This motif of stacked pishtaqs is replicated on the chamfered corner areas. The design is completely uniform and consistent on all sides of the building. Four minarets, one at each corner of the plinth, facing the chamfered corners, frame the tomb.

Craftsmen: The Taj Mahal was not designed by a single person. The project demanded talent from many quarters.

The names of many of the builders who participated in the construction of the Taj Mahal in different capacities have come down to us through various sources. Ustad Isa and Isa Muhammad Effendi trained by the great Ottoman architect Koca Mimar Sinan Agha had a key role in the architectural design of the complex. The main dome was designed by Ismail Khan from the Ottoman Empire, considered to be the premier designer of hemispheres and builder of domes of that age. Qazim Khan, a native of Lahore, cast the solid gold finial that crowned the Turkish master's dome. Chiranjilal, a lapidary from Delhi, was chosen as the chief sculptor and mosaicist. Amanat Khan from Persian Shiraz, Iran was the chief calligrapher (this fact is attested on the Taj Mahal gateway itself, where his name has been inscribed at the end of the inscription). Muhammad Hanif was the supervisor of masons. Mir Abdul Karim and Mukkarimat Khan of Shiraz, Iran handled finances and the management of daily production.

The creative team included sculptors from Bukhara, calligraphers from Syria and Persia, inlayers from southern India, stonecutters from Baluchistan, a specialist in building turrets, another who carved only marble flowers — thirty seven men in all formed the creative nucleus. To this core was added a labour force of twenty thousand workers recruited from across northern India.

Materials: The Taj Mahal was constructed using materials from all over India and Asia. Over 1,000 elephants were used to transport building materials during the construction. The white marble was brought from Rajasthan, the jasper from Punjab and the jade and crystal from China. The turquoise was from Tibet and the Lapis lazuli from Afghanistan, while the sapphire came from Sri Lanka and the carnelian from Arabia. In all, 28 types of precious and semi-precious stones were inlaid into the white marble.

Soon after its completion, Shah Jahan was deposed and put under house arrest at nearby Agra Fort by his son Aurangzeb. He spent the remainder of his days gazing through the window at the Taj Mahal. Upon Shah Jahan's death, Aurangzeb buried him in the Taj Mahal next to his wife, the only disruption of the otherwise perfect symmetry in the architecture. By the late 19th century parts of the Taj Mahal had fallen badly into disrepair. During the time of the First war of Indian Independence the Taj Mahal faced defacement by British soldiers, sepoys, and government officials who chiselled out precious stones and lapis lazuli from its walls.

At the end of the 19th century British viceroy Lord Curzon ordered a massive restoration project, completed in 1908. He also commissioned the large lamp in the interior chamber (modelled on one hanging in a Cairo mosque when local craftsmen failed to provide adequate designs). It was during this time the garden was remodelled with the more English looking lawns visible today. By the 20th century the Taj Mahal was being better taken care of. In 1942 the government erected a behemoth scaffolding over it in anticipation of an air attack by the German Luftwaffe and later by the Japanese Air Force. During the India-Pakistan wars of 1965 and 1971 scaffoldings were erected by the government to mislead would-be bomber pilots.

As of 1983 the Taj Mahal was designated a UNESCO World Heritage Site. Today it is a major tourist destination. Recently the Taj Mahal was claimed to be Sunni Wakf property, on the grounds that it is the grave of a woman whose husband Emperor Shah Jahan was a Sunni. The Indian government have dismissed claims by the Muslim trust to administer the property, saying their claims are baseless and the Taj Mahal is Indian national property.

The name *Taj* comes from Persian, the language of the Mughal court, meaning crown, and *Mahal* means palace. Most sources suggest that *Taj Mahal* is a shorter variant of *Mumtaz Mahal*, the nickname of Arjumand Banu Begum, meaning *First Lady of the Palace*. As early as 1663, the French traveller Francois Bernier referred to the place as *Tage Mehale*.

The Taj Mahal in Agra is indisputably the most famous example of Mughal architecture. Described by Rabindranath Tagore as "a tear on the face of eternity", it is in popular imagination a veritable "wonder of the world". The white-splendored tomb was built by Emperor Shah Jahan in the memory of his favourite wife, Arjumand Banu Begum, better known as *Mumtaz Mahal* ("Chosen of the Palace"). She married Shah Jahan in 1612 to become his second wife and inseparable companion, and died in childbirth at Burhanpur while on a campaign with her husband in 1629. Shah Jahan was, it is said, inconsolable to the point of contemplating abdication in favour of his sons. The court went into mourning for over two years; and Shah Jahan decided to commemorate the memory of Mumtaz with a building the like of which had never been seen before.

Craftsmen from as far as Turkey came to join in the work. The marble was quarried at Makrana near Jodhpur in Rajasthan. Precious stones were imported from distant lands. A two mile Ramp was built to lift material up to the level of the dome. It is alleged that on its completion, Shah Jahan ordered the right hand of the chief mason to be cut off so that the masterpiece could never be recreated. As one might expect, numerous other legends are associated with the Taj Mahal: thus, according to one story, Shah Jahan desired to have another Taj built across the river, this one entirely in black marble.

In a manner of speaking, the pillage of the Taj continues unabated: more recently, the fumes from the surrounding industries have started deteriorating the marble, though various court orders have resulted in industries around the Taj being moved to more distant points. The latest desecration of the monument took place, ironically, in celebration of the fiftieth anniversary of Indian independence, when the mediocre rock star Yanni, whose elevator music has attracted a worldwide audience, was allowed to give a live and certainly unprecedented performance at the Taj. The surroundings of the Taj Mahal have been restored to the original designs of Ali Mardan Khan, a noble at Shah Jahan's court. The main vista is accentuated by a red sandstone channel set between rows of cypress trees. The main entrance is from the west, but there are two other entrances—from the east and from the west. The main gateway is a large three-storey sandstone structure with an octagonal central chamber with smaller rooms on each side. The walls are inscribed with verses from the Quran.

The Makrana white marble of the Taj Mahal assumes subtle variations of light, tint and tone at different times of the day. At dawn it assumes a soft dreamy aspect; at noon, it appears to be a dazzling white, and in the moonlight the dome looks like a huge iridescent pearl. Not surprisingly, then, the Taj is today regarded all over the world as a supreme labour of love.

Though the architectural history of the Taj has received much attention, a cultural and political interpretation of the Taj has never been attempted. While it never fails to move and dazzle, one can scarcely forget that its history, like that of other monumental achievements of pre-modern (and even modern) states, is bound to oppression and slavery. Who thinks of the large force of serfs whose labour was exploited to satisfy the love of one man, and how brutal was the repression of the peasantry in order to increase the revenues of the state? Or consider this: is it not oppressive that the Taj charges an admission fee of Rs. 100, an amount that the majority of Indians still do not make in one day's work, for the luxury of viewing it by moonlight?

The monument remains the supreme icon of India to the rest of the world, along with the overpopulation, notorious poverty, and "mysticism" of this ancient land. It is one of India's largest tourist-revenue earners, and no tourist image predominates as that of the visitor snapped in front of the Taj. The image of the Taj appears in countless advertisements, and the

Mughal Art and Architecture: A characteristic Indo-Islamic-Persian style that flourished on the Indian subcontinent during the Mughal empire (1526–1857). This new style combined elements of Islamic art and architecture, which had been introduced to India during the Delhi Sultanate (1192–1398) and had produced great monuments such as the Qutb Minar, with features of Persian art and architecture. Mughal monuments are found chiefly in N India, but there are also many remains in Pakistan. This article discusses these distinctive forms of art and architecture as they developed under a succession of Mughal emperors.

Achievements under Akbar: In architecture the first great Mughal monument was the mausoleum to Humayun, erected during the reign of Akbar (1556–1605). The tomb, which was built in the 1560s, was designed by a Persian architect Mirak Mirza Ghiyas. Set in a garden at Delhi, it has an intricate ground plan with central octagonal chambers, joined by an archway with an elegant facade and surmounted by cupolas, kiosks, and pinnacles. At the same time Akbar was building his fortress-palace in his capital, Agra. Native red sandstone was inlaid with white marble, and all the surfaces were ornately carved on the outside and sumptuously painted inside.

Akbar went on to build the entire city of Fatehpur Sikri (City of Victory) in which extensive use was made of the low arches and bulbous domes that characterise the Mughal style. Built in 1571 the choice of the site of Sikri reflected Akbar's gratitude to a Muslim saint at Sikri for the birth of his son. Courtiers soon followed suit and built homes surrounding the palace and mosque. The new city became the capital of the empire, but in 1585 it was abandoned.

Under Akbar, Persian artists directed an academy of local painters. The drawings, costumes, and ornamentation of illuminated manuscripts by the end of the 16th cent illustrate the influence of Indian tastes and manners in the bright coloring and detailed landscape backgrounds. Modelling and perspective also began to be adapted from Western pictures. Basawan, Lal, and Daswanth were Akbar's most famous painters.

Jahangir (1605–27) favoured paintings of events from his own life rather than illustrated fiction. He encouraged portraiture and scientific studies of birds, flowers, and animals, which were collected in albums. Mansur and Manohar were among his famous painters. Jahangir, who resided at Lahore, built less than his predecessors but effected the significant change from sandstone to marble

Shah Jahan (1628–58) perfected Mughal architecture and erected at Agra its most noble and famous building, the tomb of his favourite wife, which is known as the Taj Mahal. A huge white marble building of simple, symmetrical plan, it is inlaid with colourful semiprecious materials and is set in an equally beautiful and symmetrical garden. The Taj Mahal continues the tradition of Mughal garden tombs, of which Humayun's tomb was the first. Shah Jahan established (1638) Delhi as his capital and built there the famous Red Fort, which contained the imperial Mughal palace.

The extensive use of precious and semiprecious stones as inlay and the vast quantity of white marble required nearly bankrupted the empire. The Taj Mahal is completely symmetric other than the sarcophagus of Shah Jahan, which is placed off centre in the crypt room below the main floor. This symmetry extended to the building of an entire mirror mosque in red sandstone, to complement the Mecca-facing mosque place to the west of the main structure.

The Taj Mahal in Agra, India and the Shalimar Garden in Lahore, Pakistan, are two sites which are on the world heritage list of UNESCO. One can see the architectural similarities and the love for water that the Mughals expressed in many of their buildings. Some high resolution pictures of the Shalimar Gardens, Badshahi Mosque and Lahore Fort can be found here. The Taj is considered to be one of the most beautiful monuments of love and is one of the Seven Wonders of the World.

The "Black Taj": A longstanding popular tradition holds that an identical mausoleum complex was originally supposed to be built on the other side of the river, in black marble instead of white. The story suggests that Shah Jahan was overthrown by his son Aurangzeb before the black version could be built. Ruins of dark marble found across the river are, the story suggests, the unfinished base of this "Black Taj".

Recent scholarship disputes this theory, and throws some interesting light on the design of the Taj Mahal. All other major Mughal tombs were sited in gardens that form a cross, with the tomb at the intersection of the vertical and horizontal pieces. The Taj Mahal gardens, by contrast, form a great 'T', with the tomb at the centre of the crosspiece. But the outline of the ruins on the other river bank would extend the design of the Taj Mahal gardens to form a cross of proportions typical of other Mughal tombs. Further, the marble in the ruins opposite the Taj Mahal, while dark from staining, were originally white. In addition, an octagonal pool in these ruins would have reflected the Taj Mahal. Scholars have called these ruins the Mahtab Bagh or "Moonlight Garden".

Agra Fort : By most estimates, the fort was taken over from the Lodis by the Moghuls in the late 16th century, by Akbar the Great. During his reign, he shifted the government of his empire from Delhi to Agra. Because of this, much of Agra flourished and the site of the old Lodis fort began changing into more of a royal estate. Akbar tended to build from red sandstone, often inlaid with white marble and intricate decorations.

It was only during the reign of Akbar's grandson, Shah Jahan, that the site finally took on its current state. Legend foretells that Shah Jahan built the beautiful Taj Mahal for his wife. Unlike his grandfather, Shah Jahan tended to have buildings made from white marble, often inlaid with gold or semi-precious gems. He destroyed some of the earlier buildings inside the fort in order to make his own.

This was also a site of one of the battles during the Indian rebellion of 1857, which caused the end of the British East India Company's rule in India, and led to a century of direct rule of India by Britain.

The walls have two gates, the 'Delhi Gate' and the 'Lahore Gate' (sometimes called Amar Singh Gate). The Delhi Gate is considered the grandest of the gates and leads into an inner gate called the Hathi Pol (Elephant Gate). Due to the fact that the Indian military (the Parachute Brigade in particular) is still using the northern portion of the Agra Fort, the Delhi Gate cannot be used by the public. Tourists enter via the Lahore Gate. Lahore Gate is named so because it faces Lahore, now in Pakistan.

Babri Mosque : The rulers of the Sultanate of Delhi and its successor Mugal Empire were great patrons of art and architecture and constructed many fine tombs, mosques and madrasas. These have a distinctive style which bears influences of 'later Tughlaq' architecture. Mosques all over India were built in different styles; the most elegant styles developed in areas where indigenous art traditions were strong and local artisans were highly skilled. Thus regional or provincial styles of mosques grew out of local temple or domestic styles, which were conditioned in their turn by climate, terrain, materials, hence the enormous difference between the mosques of Bengal, Kashmir and Gujarat. The Babri Mosque followed the architectural school of Jaunpur.

Babri is an important mosque of a distinct style, preserved mainly in architecture, developed after the Delhi Sultanate was established (1192). The square Char Minar of Hyderabad (1591) with large arches, arcades, and minarets is typical. This art made extensive use of stone and reflected Indian adaptation to Muslim rule, until Mughals art replaced it in the 17th century, as typified by structures like the Taj Mahal.

The traditional hypostyle plan with an enclosed courtyard, imported from Western Asia was generally associated with the introduction of Islam in new areas, but was abandoned in favour of schemes more suited to local climate and needs. The Babri Masjid was a mixture of the local influence and the Western Asian style and examples of this type of mosque are common in India. The Babri Mosque was a large imposing structure with three domes, one central and two secondary. It is surrounded by two high walls, running parallel to each other and enclosing a large central courtyard with a deep well, which was known for its cold and sweet water.

On the high entrance of the domed structure are fixed two stone tablets which bear two inscriptions in Persian declaring that this structure was built by one Mir Baqi on the orders of Babur. The walls of the Babri Mosque are made of coarse-grained whitish sandstone blocks, rectangular in shape, while the domes are made of thin and small burnt bricks. Both these structural ingredients are plastered with thick chunam paste mixed with coarse sand.

One of the columns of the Babri Mosque. Some Hindus say it came from a Temple under the site, particularly noting the two flowers (far top of photo) which they say are Hindu-associated lotus motifs, however this motif is common in mosques of that period.

The Central Courtyard was surrounded by lavishly curved columns superimposed to increase the height of the ceilings. The plan and the architecture followed the Begumpur Friday mosque of Jahanpanah rather than the Moghul style where Hindu masons used their own trabeated structural and decorative traditions. The excellence of their craftsmanship is noticeable in their vegetal scrolls and lotus patterns. These motifs are also present in the Firuz Shah Mosque in Firuzabad (about 1354) now in a ruined state, Qila Kuhna Mosque (about 1540). The Darasbari Mosque in the Southern suburb of the walled city of Gaur, and the Jamali Kamili Mosque built by Sher Shah Suri this was the forerunner of the Indo Islamic style adopted by Akbar. The Babri Masjid with its bold and graceful style was universally praised and widely followed.

> *"A whisper from the Babri Masjid Mihrab could be heard clearly at the other end 200 feet [60 m] away and through the length and breadth of the central court" according to Graham Pickford architect to Lord William Bentinck (1828–1833) The Mosque's acoustics were mentioned by him in his book 'Historic Structures of Oudhe' he says "for a 16th century building the deployment and projection of voice from the pulpit is considerably advanced, the unique deployment of sound in this structure will astonish the visitor".*

Modern Architects have attributed this intriguing acoustic feature to a large recess in the wall of the Mihrab and several recesses in the surroundings walls which functioned as resonators, and gave our sounds back to the worshippers, this design helped everyone to hear the speaker at the Mihrab. The sandstone used in building the Babri Mosque also had resonant qualities which contributed to the unique acoustics. The Babri mosque's Tughluquid style integrates other indigenous design components and techniques (air cooling systems) disguised as recognizably Islamic design elements (arches, vaults and domes) In the Babri Masjid the high ceiling, domes, and six large grill windows (see picture) all served as a passive environmental control system that brought down the temperature and also allowed in natural ventilation as well as daylight.

Legend of the Babri Mosque's Miraculous Well: The reported medicinal properties of the deep well in the central courtyard have been featured in various news reports such as the BBC report of December 1989 and in various newspapers. The earliest mention of the Babri water well was in a two line reference to the Mosque in the Gazette of Faizabad District 1918 which says "There are no significant historical buildings here, except for various Buddhist shrines, the Babri Mosque is an ancient structure with a well which both the Hindus and Mussalmans claim has Miraculous properties."

Ayodhya, a pilgrimage site for Hindus has an annual fair attended by over 500,000 people of both faiths, many devotees came during the annual Rama festival to drink from the water well in the Babri Courtyard. It was believed drinking water from this well could cure a range of illnesses. Hindu pilgrims also believed that the Babri water well was the original well in the Rama Temple under the mosque. Ayodhya Muslims believed that the well was a gift from God. Local women regularly brought their new born babies to drink from the reputedly curative water.

The 125 foot (40 m) deep well in question was situated in the South Eastern Courtyard of the large rectangular courtyard of the Babri Mosque. There was a small Hindu shrine built in 1890 joining the well with a statute of Lord Rama. It was an artesian well and drew water from a considerable distance below the water table. Eleven feet (3 m) in radius the first 30 feet (10 m) from ground level were bricked. It drew water from a reservoir trapped in a bed of shale sand and gravel; this could explain the unusually cool temperature of the water. The water contained almost no sodium explaining its reputation that the water was 'sweet.' To access the well one had to climb onto a three foot (1 m) platform, the well was covered with planks of thick wood with an unhinged trapdoor. Water was drawn by means of a bucket and long lengths of rope and due to its claimed 'spiritual properties' used only for drinking.

Badshahi Masjid : The mosque was built under the patronage of the sixth Mughal Emperor, Aurangzeb Alamgir. It was completed in 1673 under the supervision of Aurangzeb's foster brother Muzaffar Hussain (also known as Fidaie Khan Koka) who was appointed governor of Lahore in May of 1671 and held this post until 1675. He was also Master of Ordnance to the emperor. The construction of the mosque took about two years from May, 1671 to April 1673. The mosque was built opposite the Lahore Fort, illustrating its stature in the Mughal Empire, and in conjunction to the building of the mosque, a new gate was built at the fort, named *Alamgiri Gate* after Aurangzeb.

From 1850 onwards piecemeal repairs were carried out frequently, but under the supervision of the *Badshahi Mosque Authority,* thorough repairs were carried out from 1939 to 1960 at a cost of about 4.8 million rupees, which brought the mosque to its original shape and condition. The blueprint for the repairs was prepared by the late architect Nawab Zen Yar Jang Bahadur.

In 2000, the relief work of marble inlay in the main vault was repaired under the supervision of Saleem Anjum Qureshi. On the occasion of the second Islamic Summit held at Lahore on February 22, 1974, thirty-nine heads of Muslim states offered their Friday prayers in the Badshahi Masjid, led by Maulana Abdul Qadir Azad, the Khatib of the mosque. Recently a small museum has also been added to the mosque complex. It contains relics of Muhammad, his cousin, and his daughter, Hazrat Fatimah.

Like the character of its founder, the mosque is bold, vast and majestic in its expression. It was the largest mosque in the world for a long time. The interior has rich embellishment in stucco tracery (Manbatkari) and panelling with a fresco touch, all in bold relief, as well as marble inlay. The exterior is decorated with stone carving as well as marble inlay on red sandstone, specially of Loti form motifs in bold relief. The embellishment has Indo-Greek, Central Asian and Indian architectural influence both in technique and motifs.

The skyline is furnished by beautiful ornamental merlons inlaid with marble lining adding grace to the perimeter of the mosque. In its various architectural features like the vast square courtyard, the side aisles (dalans), the four corner minars, the projecting central transept of the prayer chamber and the grand entrance gate, is summed up history of the development of mosque architecture of the Muslim world over the thousand years prior to its construction in 1673.

The north enclosure wall of the mosque was laid close to the Ravi River bank, so a majestic gateway could not be provided on that side and to keep the symmetry the gate had to be omitted on the south wall as well. Thus a four aiwan plan like the earlier Delhi Jamia Masjid could not be adopted here. The walls were built with small kiln-burnt bricks laid in kankar, lime mortar (a kind of hydraulic lime) but have a veneer of red sandstone. The steps leading to the prayer chamber and its plinth are in varigated marble. The prayer chamber is very deep and is divided into seven compartments by rich engraved arches carried on very heavy piers. Out of the seven compartments, three double domes finished in marble have superb curvature, whilst the rest have wagon shaped curvilinear domes with a central rib in their interior and flat roof above. In the eastern front aisle, the ceiling of the compartment is flat (Qalamdani) with a curved border (ghalatan) at the cornice level.

The original floor of the courtyard was laid with small kiln-burnt bricks laid in the Mussalah pattern. The present red sandstone flooring was laid during the last thorough repairs (1939-60). Similarly, the original floor of the prayer chamber was in cut and dressed bricks with marble and Sang-i-Abri lining forming Mussalah and was also replaced by marble Mussalah during the last repairs.

Quranic Inscriptions: There are only two inscriptions in the mosque:

(i) one on the gateway

(ii) the other of Kalimah in the prayer chamber under the main high vault.

Bibi Ka Maqbara was built by Prince Azam Shah, son of Emperor Aurangzeb, in the late 17th century as a loving tribute to his mother, Dilras Bano Begam. The monument's name translates literally to 'Tomb of the Lady', but has earned the nickname 'poor man's Taj' because of its resemblance to the Taj Mahal.

Hiran Minar is set in peaceful evirons near Lahore in Sheikhupura, Pakistan. It was constructed by Emperor Jehangir as a monument to Mansraj, one of his pet antelopes. Its structures consist of a large, almost-square water tank with an octagonal pavilion in its centre, built during the reign of mughal emperor Shah Jahan; a causeway with its own gateway connects the pavilion with the mainland and a 100-foot-high minar, or minaret.

At the centre of each side of the tank, a brick Ramp slopes down to the water, providing access for royal animals and wild game. The minar itself was built by Emperor Jahangir in 1606 to honour the memory of a pet hunting antelope named Mansraj. Unique features of this particular complex are the antelope's grave and the distinctive water collection system. At each corner of the tank (approximately 750 by 895 feet in size), is a small, square building and a subsurface water collection system which supplied the tank; only one of these water systems is extensively exposed today.

Hiran Minar and its location and environment are other important features : the top of the minar is perhaps the best place in the province of Punjab to get a feel for the broader landscape and its relationship to a Mughal site. Looking north from the top of the minar, one can see a patch of forest which is similar to the scrub forest vegetation of Mughal times, while to the west are extensively-irrigated fields, a product of the late nineteenth and early twentieth centuries, but similar in size and appearance to the well-irrigated fields of the Mughal period.

Itmad-Ud-Daulah's Tomb is a Mughal mausoleum in the city of Agra in the Indian state of Uttar Pradesh. Often described as 'jewel box', sometimes called the *Baby Taj*, the tomb of Itmad-Ud-Daulah is often regarded as a "draft" of the Taj Mahal. Along with the main building, the structure consists of numerous outbuildings and gardens. The tomb, built between 1622 and 1628 represents the transition between the first phase of monumental Mughal architecture-primarily built from red sandstone with marble decorations, as in Humayun's Tomb in Delhi and Akbar's tomb in Sikandra-to its second phase, based on white marble and pietra dura inlay-most elegantly realised in the Taj Mahal.

Nur Jahan, the wife of Jahangir, commissioned the mausoleum for her father Mirza Ghiyas Beg, who had been given the title of *Itimad-ud-Daula* (pillar of the state). Mirza Ghiyas Beg is also the grandfather of Mumtaz Mahal (originally named Arjumand Bano, daughter of Asaf Khan), the wife of the emperor Shah Jahan, responsible for the building of the Taj Mahal.

Located on the left bank of the Yamuna river, the mausoleum is set in a large cruciform garden criss-crossed by water courses and walkways. The mausoleum itself is set on a base about 50 meters square and about 1 meter high. The mausoleum is about 23 meters square. On each corner are hexagonal towers, about 13 meters tall. The walls are white marble from Rajasthan encrusted with semi-precious stone decorations-cornelian, jasper, lapis lazuli, onyx, and topaz in images of cypress trees and wine bottles, or more elaborate decorations like cut fruit or vases containing bouquets. Light to the interior passes through delicate *jali* screens of intricately carved white marble.

Many of Nur Jahan's relatives are interred in the mausoleum. The only asymmetrical element of the entire complex is that the cenotaphs of her father and mother have been set side-by-side, a formation replicated in the Taj Mahal.

Lahore Fort: The Lahore Fort, locally referred to as Shahi Qila is the citadel of the city of Lahore, in modern day Pakistan. It is located in the northwestern corner of Lahore, adjacent to the Walled City. Some of the famous sites within the fort are: Sheesh Mahal, Alamgiri Gate, Naulakha pavilion, and Moti Masjid. The fort is 1,400 feet long and 1,115 feet wide. In 1981, the fort was added to the UNESCO World Heritage List of culturally important sites.

Historically, the origin of Lahore Fort is obscure. Traditionally the foundation of Lahore and its fort is attributed to Loh, the son of Rama, Avatara of Lord Vishnu of Hinduism, and hero of the Ramayana of epic age (1200-800 B.C.). However, during the execution done in the year 1959 A.D. by the Department of Archaeology, in front of Diwan-e-Am, a gold coin of Mahmud of Ghazni dated A.H. 146 (1025 A.D.) was found at a depth of 25 feet from the level of the lawns. Cultural layers continued to a further depth of 15 feet, giving strong indications that people had lived here, long before the conquest of Lahore by Mahmud in 1021 A.D. Further mention of the fort is traceable in connection with Shahab-ud-Din Ghori's successive invasions of Lahore from 1180 to 1186 A.D

The Naulakha pavilion is a marble building located at the Sheesh Mahal courtyard, which is itself located at the Lahore Fort in Lahore, Pakistan. Its western face provides a panoramic view of the ancient city of Lahore. When it was built in 1631 A.D. by the Mughal emperor Shahjahan, it cost Rs. 900,000 an exorbitant amount at the time. It is called Naulakha because that word in Urdu means 'worth 9 lakhs' (one lakh equals 100,000).

Nizamuddin Dargah is the mausoleum of Delhi's most famous Sufi saint Nizamuddin Auliya. It is visited daily by many of people of all religions. The tomb of Amir Khusro is also located within the Nizamuddin Dargah Complex. The neighborhood of Delhi where the mausoleum is located is called "Hazrat Nizamuddin" or simply "Nizamuddin" because of this.

Omar Hayat's Mahal is a 19th century wooden architectural wonder of Chiniot, a tehsil of the district of Jhang in Pakistan. It is also known as Gulzar Manzil. Omar Hayat's Palace is a three storey building which stands in the heart of the city. It is a great tourist attraction both local and foreign visitors. Members of sheikh family migrated from Calcutta to Chiniot in the 18th or 19th century A.D.

Sheikh Omar Hayat who was a successful trader was born in a middle class family. He decided to construct a magnificient palace for his newborn son in 1923. Syed Hassan Shah was assigned the task of palace's construction. He gathered many famous artisans from different places who continued working day and night for 10 ten years. Rahim Bakhsh Pirjha and Elahi

Bakhsh Pirjha who were masters in *manabat kari* did wood carving. Gazeteer Vol XXXII, Jhang district 1929 states, *"The house built by Sheikh Omar Hayat's is a sort of local wonder, as it cost more than Rs. 200,000 to make and rises high above all other buildings of area"*. The construction of the palace completed in 1935 and Mr. Hayat expired in same year just a couple of months before its completion.

History claims that Mr. Hayat's only son Gulzar Muhammad's marriage in 1938 brought an ironic twist of fate in the shape of death. He (Gulzar) was found dead in the palace the very next day of his marriage. The news of son's death lofted loads of grief on mother who died remembering him. Both the mother and the son were buried in the courtyard of the ground floor of the palace.

Mr. Hayat's relatives left the palace thinking it as a subject to bad luck, while servants continued living for a couple of years and then parted from it. An orphanage was established by some religious leaders and then it was evacuee when its top story collapsed. Next came the Qabza groups who got shops and houses constructed on the piece of land lying next to it. The palace's building is the last of Mughal's architectural style. Unique carving cuts on the doors, windows and jhirokas reflect a colour of their own. The roofs, balconies, stairways, terrace and the stucco designs make a perfect interior. The facade of the building is decorated with a fine inlay of bricks, the dazzling shine of marble and picturesque shades help it rank among the great palaces of Mughal era landlords. Later on, this placed was occupied by Qabza mafia who destroyed most of the building However seeing death of its glory in 1989, Athar Tahir, the then deputy commissioner of Jhang, took the palace into his custody. He removed the encroachments and started its renovation with an expenditure of Rs. 900,000.

Period of Babur, Humayun and Sher Shah

A political vacuum-this phrase can best summarise the state of affairs in north India in 1526 AD. The last of the Lodi sultans had succeeded in alienating the majority of his nobles by his arrogant posturing. Ibrahim Lodi's pretensions were to prove his downfall in a land where class and clan loyalties were precarious at best. And yet the Delhi sultanate had, in the last three centuries, left an undeniable mark on the subcontinent. Firstly it introduced Islam along with its culture-literature, painting, philosophy. Secondly the sultans put into place a system of administration-revenue collection, taxes and minting-that would serve as the base for their successors the Mughals.

And lastly, and important as far as we are concerned, they established firmly the principles of Islamic architecture-which from its Persian and Turkish origins was to evolve into many regional prototypes. The Lodi dynasty was thus fated to be the last in the Delhi Sultanate. After the extinction of the Tughlaq dynasty at the hands of Tamerlane, the Lodis finally assumed power at Delhi. In spite of the empire building efforts of the first two of the line, Bahlol and Sikander, Ibrahim Lodi frittered away their gains by his imperious manner. This he did largely forgetting that the Sultan's power base was eventually his nobles, that he was at best first among equals.

Thus, the Afghan nobles found themselves allied, along with certain Rajput chieftains-chief among whom was Rana Sanga of Chittor-with the disinherited Timurid prince Babur, from Ferghana. In search of a new land to claim for his own, Babur was a young, ambitious and ruthless warrior who knew an opportunity when he saw one. And so came about the first battle of Panipat. This was to be the ground for many a decisive battle afterwards, its fertile plains proving ideal ground for the massing of armies. The Sultan's 100,000 horsemen and 1000 elephants far outnumbered Babur's troops, but it was his use of artillery, for the first time in India, that won him the day.

The Delhi Sultanate, and the seat of power at Delhi since the 12th century, thus finally came to an end. Never controlling more than a part of north India, it left behind a fractured and divided subcontinent characterised by the lack of central power, and numerous princes and would-be sultans. Winning and keeping control of an empire here would require finesse and tact, brutality and astuteness.

The Mughal Empire: Starting

Periodically, this stage is chiefly taken as the end of the Delhi Sultanate, and the beginning of the Mughal period. However, Mughal supremacy in India was not established till the reign of Akbar and before that there were times when the Mughals were in danger of extinction. This danger came from the brief reign of the Afghan Sher Shah Sur, of Sasaram in Bihar.

For a while he succeeded in chasing Humayun from the subcontinent, and were it not for his accidental death, the Mughal destiny in India might have ended before it begun. This period in history thus show a flux in political power at Delhi, with the short reign of Babur giving way to Humanyun. He in his turn was defeated by Sher Shah, only to return after the latter's death. Thus with war taking precedence, architectural activity was sporadic at best. Yet a number of notable changes came about, mainly with the Timurid and Safavid influences which came along with Babur. The founder of the Mughal empire did not have much time for architectural construction. The Rama and Zahara Bagh at Agra is a garden that ameliorated the climate that Babur so detested, and also a talar before the Lodi palace.

The Purana Qila: The main citadel of the time, which can be attributed to both Humayun and Sher Shah, is the Purana Qila at Delhi, with its associated structures. Though the walls are crumbling in places, the massive portals of the Qila are still for the most part intact and show a fine sense of proportion combined with a judicious mix of local red sandstone, Persian-inspired encaustic tile work and marble mosaic. Of the structures inside the Qila, two of the most notable are the Sher Mandal, the octagonal library-this was to prove ill-fated as it is from its steps that Humayun died.

Another is the superb Qila-i-Kuhna mosque. This should also be compared with the Jamali Masjid of roughly the same period near the Qutb Minar complex. Both these mosques are of similar pedigree, with five frontal arches of which the central one is made the most prominent. However, in the Qila-i-Kuhna, the subtle variations of the arch heights are among the features that mark this as the high point of mosques of this plan type.

Tomb of Sher Shah

A word should also be added here for the fine tomb of Sher Shah Suri at Sasaram in Bihar. This tomb was the apogee of the octagonal type which found its beginnings in the Tughlaq and Lodi dynasties. Situated in the middle of a lake, the tomb obeys all the principles of octagonal tombs-arched side openings, buttressed walls and chhattris, but takes them to a previously unsurpassed level of grandeur not only in size, but also cohesiveness of concept. The magnificent setting of the tomb is eloquent, and speaks of the quirks of fate. But for a cannon exploding ahead of time which caused Sher Shah's death, the Mughal empire that came after him may never have been able to take root.

Shah Jahan's Asymmetric Tomb

Aurangzeb had Shah Jahan's tomb and cenotaph placed in the Taj Mahal rather than building him a separate mausoleum such as other emperors had. He thus destroyed the symmetry of the Taj Mahal design. A variation on the Black Taj legend suggests that Aurangzeb's decision was made from malice or parsimony. In Itmad-Ud-Daulah's Tomb however, which was a major influence on the Taj Mahal design, Aurangzeb's grandparents were interred in a similar asymmetric fashion.

Aurangazeb was a pious man, and Islam discourages all kinds of ostentation-least of all in death. That is why they do not use box-coffins but rather bury their dead in a white shroud. Islamic books describe burying in coffins or boxes as 'wasting wealth that can be used in good deeds like feeding the hungry or needy' Shah Jahan's building itself was thus a waste of money according to Aurangazeb's worldview. Thus he just buried his father next to his mother's tomb without much ado.

A seemingly endless number of stories describe, often in horrific detail, deaths, dismemberments and mutilations which Shah Jahan inflicted on various craftsmen associated with the tomb. Perhaps the most common story prevailing is that Shah

Jahan had the finest architects and sculptors at his disposal. After the completion of the work, Shah Jahan had their hands cut off so that they would never build a monument in greater splendour, and their eyes pulled out so that they would never witness anything more beautiful. No respected authorities find these legendary horrors credible.

Legends abound concerning items originally attached to the Taj Mahal which were stolen. Some original items have been removed over time, but many are mere legends only. These legends include:

- Gold leaf, supposed to have covered all or part of the dome.
- A golden railing supposed to have circled the cenotaphs (suggested perhaps by a temporary enamel railing that was replaced after completion of the marble jali)
- Diamonds supposedly inlaid in the cenotaphs
- A blanket woven of pearls supposedly covering Mumtaz's cenotaph

Numerous items from the Taj Mahal *have* gone missing however; these include the following:

- An entrance door of carved jasper
- Gold leaf that adorned the cast iron joints of the jali screen around the cenotaphs
- Numerous rich carpets that covered the interior of the tomb
- Enamelled lamps from the interior of the tomb

Fort Architecture

Fort at Jaisalmer: Rajput architecture is in some sense an anomaly because it is a "Hindu" art dating from a time that is usually described as an "Islamic" period. The Rajputs were a group of warrior clans who lived in what is now Rajasthan and Madhya Pradesh. As *Kshatriyas* (members of the warrior caste) they considered it their *dharma*, or divine duty, to fight, and stories of their extraordinary courage on the battlefield are legion. Despite their preoccupation with war, the Rajputs were great patrons of art and architecture, the finest examples being their forts and palaces. In contrast to the perfect symmetry of Mughal architecture, Rajput palaces are complex compositions.

Bikaner was founded in 1488 by Bikha. The city is encircled by a three and a half mile long stone wall in rich pink sandstone. There are five gates and three sally-ports. Junagarh fort was built between 1588 and 1593 by Raja Rai Singh, one of Akbar's generals. The fort has an excellent library of Persian manuscripts and ancient Sanskrit books and an impressive armoury. The fort at Jodhpur dominates the city and can be seen for miles across the bare desert. The old city is surrounded by a huge wall with 101 bastions, nearly six miles long. The Meherangarh fort stands on a cliff with a sheer drop of over 120 feet. The foundation of Jaipur, the fabled "pink city", in 1727 represents the final phase of Rajput architecture. Built by Jai Singh, Jaipur represents a fusion of Eastern and Western ideas of town planning. A huge battlemented wall with bastions and towers at regular intervals, loopholed for musketry, encloses the city.

The City Palace is at the center of the walled city and is a spectacular synthesis of Rajput and Mughal architectural styles. The *Hawa Mahal*, or Palace of Winds, (1799) is the building that put Jaipur on the tourist map. The five storey symmetrical facade is composed of 953 small casements in a huge curve each with a projecting balcony and crowning arch. The fact that it is no more, in architectural terms, than a facade points to the continued Indian fascination with dissimulation. This dialectic of illusion and reality is also to be found in the *Jantar Mantar*, the largest of five observatories built by Jai Singh II in the early eighteenth century. The Jantar Mantar, a scientific and yet playful array of astronomical buildings, is truly the abode of magic.

Water has played an important role in the architectural heritage of western India from the earliest times. One of the most characteristic features of the early Harappan towns (3000 BC) was the presence of a sophisticated system of drains, wells and tanks. The practice of making wells into an art form was begun by the Hindus but it developed under Muslim rule. The *vavs* or *baolis* (step-wells) of Gujarat consist of two parts: a vertical shaft from which water is drawn and the surrounding inclined subterranean passageways, chambers and steps which provide access to the well. The galleries and chambers surrounding these wells were often carved profusely with elaborate detail and became cool, quiet retreats during the hot summers.

One of this is the Mata Bhavani's *vav* at Ahmedabad, built in the eleventh century. The water is approached by a long flight of steps above which rises a sequence of two, three and four storey open pavilions. The elaborate ornamentation of the columns, brackets and beams, and the friezes of motifs are in the Solanki school of temple architecture.

The *Rani Vav* (Queen's well) at Patan, built during the late eleventh century, is probably the most magnificent step-well in Gujarat. Multi-storey colonnades and retaining walls link a stepped tank to a deep circular well. Throughout, the ornamentation is sumptuous. Columns, brackets and beams are encrusted with scrollwork and the wall niches are carved with figures. Hindu deities alternate with alluring maidens on the walls flanking the staircase.

The Dada Harir's *vav* at Ahmedabad, together with the *vav* at Adalaj, is the finest example of the Muslim period. The Dada Harir's *vav* is modeled on the earlier Mata Bhavani's *vav*, though it has an additional domed pavilion at the entrance. One striking feature of this *vav* is the complete absence of figural themes. The motifs in stylised scrollwork that adorn the wall niches may be compared with those that appear in Islamic architecture. The *vav* at Adalaj, located 12 miles north of Ahmedabad, is octagonal.

Fort Wall at Gwalior: The oldest surviving palaces date from the mid-fifteenth century and are found at Chitor and Gwalior. The Man Mandir is the largest palace in Gwalior and was built by Raja Man Singh Tomar (1486-1516). Each of these palaces is a complex grouping of small spaces enclosed by a fortified wall. The Man Mandir has two storeys above, and two below, ground level overhanging a sandstone cliff. Here in the underground chambers, royal prisoners were tortured and killed.

This gigantic cliff is punctuated by five massive round towers, crowned by domed cupolas and linked by delicately carved parapets. The whole facade is enriched with brilliant blue tiles. The palaces of Jaisalmer, Bikaner, Jodhpur, Udaipur and Kota represent the maturity of the Rajput style.

All of these palaces were built predominantly in the seventeenth and early eighteenth centuries. The huge fortified city of Jaisalmer is situated far out in he Thar desert. The buildings are constructed with the local yellow-brown stone and they have been remarkably preserved owing to their remote location. The fort is enclosed by an imposing 30 feet high sandstone wall. Wells within the fort provided a regular source of water. The fort at Jaisalmer has now acquired another kind of history, becoming a favourite locale for film shooting: even Satyajit Ray shot *Sonar Kela* (The Golden Fortress) here.

The Delwara Templesat Mount Abu: There are many followers of Jainism in West India. However, since Jainas account for only 0.5% of the total Indian population, they are still a minority. The most important teaching of Jainism is "Ahimsa," meaning non-violence or non-killing. Ahimsa is applied not only for humans, but also for all sentient beings. Jainas even avoid claiming the lives of insects. The precepts that Jain monks should follow are very strict. When they travel on foot for ascetic practices and preachment during the dry season, they carry brushes in their hands and wear masks. They make it a rule to brush away surfaces of stones before sitting down on them in order to avoid stamping on insects. To wear a mask is for fear of biting small flying insects unwittingly when opening their mouths carelessly. Lay followers, however, seldom keep such harsh precepts. Incidentally, Gujarat is the birthplace of Mahatma Gandhi. Although he was not a Jain, he was deeply influenced by the thought of Jainism and persistently observed the teaching of "ahimsa" while he was struggling to achieve independence of India.

There are lots of Jain temples in both states of Gujarat and Rajasthan in West India. The most famous ones among them are the Delwara temples. They are situated at Mt. Abu, which is 170km north of Ahmadabad and 1,200m above sea level. The mountain has been worshipped by Hindu Shivaites and Jainas since ancient times. After the construction of this group of temples, Mt. Abu became a very significant pilgrimage site for Jainas as well as Mt. Satrunjaya. The Delwara temples consist of four temples of similar size and one small temple. Although each temple has symmetrical plan, there is no axis that runs through this group of temples as a whole. Space surrounding the temples seems just a residuary, and does not form a public square.

Plan of the Derwara temples In addition to that, since most of the temples are single-storied structures, there is not a tall tower which can be seen from outside, and the surrounding walls of each temple are not attractive at all. In short, it does not show any beauty in external appearance. One might feel dubious if these are the famous Jain temples. But upon entering the temples, there is another world that takes our breath away. Two temples are especially stunning.

One is Vimala Vasahi, which is dedicated to Adinatha, the first Tirthankara or Jina. The other is Luna Vasahi, dedicated to Neminatha, the 22nd one. The interior space of both temples is made of white marble. Everywhere except the floors, from walls to ceilings as well as columns and beams, are covered with extremely delicate engravings. This white and pure space is so gorgeous that it makes us feel as if we are out of this world. Above all a Domical ceiling of "Ranga mandapa" (open-type hall) is carved concentrically with utmost intricacy. The central part of it is sagging like a chandelier made of stalactite. Sixteen bodies of "Vidyadevi" (goddesses of knowledge) are also engraved on the vault. It is hard to believe that all of them are made of stone. A block of ceiling at Cloisters in Vimala Vasahi.

It is a feast for the eyes to watch from amongst pillars, each one of them carved with different designs, the intertwined interior and exterior space lit up by reflecting sunlight that comes from courtyards. Every part of ceiling at "bhamati" (cloisters) which surrounds "Vimana" (main shrine) is also covered with carvings such as lotuses, gods, and abstract patterns. In each external "deva-kulikas" (small shrines) that face the bhamati, a statue of Tirthankara (Jina) is installed.

According to a legend, sculptors conducted their jobs with ultimate delicacy because they were paid by the weight of stone refuse. Standing in the luxurious space that tells the plausibility of this tale, one would also be reminded of Alhambra Palace in Spain that is far away from here. Like this temple, that masterpiece of Islamic architecture has an extremely gorgeous interior space that is unimaginable from its plain exterior.

Although there are lots of great works of architecture in the world, these Jain temples and Patio of Lion at Alhambra Palace would be the world's two equals, not in the fact that they boast of their large size or splendid sculptural appearance in exterior, but in the fact that they express highly polished microcosm by covering rather small-scale interior spaces with extremely minute engravings. If Alhambra Palace was aimed for the actualisation of Earthly Paradise, the Delwara temples would be the realisation of the Pure Land after emancipation.

Therefore the Delwara temples had come to be visited by a lot of people. Historically, Jain architecture had followed the development of Buddhist and Hindu architectures. But in time, it established its originality and reached its highest peak in Ranakpur. The temples at Mt. Abu can be regarded as the most excellent works at the stage just before attaining to the peak. Here we will go through the temples at Mt. Abu. Base carving of a pillar in Luna Vasahi Vimala Shah, who served as a minister at the time of the Solanki Dynasty, established the Adinatha temple in compensation for committing political murder.

The temple came to be known accordingly as Vimala Vasahi (temple). At that time, however, he built only "Garbhagriha" (sanctum), "Gudha mandapa" (closed hall) and "Trika mandapa" (vestibule). It is said all of them were made of black marble produced at a nearby quarry. Thus it was nothing but a temple similar to those of ordinary Hindu temples. Pittalahara temple, which had not been completed, still retains such traces of the old times. But in the 12th century, the premises were surrounded by cloisters and the "Ranga mandapa" was built in connection with the cloisters.

At this stage, the whole situation changed dramatically and most part of the courtyard was turned into an interior space. Apart from cave temples, Indian architecture had an inclination to make external appearance as a grand sculpture, while interior space was left humble. In this context, it was the first time that Indians developed an architecture that put stress on the interior space rather than external expression. Furthermore, all the buildings were made of white marble which was carried all the way to the top of the 1,200 m-high mountain from a quarry near Kumbharia, and that finally resulted in establishing the new style of Jain architecture.

In the 13th century, two brothers, Tejahpala and Vastupala, who are described as the Medici for Jainas, built Neminatha temple in following the same style with more delicate carvings. It is also called Luna Vasahi, from the name of Luna, Tejahpala's son. Although a major part of the temple was destroyed by the attack from the Khalji Dynasty of Islam in 1311, it had been constantly reconstructed and developed with sculptural precision until the 19th century. Main Dome of magnificent carving in Luna Vasahi Right: One of corner sculptures of ceiling in Luna Vasahi However, even these unsurpassed pieces of architecture have flaws. Since architects and masons in those days did not know the construction method of a true arch, and consequently did not know that of a true dome, they made corbelled domes by laying stones not radially but horizontally.

As a result, they could not make a large-scale dome that was seen in later Islamic architecture in India. Even the biggest dome of Vimala Vasahi is merely 7.5 meters in diameter, while that of Gol Gumbaz in Bijapur is carried out 38 meters. In addition to that, if we observe closely the abundant sculptures in the temple, each of them seems to be inferior to the expressive and dynamic ones found in Hindu temples. However, these are the engravings devoted to the architecture as its elements, and the purpose of all the energy infused here lied in the realisation of a space as Pure Land. The most important value of the Delwara temples would be the introduction of the sense of interior space to Indian architecture, and this viewpoint would arouse a strong interest among the architects of our times. This aspect was developed later into the new form of Kharatara temple, and further developed into the style of the Adinatha temple at Ranakpur. We will observe this development later in this report.

Mughal Decline and Princely Architecture

If Jaisalmer is famous for its havelis, Jaipur is known for its town planning inspired from ancient texts. The death of the Mughal emperor Bahadur Shah accentuated the influence of Maharaja Jai Singh II of Amber, who then embarked upon the construction of a modern capital in the plains – a metropolitan fort inspired by Kautilya's *Arthashastra*. Like Kautilya's ideal towns too, Jaipur is regularly planned. Its original regular nine-square geometry was however disturbed by military and esthetic considerations the plan had to be modified to incorporate an existing garden palace at the ruler's direction, and by displacing the north-west zone to integrate the defences with the hills there, extending to Jaigarh and Amber.

Within the walls, the original garden palace was follows the precepts of an ideal Kautilyan complex. The uniform pink colour of the construction and the fantastic observatory built by Sawai Jai Singh contribute to give Jaipur its distinctive flavour. The famous nine-square pattern of Jaipur is again much celebrated and has once again inspired modern buildings – the most famous being Charles Correa's Jawahar Kala Kendra in the same city.

The Portuguese and the Estada da India: The control of the Mediterranean by the Turks and the Egyptians, and their subsequent domination of cities in the Middle East holy to both Christianity and Islam, prompted the orthodox Portuguese kings to find a way to the Indies, both to menace the Muslims along another front as well as to supplement trade.

1498 AD – Vasco da Gama was the first to round the Cape of Good Hope, South Africa, and, with the help of a Gujarati navigator, to eventually sail and drop anchor off the port of Calicut. In his log, Vasco da Gama records his first meeting, and answers to a query that he comes in search of 'Christian and Spices'. In fact, the Portuguese first mistook the Hindu inhabitants of Calicut for Christians. In Vasco da Gama's words:

> *The city of Calicut is inhabited by Christians. They are of tawny complexion. Some of them have big beards and long hair, whilst others clip their hair short or shave the head, merely allowing a tuft to remain on the crown as a sign that they are christians.*

This first encounter was the beginning of the Portuguese adventure with India which lasted till 1961, when the Indian Army took over Goa, Daman and Diu. In the 15th and 16th centuries, the Portuguese established trading bases all along the Malabar coast, and became an important political force in the hinterland. Their powerful naval fleet controlled commerce in the Indian Ocean and broke up the hegemony enjoyed till that point by Gujarat. The Portuguese would remain powerful till their domination was broken by two events – the defeat and subsequent vassal status of Portugal itself by the Spanish, and the arrival of other European powers, namely the French, the English and the Dutch in the Indian Ocean. This did not mean, however, that the Portuguese culture has not contributed substantially to the region.

The Portuguese did not take their women with them when they travelled across the sea; and so to maintain the small garrisons in India, the sailors were encouraged to marry Indians and this phenomenon gave birth to another class of mixed blood people who were Christians and spoke Portuguese, but in many ways retained the culture and customs of their maternal ancestors. Goa also became cosmopolitan – its status as a trading centre attracted people from all over India and at one time the university had students from all over the subcontinent speaking 18 different languages, and the printing presses were amongst the first to print in vernacular.

The Jesuits were asked to send two representatives to Akbar's discussions on various religions that were taking place contemporaneously at Fatehpur Sikri. The architecture of the imperial Portuguese presence is marked by its many churches and cathedrals, which faithfully document in their turn European post-Renaissance architecture, though to Classicism and its Mannerist and Baroque branches. There also still exist old mansions, dating mainly from the 18th century, as well as numerous remains of fortifications and defences, but in the main it is Portuguese churches and monastic buildings which take pride of place.

Goa – St. Francis of Assisi : The Cathedral of St. Catherine (Se Cathedral) was built by the colony's Chief Engineer Julio Simao is a style which would later be very popular and was further developed and refined by the French at Pondicherry, as well as more modest 18th century Portuguese works such as the Church of Our Lady of the Rosary, Nellitope, Madras.

The rich facade of the Bom Jesus incorporates much leathery scroll-work and oddly proportioned pilasters at variance with the canonical four-storey sequence from Doric at the base to Composite at the top. This cathedral is also famous for housing the mortal remains of St. Francis Xavier, whose extremely floral tomb rests in one niche of the building.

5

Architectures of Rajputs

Vibrant and striking land of Rajasthan which was the home of the Rajput warrior clans who had ruled here for many years has many architecture. The desert state has some of India's most romantic cities like Udaipur, Jaisalmer, Jodhpur, Jaipur and the list is endless. The vast area of Rajasthan is dotted with the most imposing and magnificent forts and palaces in the world. The Rajputs were prolific builders and today these magnificent structures tell the story of gallantry, courage and tragedy of that bygone era.

The majestic forts, intricately carved temples, and decorated havelis are part of the architectural heritage of Rajasthan. Many tourists visit Rajasthan to explore this traditional art. These Forts and Palaces of Rajasthan can be an inspiration for an architecture lover. When we talk about the architecture of Rajasthan the names, which strike our mind, are Jantar Mantar, Dilwara Temples, Chittorgarh Fort, Lake Palace Hotel, City Palaces, and Jaisalmer Havelis.

Jaisalmer Havelis depict a true picture of the royal heritage of Rajasthan. The Nathmal Ji Ki Haveli in Jaisalmer was built in the 19th century by two architect brothers. The interesting fact about the construction of this Haveli was that the two brothers concentrated on either side separately, which could give a proper symmetry to the structure. Paintings in miniature style monopolize the walls in the interior. Mighty tuskers carved out of yellow sandstone stand guard to the Haveli.Another popular Haveli in Jaisalmer is Salim Singh Ki Haveli, which was built about 300 years ago and has a beautifully arches roof with superb carved brackets in the form of Peacocks. The architecture of Rajasthan is basically secular and draws a lot of inspiration from the Mughals, while the later day architecture also embraces European interiors. The structures like those of mahals, zenanas, diwan-I-aam, diwan-I-khas, sils, mandir, bagh chatris, and ramparts all display these art forms. One can trace the historic interventions in the Lodhi and Mughal periods and their absorption into the traditional architecture of Rajasthan.

Most of Rajasthan's early architecture was damaged or destroyed by the first waves of Muslim invaders. Many such buildings dating from the 10th to 15th centuries still exist today.

The mixture and brilliance of Rajasthan's architectural heritage can amaz. Majestic forts, intricately carved temples and havelis (meaning mansion) and even step well make Rajasthan a paradise for an architecture buff. The desert state of Rajasthan is a land of irony and extremes. This vibrant and striking region is the home of the Rajput warrior clans who had ruled here for many years. Rajasthan is also home to some of India's most romantic cities. The Rajputs were prolific builders and have dotted the arid Aravali landscape with their legacy of some most imposing and magnificent forts and palaces in the world. Today the structures defy time to tell the story of gallantry, courage and tragedy of the bygone era and its story of survival in the harsh Thar Desert.

Forts & Palaces

The architecture is basically secular and draws a lot on stimulation from the Mughals, while later day architecture also embraces European interiors. These structures encompass mahals (palaces), zenanas (women's quarters), diwan-I-aam (public audiences), diwan-I-khas (private audiences), sils (galleries), mandir (temples), bagh (garden) chatris and ramparts for display and parades.

Moti Dungari, Jaipur

In the middle of Jaipur rises a small hill Moti Dungri meaning pearl hill, because it looks hill a drop of pearl. An exotic palace is parched which is a replica of Scottish castle once occupied by Maharaja Madho Singh's son. From There on remained as a private property of the ruling family. In the recent past it served as a home for Rajmata Gaytri Devi and her estranged son Jagat Singh. The mere view of this castle is exotic enough. The highlight of this place is the famous and auspicious temple of Lord Ganesh, which is frequently visited by almost whole of Jaipur and people from outside.

Hawa Mahal

The Hawa Mahal, or the "Palace of Wind" built by Maharaja Sawai Pratap Singh in 1799 A.D. is characterised by elaborate and fanciful architecture. The broad pyramidical facade comprises five storeys of semi octagonal overhanging windows with perforated screens, domes and spires.

Jaigarh Fort, Jaipur

The Jaigarh fort is the most spectacular of the three-hilltop forts that overlook Jaipur. In Mughal times, the Jaipur region was a major weapon-producing centre for the Mughal and Rajput rulers, several of which are on display in the fort's museum. It is one of the few military structures of medieval India preserved almost intact, containing palaces, a granary, a well-planned cannon foundry, several temples, a tall tower and a giant mounted cannon-the Jai Ban (Jaivan) which is the largest cannon in the world. Jaigarh Fort is also known as the fort of victory. The display includes a collection of canons, many of which are exquisitely decorated and were used in the Mughal campaigns led by the Rajput King, Raja Man Singh.

Of the Jaipur's three forts, Jaigarh is perhaps the most motivating. It does not have those delicate structures or palaces like that of Amber but if you want a quick look at a hard-core fortress, this is it. Jaigarh means 'Victory Fort' and was built between the 15th and the 18th century, and stands 15 km from Jaipur, amidst rock-strewn, thorn-scrub covered hills, its forbidding stone ramparts are visible from the Jaipur town. A steep road goes up to the main gate, the Dungar Darwaza, from where the view is stupendous.

It was the royal treasury for several years. It was one of the few ancient Indian military structures to be kept intact through the ages. There are passageways among the palaces and you can see a collection of coins and puppets. This fort is open to public since a few years only. It was sealed for seven years, due to a rumour, that an enormous treasure in gold was buried, in the fort area. The government ransacked the fort, emptied the reservoirs of water but found nothing. Jaigarh was once responsible for the security of both Jaipur and Amber, is a huge moated fort and contains all the accoutrements of a full-fledged citadel.

Nahargarh Fort, Jaipur

Nahargarh Fort is located on the sheer rugged ridge of Aravali Hills and it forms an impressive northern backdrop of Jaipur. It looks most classy when floodlit at night. The fort overlooks the city and presents a glittering view of the city lights. It was built in 1734 and extended in 1868. Nahargarh meaning abode of the tigers was built by Jai Singh to bolster the defence of Amber. The legend also have it that it was named Nahargarh after Nahar Singh a prince whose spirit would destroy the construction and not allow its progress further. So after a tantrik prayer to the spirit it agreed to leave on condition that the fort is named after him.

The Madhavendra Bhawan, built by Sawai Ram Singh II has uniquely a cluster of 12 identical suits for queens and at the head is a suit for the king himself. The rooms are linked by corridors and retain some delicate frescos as well as toilets and kitchen hearths. It was used by members of the royal family for excursion in summers and is now even a favoured picnic spot. Durg Cafeteria just above the entrance sells meals and refreshments, while Padao Restaurant on the west sells drinks around sunset.

Amber Fort, Jaipur

Amber (pronounced Amer) is situated about 11 kilometres from Jaipur and was the ancient citadel of the ruling Kachhawa clan of Amber, before the capital was shifted in the plains to present day Jaipur. The Amber Fort set in picturesque and rugged hills is a fascinating blend of Hindu and Mughal architecture. Constructed by Raja Man Singh I in 1952 and completed by Sawai Jai Singh I the fort is made in red sand stone and white marble. The rugged forbidding exterior belies an inner paradise with a beautiful fusion of art and architecture. Amber is the classic and romantic fort—palace with a magnificent aura. The interior wall of the palace depicts expressive painting scenes with carvings, precious stones and mirror settings. In the foreground is the Maota Lake providing a breathtaking look. Built mainly for the warring enemies as a safe place, the heavily structured walls could defend the residents within the ramparts of the fort.

All the means of survival & luxuries for the royal families and the people who were concerned with the functioning of this small kingdom of the Kachhawas were well provided. The Rajputs who had apparently won a small structure passed on by Meena tribes, later on renovated it into the grand Amber Fort. Holding a history so old as 7 centuries, this place vibrates with its legendry past, in the archaeological history. Although many of the early structures have been literally ruined but at the same time, those dating from the 16th century on are remarkably preserved by sincere efforts The fort has 4 sections; each with the premises and one has to climb up through the imposing stairway or else the broad aisle, where one can ride on the elephant back for royal feel. The main gate Surajpol that leads to the Jaleb chowk, which is the main courtyard from where one can walk up the stairway that leads to the palace. Jaleb Chowk was also the area where returning armies were welcome and they would display their war earnings to the population at large.

Before you enter the palace just towards the right is a sleep aisle and a narrow staircase reaching up to Kali Temple also called Shila Devi Temple famous for its mysterious history and the huge silver lions. It is a gorgeous temple featuring silver doors with raised relief. According to a legend, Maharaja Man Singh I had worshipped the Goddess for a victory over the rulers of Bengal. The Goddess appeared in the Maharaja's dream and ordered him to recover her statue lying under sea near Jessore (now in Bangladesh) and install it in a befitting Temple. True enough, after subjugating the enemies the Maharaja recovered the statute from the bed of the sea. The temple is called after Shila Devi, "shila" meaning stone slab. Like all temples this too has an image of Ganesha on the doorway, but carved from a single piece of coral

Getting back from the temple the main stairways lead to the second courtyard of the fort. Here situated is the imposing Diwan-i-Aam, the hall of public audiences where the Maharaja received the populace and their petitions. This is a pavilion of double row of columns each capped by an elephant shape. There is a lattice gallery also.

Behind the exquisite and fabulous Ganesh Pol, "pol" meaning gate are located in the residential apartments of the Maharaja. The Jai Mandir, the Hall of Victory is famous for its inlaid panel and dazzling mirror ceiling. Much of it had deteriorated with neglect and is under restoration.

On the other side is Sukh Niwas, the residence of pleasure or pleasurable residence. The palace has an ivory inlaid sandalwood door. A channeled lay for flow of water is an inventive system of cooling. The water flowing from the channel wasn't wasted as it was allowed to flow in the garden. From there you can also take pleasure in viewing of the fort rampart and its reflection in the Moata Lake.

The Zenana or the palace of the women are in the forth courtyard. The rooms are though connected through a common corridor are cleverly designed to give each room privacy so that the Maharaja can have nocturnal visits to his various Maharanis without notice of the other.

City Palace, Jaipur

Located in the heart of the walled city, The City Palace Complex gives you an idea about the farsightedness of the founder of Jaipur Sawai Jai Singh. He left behind a legacy of some of the most imposing and magnificent architecture, art and craft structure in the city. Sawai Jai Singh built its many buildings but some of some of the structures were also built by later rulers and some of them are even dated in the in the twentieth century too. The palace is a blend of Mughal and Rajasthani architecture and the royal family still lives in a part of the palace.

On entering the complex and before the palace proper lies the Mubarak Mahal, the palace of welcome or reception. Sawai Madho Singh built the palace in the nineteenth century. It was used as a reception centre for the visiting personage. The building now forms the Maharaja Sawai Man Singh II Museum and on display here are a wide array of royal costumes, some very exquisite and precious Pashmina (Kashmiri) Shawls, Benaras silk saris, Sanganeri prints and folk embroidery. An unusual display is that of voluminous clothes worn by Maharaja Sawai Madho Singh I (ruled 1750-68).

The Maharani's Palace, the palace of the Queen paradoxically puts a display of the Rajput weaponry. The inestimable collections of weapons date back to even 15th century and are in a remarkable state of preservation. Remarkable amongst them is scissor-action dagger. This deadly weapon when thrust in bodies the handles was release to spread the blades. The dagger was then withdrawn tearing limb from limb of the body of the hapless victim into certain fatality. Other exhibits include protective chain armours, pistols, jewelled and ivory handled swords, a belt sword, small and assorted cannons, guns, poison tipped blades and gun powder pouches. The frescos on the ceiling are amazing and well preserved.

The art gallery is located in the Diwan-I-Aam, which literally mean the Hall of public audience. The exhibits here included some very precious and ancient handwritten original manuscripts of Hindu scriptures. Particularly intriguing in miniature copies of Bhagwat Gita made in this manner so that it can be concealed out of sight of Emperor Aurangzeb's onslaught on Hindu scriptures. Some very delicate miniature paintings in Rajasthani, Mughal and Persian schools on various themes including the Ramayana are very engrossing displays. Visitors must also take a good at preserved painted ceilings. Also on display are elephant saddles called "haudha".

The Chandra Mahal Palace is still occupied by the royal family but visitors can visit the ground floor where some exhibits are on display. However the visit here is worthwhile for the exquisite Peacock in the courtyard outside.

The present day royal family that takes charge of the museum has done exceptionally well in preserving this legacy in fine state maintenance and presentation. A visits to the palace is enlightening one for its extraordinary occurrence.

Umaid Bhawan Palace, Jodhpur

Maharaja Umaid Singhji who built this palace was fascinated with western lifestyles so he marshalled the services of a well-known Edwardian architect, Henry Vaughan Lanchester, a creditable equal of Edward Lutyens (architect of New Delhi) to construct a three hundred and forty seven roomed Umaid Palace. This was to become India last of the great palaces and the biggest private residence in the world. Spectacular Central Rotunda, the cupola rises to a hundred and five feet high; the Throne Room with its exquisite Ramayana murals; an elegant wood-panelled library, and even a private museum; an indoor swimming pool, a Billiards Room, tennis courts and unique marble squash courts makes Umaid Bhawan Palace is unabashedly the most magnificent. The palace was also built with superficial intentions of providing employment to famine stricken farmers.

The Palace now is a five star deluxe palace hotel. The museum of the palace is highly recommended for its display of weapons, an array of stuffed leopards, a huge banner presented by Queen Victoria and an incredible collection of clocks.

Mehrangarh Fort, Jodhpur

Perched on a 150 m high hill its sprawl is the most formidable and magnificent fort in Rajasthan. Rao Jodha founded it in 1459 but subsequent rulers of Jodhpur have also added to it over the centuries. A meandering road leads to the from the city 5 kms below. Battle scars of canon ball hit by attacking armies of Jaipur can still be seen on the second gate. To the left is chhatri of Kirat Singh Soda, a soldier who fell on the spot while defending the fort against the armies of Amber. There are seven gates, which include Jayapol meaning victory built by Maharaja Man Singh to commemorate his victories over Jaipur and Bikaner armies. Fattehpol also meaning victory gate was built by Maharaja Ajit Singh to mark the defeat of Mughals.

And Lohapol meaning Iron Gate has a moving memorabilia on palm print of the queens of Maharaja Man Singh who threw themselves on his funeral pyre in an act of sati [self-immolation]. The palm imprints still attract devotional attention and are covered by vermilion paste and paper-thin silver foil.

Fort Museum

This is one of the finest museums in Rajasthan and certainly the best layed out. In the palanquin section of the fort museum, you can see an interesting collection of old royal palanquins including the elaborate domed gilt Mahadol palanquin, which was won in a battle from the Governor of Gujarat in 1730. The museum exhibits the heritage of the Rathores in arms, costumes, paintings and decorated period rooms.

Phool Mahal

The grandest of Mehrangarh's period rooms, the Phool Mahal was in all likely hood a private and exclusive chamber of pleasure dancing girls once swooned in exhaustion here under a ceiling rich in gold filigree. The Phool Mahal was created by Maharaja Abhaya Singh (1724-1749) and the gold came from Ahmedabad in Gujarat as war booty after his famous victory over the rebellious Mughal governor, Sarbuland Khan. The paintings, royal portraits and the ever-popular raga mala, came much later, in the reign of Jaswant Singh II.

Janki Mahal

The Jhanki Mahal, from where the royal ladies watched the official proceedings, in the courtyard, today houses a rich collection of the royal cradles. The cradles are decorated with gilt mirrors and figures of fairies, elephant and birds.

City Palace, Udaipur

City Palace towers over the Pichola Lake. Maharana Uday Singh initiated in the construction of the palace but succeeding Maharanas added several palaces and structures to the complex retained a surprising uniformity to the design. The entry to the Palace is from the Hati Pol, the Elephant gate. The Bari Pol or the Big gate brings you to the Tripolia, the Triple gate. It was once a custom that the Maharana would weigh under this gate in gold and silver, which was distributed to the populace. It is also now the main ticket office. Balconies, cupolas and towers surmount the palace to give a wonderful view of the lake. Suraj Gokhada or the balcony of the sun is where the Maharana would grant public audiences mainly to boost the morale of the people in difficult times. The Mor Chawk is the peacock square and gains its name from the vivid blue mosaic in glass of a peacock that decorates its walls.

The main part of the palace is now preserved as a museum displaying a large and diverse array of artefacts. Down steps from the entrance is the armoury museum exhibiting a huge collection of protective gear, weapons including the lethal two-pronged sword. The City Palace museum is then entered through the Ganesh Deori meaning the door of Lord Ganesh. This leads to the Rajya Angan, the royal courtyard that is the very spot where Maharana Udai Singh met the sage who told him to find a city here.

The rooms of the palace are superbly decorated with mirror tiles and paintings. Manak Mahal or the Ruby Palace has a lovely collection of glass and mirror work while Krishna Vilasdisplay a rich collection of miniature paintings. Moti Mahal or the pearl palace has beautiful mirror work and the Chini Mahal has ornamental tiles all over. The Surya Chopar or the sun square depicts a huge ornamental sun symbolising the sun dynasty to which the Mewar dynasty belongs. The Bari Mahal is a central garden with view of the city. Some more beautiful paintings can be seen in the Zenana Mahal or the ladies chamber, which leads to Lakshmi Chowk a beautiful white pavilion.

Chowk, are the Shiv Niwas and Fateh prakash Palace, which are now run as hotels. The Sunset view terrace and gallery restaurants, the crystal gallery and the boat wharves for trips to Jagmandir and the Lake Palace.

Fateh Prakash Palace, Udaipur

It's like being cocooned in authentic royal luxury at the Fateh Prakash Palace, the grand heritage palace of the HRH group. The warmth of royal hospitality greets you as you walk along the corridors lined with large paintings of the Mewar school that flourished in the seventeenth through nineteenth century.

The lake facing suites in the turrets are suitably appointed with four poster beds and period furniture, festooned with maroon velvet curtains and delicate silk tassels. It's a legacy kept alive since the early decades of the twentieth century when Maharana Fateh Singh (period of reign : 1884—1935) used to be the royal occupant of this palace. Till date the formality of royal occasions are maintained..

Crystal Gallery: It is situated in the Fateh Prakash Palace is a breath taking collection of crystals. Maharana Sajjan Singh mainly ordered these crystals from F & C Osler England. But he could not see the crystals because of his untimely death. The crystal item includes tables, sofa sets, dinning table, dressers, fountains and even beds besides a whole array of washing bowls, decanters and perfume bottles. There is also an exquisite jewel studded carpet, which is beyond description.

Durbar Hall: In India the Durbar Hall is generally a place where state banquets are held and is also used for formal and informal meetings. The Durbar Hall at the Fateh Prakash Palace is undoubtedly the most lavish Durbar Hall in India. It is one of the grandest chambers in Udaipur and its sheer size makes one gasp in awe.

The chandelier in the middle is the most impressive and is complimented with paintings of Maharanas and various weapons adore the walls. The hall has an exquisite ceiling and is surrounded by viewing galleries from where the ladies of the palace could get a view from the privacy of their veils. Lord Minto, the Viceroy of India laid the foundation stone for the Durbar hall in 1909.

Lake Pichola: Pichola Lake derives its name from Pichola Village was submerged and Maharana Udai Singh enlarged the lake after he founded the city. He built a masonry dam known as Badipol and lake is now 4 km long and 3 km wide. This picturesque lake encloses the Jag Niwas Island and the Jag Mandir. And, the City Palace extends along its eastern banks.

Sajjangarh, Udaipur

High on a hilltop just outside Udaipur lies this dramatic 18th century palace, with a breathtaking view of the Mewar countryside. Originally intended to be a towering five-story astronomical centre, it was later abandoned and used as a monsoon palace and hunting lodge. It was built by Maharana Sajjan Singh to house and observatory and was planned as a nineteen-storied structure. However the Maharana died prematurely & the plans were curtailed. The now derelict palace dominates the skyline 2468 feet high on top of Bansdara Mountain. It is visible from a great distance & affords splendid scenic views.

Kumbhalgarh Fort, Udaipur

Located 64 kms north of Udaipur in the wilderness, Kumbhalgarh is the second most important citadel after Chittorgarh in the Mewar region. Cradled in the Aravali Ranges the fort was built in the 15th century by Rana Kumbha. Because of its inaccessibility and hostile topography the fort had remained un-conquered. It also served the rulers of Mewar as a refuge in times of strife. The fort also served as refuge to the baby king Udai of Mewar. It is also of sentimental significance as it is the birthplace of Mewar's legendary King Maharana Partap.

The fort is self-contained and has within its amalgam almost everything to withstand a long siege. The fort fell only once that too to the combined armies of Mughal and of Amber for scarcity of drinking water. Many magnificent palaces an array of temples built by the Mauryas of which the most picturesque place is the Badal Mahal or the palace of the clouds. The fort also offers a superb birds view of the surroundings. The fort's thick wall stretches some 36 kms and is wide enough to take eight horses abreast. Maharana Fateh Singh renovated the fort in the 19th century. The fort's large compound has very interesting ruins and the walk around it can be very rewarding.

Tower of Fame: Kirti Stambh

Dedicated to Adinathji the 1st Jain Teerthankar adorned by the naked figures of the Digambars [Adherents of the Digambar sect who does not believe in covering the natural body] A narrow stairway goes through seven stories of the tower to the top. The 22 metres high tower was build by a wealthy jain merchant in the 12th century A.D.

Junagarh Fort, Bikaner

It is an unassailable fortress, which has never been conquered. Built in 1593 A.D. by Raja Rai Singh, one of the most distinguished generals in the army of Emperor Akbar, the fort is a formidable structure encircled by a moat.

Lal Garh Palace, Bikaner

This grand palace is an architectural masterwork in red sandstone, and was built by Maharaja Ganga Singh Ji in the memory of his father Maharaja Lal Singh Ji in 1902. Sir Swinton Jacob designed this oriental fantasy.

This architecture is a fusion of Rajput, Mughal and European architecture. The exterior contrasts dramatically with the oriental interiors and amenities. The palace has beautiful latticework and filigree work, which are hallmarks of a great craftsmanship.

The Palace has an amazing collection of well-maintained paintings and hunting trophies. Sprawling lawns with blooming bougainvillea and dancing peacocks make a visual extravagance.

Taragarh Fort, Ajmer

The giant fort stands guarding the city. It has six gates. The fort also has Miran Saheb ki Dargha who was the governor of the fort and laid down his life in an encounter. It gives a panoramic view of the city situated in Nagpahari of Aravalli ranges, this fort has immense archaeological and historical importance.

Man Mahal, Ajmer

Raja Man Singh I of Ajmer built this largest royal house in Pushkar Located on the east of Sarovar, the sacred lake. It gives view of the banks and temples located around the lake. It was built as a royal guest house for Raja Man Singh I on his Trips to the holy town. This traditional guest house has now been converted into a hotel.

Jaisalmer Fort, Jaisalmer

Known as SONAR QUILA, rising from the sand, the mega structure merges with the golden hues of the desert ambience and the setting suns in its most colourful shades gives it a fairy tale look.

Its simply a magic, the bastions envelops a whole townships that consist of palace complex various security sources and the havelis of rich merchants carved with an incredibly light touch, several temples and the residential complexes of the armies and traders placed strategically on the trade route, from where the ancient caravans passed en-route passing all the riches for the prosperity to an otherwise non source full kingdom. These merchants served and acquire a great deal of power and noble status in the royal courts of Bhatti Rajputs who founded the state in the 12th century and proceeded further.

But the rich merchant inspired by the classic style of the royals, constructed huge mansions (havelis) adjacent to each other in the nature of medieval culture and profusely decorated walls and ceilings and intricately carved outdoors and interiors.

The colourful art forms and some how side kind the royal heritage and made it appear more pale in comparison. The craftsmen were usually muslims who were induced on their journey to exhibit their skills. The results was architectural purity that cannot be seen elsewhere.

Sukh Niwas Palaces, Bundi

Sukh Niwas Palaces evokes memories of *Rudyard Kipling* who not only stayed here but found inspiration for his famous work *Kim*.

Sar Bagh, Bundi

Sar Bagh has 66 royal cenotaphs. Step wells (Bawari) are another prominent highlights of Bundi, these served as water reservoirs in the months of summers, there were over 50 wells but many of them had to suffer the ravages of the time. The *Chhatar Mahal* is adorned with beautiful wall paintings of the famous Bundi School. And so are the *Zanana Mahal* (palace for the queens) and BADAL MAHAL.

Taragarh Fort, Bundi

It was built in 1345 and is great ramble around at leisure. This is rather a ramshackle fort, with its overgrown vegetation.

The view over the town and surrounding countryside from the top are magical, especially at sun set. Inside the ramparts are huge reservoirs carved out of solid rock, and the Bhim Burj, the largest of the battle-fields, on which there is mounted a famous cannon. Taragarh is reached by steep road leading up the hillside to its enormous gateway. Take a path up behind the chitra Shala, go east along the inside of the ramparts then left up the steep stone ramp just before the Dudha Mahal, a small disused building 200m from the palace.

Achalgarh, Mt. Abu

Medieval monument of Mt. Abu, is the Achalgadh fort commissioned by Rana Kumbha, who was responsible for dozens of gigantic fortresses in southern Rajasthan, with massive battlemented walls and a situation on a mountain peak offering great views. A steeply winding path leads up to the 15th century fortress and the temples within the fortified walls, great for a view of the countryside.

The carved Jain temples are a 10 minute climb, worthwhile for the view and the sculpture. Below the path is the Achleshwar temple, with a Nandi said to be made of the five metals-gold, silver, copper, brass and zinc, called Panchadattu, and weigh more than 4 tons. The temple is believed to have been built in the 9th century around a toe print of lord Shiva, with a hole claimed to reach the netherworld, a natural Shivalinga and idols of a crystal like stone, which looks opaque, but when a candle is placed behind it sparkles like crystal. Nearby is the pleasant looking Mandakini Lake, enclosed by rocky hills, with images of a Rajput king and buffaloes. According to legend, the tank was filled with ghee and the watering hole of demons disguised as buffaloes until they were shot by Raja Adi Pal.

Temples

The great architectural movement which swept Rajasthan from the 8th to the 11th century was really a later flowering of the virile development inspired by the Guptas during the 4th, 5th and 6th centuries. The 8th and 9th century also saw new styles of temples emerging from the Gurjara Pratihara dynasty from Mandore.

Temples built around this time also include temples at Chittorgarh and Osiyan in western Rajasthan. The familiar feature of these temples is single sikhara or spire and intricately carved outer chamber called the mand-up before the inner sanctum. In many temples the main temple would be surrounded by series of small and finely carved temples. Good examples of these are Kalika Mata Temple and Kumbha Shyam temples in the Chittorgarh fort. Temples at Kiradu in western Barmer known as Solanki style are known for sculptured frescos. The best example in this is the Someshvara Temple, which has fine sculptured fresco, and a multi tiered spire.

The 10th century saw the constructions of many splendid Jain Temple, notable amongst them are the Dilwara Temples at Mt. Abu, Mahavira Temple at Ghanerao in southern Rajasthan and Ranakpur near Udaipur. At Ranakpur the Chomukha meaning four faced is the finest. It features a series of mandupas decorated with intricate carving giving a breath taking symmetry. A group of Jain Temples at Jaisalmer are also noteworthy.

A great deal of this fine architecture, however, was destroyed during the earlier Muslim invasions.

Havelis

The Merchants of Rajasthan built sumptuously decorated mansions as residences known as havelis. The merchants had commissioned artisans to ensure that they construct and decorate the havelis in a manner that befits the prosperity of the owner. Havelis are common everywhere in Rajasthan but havelis at Shekhawati and Jaisalmer are worth visiting.

Havelis of Shekhawati: Shekhawati as a region is known for its beautifully painted Havelis that spreads over Jhunjhunu, Sikar and Churu districts in north-western Rajasthan. Built by rich Marwari merchants of the region, Shekhawati's magnificent mansions display a unique architectural style that evolved around the courtyards to ensure safety and privacy of the womenfolk and protection from the heat of the long and harsh summers.

Painted predominantly in blue, maroon, yellow, green and indigo, the Havelis of Shekhawati have beautiful frescoes that adorn their walls. Earlier wall paintings were largely based on the mythological themes, depicting gods, heroes, epics and local legends; animals, portraits of hunting and wrestling scenes and glimpses of every day life.

The turn of the 19th century saw the appearance of new motifs, an outcome of the British Raj's influence upon the Indian Culture. The paintings continued with the mythological themes, but the new entries included European oleographs, lithographs and photographs. Trains, cars, balloons, telephones, gramophones, English men in hunting attires and portraits of Haveli owners primly dressed were painted profusely.

Jaisalmer Havelis: Patwon ki Haveli is the most elaborate and magnificent of all the Jaisalmer havelis. Salim Singh ki Haveli was built about 300 years ago and is still partially lived in.

Salim Singh was the prime minister of the princely state and his mansion has a beautifully arched roof with superb carved brackets in the form of peacocks. The mansion is just below the hill and, it is said that it once had two additional wooden storeys, in an attempt to make it as high as the Maharaja's Palace.

The Maharaja of Jaisalmer had the upper storey torn down. The late 19th century Nathmal ki Haveli was also a prime minister's house. The left and right wings of the building were carved by brothers and are very similar but not identical. Yellow sandstone elephants guard the building and the front door alone is a work of art.

Well & Tanks

The importance of a water source in a water scarce area like Rajasthan can be hardly exaggerated. So it is hardly surprising that wells and tanks or 'sagar' (lakes) were decorated ornamentally with beautiful edifices. Water table was found very low and step wells (locally known as 'baodi') leading to the water table are beautiful examples of architecture. Some excellent pavilion can be seen on the banks of lakes also.

Jantar Mantar

One of the five observatories of India built by Sawai Jai Singh, the leading astronomer of his times and the founder of Jaipur, Jantar Mantar of Jaipur is one of the largest and the best preserved. The collection of giant masonry astronomical instruments continues to provide accurate information even today and is comparable with the most sophisticated instruments of today. The Brihat Samrat Yantra Sundia is said to be the most imposing of all instruments and is 27 m high. It helps in the calculation of local time as its shadow moves up to 4 m in an hour. It also helps in ascertaining the various attributes of the heavenly bodies and is definitely the highlight and center of attraction of the observatory. 'Jantar-Mantar' in Sanskrit means, 'Magical Device'. It was built between 1728 and 1734 based on the blueprints drafted by Maharaja Jai Singh.

6

Monuments of South India

Temple Styles of Kerala and Coastal Karnataka

Karnataka has innumerable sites in the Temple Map of India, with its some of its still surviving monuments going back to the 7th century. The Badami Chalukyas were the builders of rock cut caves and ancient temple complexes. At Pattadakal, there are Temples in the Dravidian style along with Temples in styles that were later adopted in Eastern and Central India. The sculptural quality in these temples is outstanding. The subordinate rulers of the Chalukyas were the Gangas and the Kadambas.

The colossal monolithic statue of Gomateswara was built by the Gangas in the 10th century. The Badami Chalukyas were succeeded by the Rashtrakutas and the Kalyani Chalukyas. In Southern Karnataka, the Hoysalas reigned supreme. The Hoysalas (12th century CE) were great builders and they built great temples at Halebidu, Belur and Somanathapura. The Hoysalas built temples on raised complex star shaped platforms. This star shaped plan is carried all the way from the platform to the shikhara. Horizontal bands of sculptural motifs and monolithic pillars adorn these temples.

There is a profusion of sculptural work in the Hoysala style of temple building. Also in Southern Karnataka, are temples which benefited from the patronage of the Chola rulers of Tamil Nadu. A notable example is the Kolaramama temple at Kolar. Next, the Vijayanagar Empire founded in the 14th century marks the period of great Temple building activity in Karnataka and these temples are characterised by the building of pillared mandapas and lofty entrance towers. Vijayanagar temples have several of the features exhibited by the temples of Tamil Nadu, such as a covered pradakshinapatha (circumambulatory path) around the sanctum, and a mahamandapam in front. The ornate pillars are a distinctive mark of the Vijayanagar style. Several of the monuments in the capital Vijayanagar-now in ruins at Hampi are attributed to Harihara II, Sadasiva and Krishna Deva Raya.

The Vijayanagar Empire was destroyed by the Deccan Sultanates in the 16th century and the ruins can be seen at Hampi. The Mysore Maharajas (Wodeyars) who ruled from around 14th through the British period, with the brief lapse during Tipu Sultans rule, have also made contributions to temples in this State, the Chamundeswari temple near Mysore being a point in illustration. The temples of the southern coastal/ ghat region of Karnataka (such as Kollur) are markedly different in architectural styles and they resemble the Keralite temples to a larger extent.

The history of ancient Kerala is closely related to that of the neighbouring state of Tamil Nadu. The State of Kerala was by and large a part of the Tamil cultural domain, during the rule of the *Cheras*, up to the 3rd century.

The earlier cave temples of Kerala were influenced by the rock cut temple styles of the Tamil region. An indigenous temple architecture based on the utilitarian residential types of Kerala and the Konkan region originated later in Kerala. Finding expression in a mixed medium of stone, brick, laterite and wood this unique approach to temple building resulted in a distinctive form of architecture, laying stress on sanctity, simplicity and a prevailing naturalism which marked the worship in temples. This approach naturally leads to an old-world charm, not seen elsewhere in the Indian subcontinent.

Bhagawati and Sastha are the most popular of the deities enshrined in temples. So is Sankaranarayana-the Hari-Hara manifestation of Shiva and Vishnu. Bhagawati is considered to be Narayani-or the Vishnu-Maya. Sastha is considered to be the son of Hari and Hara. Shiva and Vishnu are worshipped with equal devotion in Kerala, and there are no distinctions based on the sub religions such as Saivism and Vaishnavism as seen elsewhere. In fact, Anantasaayi, or Vishnu enshrined in a reclining posture, is depicted with a Shiva lingam below his extended right arm, unlike in Tamil Nadu.

The Shiva Vishnu synthesis in general modes of worship based on earlier Indian societies of the pre Christian era has been preserved in Kerala. The temple culture of Kerala also stresses the importance of the ancient Indian epics.

The temple culture in Kerala is based on Vedic moorings, in contrast to the Agamic traditions of Tamil Nadu. The sustenance of ancient practices of worship, causes devotees to step into a different world upon entering the temple precincts. For instance, the use of oil lamps in contrast to electric lamps, lends an air of serenity and mysticism to all Keralite temples.

In contrast to Tamil Nadu, the Keralite temple tradition focuses only on the deity enshrined in the sanctum (moola bhera) and has no importance laid on processional deities (utsava bhera). Most temples do not have shrines to the consorts of the presiding deities, although the concept of *Bhoga Shakti* prevails.

The earlier temples of Kerala were primarily for Shiva and Vishnu or their manifestations (Krishna, Parasurama, Rama, Vamana). Shiva is worshipped both in the iconic and the aniconic Linga form. *Swayampradhana* shrines to Ganesha, Kartikeya are of later origin, and are seen more in the temples of the peripheral regions of Kerala adjoining Tamil Nadu or Karnataka.

Inscriptions in Kerala are mostly in the ancient *Vattezhuttu* script of Tamil Nadu. Malayalam inscriptions are seen from the 16th century onwards. Temples have been constantly rebuilt and renovated, unlike in Tamil Nadu where more permanent structures of granite were built and engraved upon.

The temples of Kerala are referenced in the works of the Tamil *Alwar* Saints and the *Nayanmar* Saints. *Kulasekhara Alwar* and *Cheraman Perumaal* (one of the Nayanmaars) belonged to the Cheras of the ninth century. There are several works on temple architecture written in Kerala during the 15th and the 16th centuries. The Bhakti literature of the 16th century played an important role in the temple culture of Kerala. The Maharajas of Travancore were ardent patrons of temples.

Temple architecture in Kerala is different from that of other regions in India. Largely dictated by the geography of the region that abounds in forests blessed with the bounties of the monsoons, the structure of the temples in Kerala is distinctive. The roofs are steep and pointed, and covered with copper sheets. The Kerala roof resembles those found in the Himalayan regions and those in East Asia. The shape of the roof is in accordance with the plan of the sanctum below. With a circular plan, one sees a conical roof, while with a square plan the roof is pyramidal. The roof is constructed with wood and is covered with copper plates. Most of the temples seen in Kerala today, have undergone several phases of renovation, given the perishable nature of the construction materials.

The central sanctum of a Keralite temple is referred to as the *Sree Kovil*. It is surrounded by a cloistered *prakara*, pierced at one or more cardinal points with a *gopuradwara*. The cloistered prakarama has a *namaskara mandapam* located directly in front of the sanctum. This prakarama also houses subsidiary shrines. A kitchen is located in the south eastern corner of the cloistered prakarama. The *mukha mandapam* is integrated with the gopura entrance. The flagstaff or *dwaja stambham* is located outside of the dwajastambham. The balipitham may be located in the mukhamandapam or in the outer courtyard. The outer prakarama or courtyard houses other subshrines, and optionally a temple tank.

The *Kuttambalam* or the theater hall of the Keralite temple is located either as a part of the inner prakara, on the south east corner facing north, or as a separate hall outside the innermost prakarama, either facing into the temple or facing north. This has a stage, raised from the rest of the floor, and a backstage area. This is the site of the performance of *Kathakali* or *Chakkiyar koothu* recitals. Thus the kuttambalam plays a role in educating visitors on the rich legends of the Indian cultural fabric.

The Keralite temple is an amalgam of stonework, wood work, stucco work and painting-harmoniously blended into a structure vibrant with traditions of the region. The wood work here is of great importance, and it gives the essential verve and character to the Kerala temple silhouette. The inner skeletal framework of the temple is of wood, although the base and the structure above are of granite and laterite respectively. The roof projects out at several levels, in order to protect the inner skeletal framework from the vigorous monsoons that inundate the region.

The Kerala temple walls are of coursed laterite stone masonry plastered in mud and lime. Murals are seen on several of these temple walls.

Another desiccative feature of Keralite temples is the use of vilakku maadam, or the multi-tiered brass lamps in front of temples. Lakshadeepam is a spectacular celebration of traditional lighting where tiers of small oil lamps lining the outer walls of the inner prakarama are lit.

Temples have held an important place in the life of Keralites. Several temples in Kerala trace their origins to antiquity. However, they were renovated frequently and the current structures that are seen are vastly a result of the numerous renovations.

Temple styles in these areas real another facet of the impact of the environment. The heavy tropical rainfall in these regions has led to the creation of unique roof systems, consisting of low and overhanging eaves with a series of diminishing gables covered with tiles. The plans for these temples have a variety of shapes-square, circular and apsidal-ended.-sometimes in combination with columned halls. The Ayyappa and Krishna shrines at SSVT are examples of this style of architecture.

Muslim invasion since the sixteenth century saw a mix of suppression of Hindu temples and tolerance or reverence by some enlightened Muslim rulers. The British, on the other hand, had a policy of benign neglect. In either case temple architecture did not flourish to any significant extent. Since Independence and more recently in the past few decades, a vigorous return to this art form is discernible; many temples are being constructed or renovated in India and overseas, and architectural talent is again being nourished.

Khajuraho-The Style of South: The classic central Indian style of temples of Khajuraho, according to historical inscriptions were built exactly 1000 years ago by the Chandella dynasty. Unfortunately, human history, this past millennium, has been one of bloodshed and greed, of terrible wars to establish unstable, petty, provincial identities.

Surely this millennium will have to be dedicated to caring for our common human heritage and our common human future. What is this heritage and future that all human beings share? A beautiful little jewel-like planet, with its waters, air, exquisitely diverse landscapes and all the species that inhabit and share it with us. The varied cultures of the world, the architecture, sculpture, painting, music, dance, theatre and crafts are examples of the enormous creativity that distinguish the human race from all other species.

In a world shattered by human destruction the arts of the world are enduring symbols of human creativity. We need to preserve our collective heritage as a reminder that human beings can be creative, caring and productive. The temples of Khajuraho, like all world heritage sites across the globe, remind us of the heights of imagination, skill and aesthetic beauty that human beings have achieved during the last few millennia.

A perception of what our heritage has to do with our future is, therefore, critical. Any investment in education about our common concerns, about the conservation of our little planet, will ensure the well-being of our species and also that of others. Education in the arts and creative activities are now crucial for every child. We need to nurture creativity to enable the young to find ways of making this a more beautiful world to live in. If we don't, we will break and destroy it.

Khajuraho is a well-known historical site, famous for its architecture and infamous for its erotic sculptures. Khajuraho was rediscovered by a British officer in 1838. He had said that this site had been abandoned and neglected for centuries. It was Captain Burt who also began the debate on the meaning and purpose of the erotic sculptures on religious architecture. This debate continues after 16 years.

Is it not pertinent to ask why the Government of India, indeed, why the citizens of India have not sponsored a thorough debate on the meaning and purpose of their culture. Why has there been so little discussion on how our culture should be interpreted, how it should be presented to the world? The Archaeological Survey of India, under whose protection these monuments of national importance are placed, remains closed to any debate. The ASI is the custodian of our monumental heritage not its owners-we are and we have the right to determine how our culture is being cared for.

India is one of the wealthiest countries in the world, its cultural assets both in terms of the past and of skilled living artists, far exceeds several nations. But this country chooses to neglect and ignore its true value and that is the tragic story of India. The need of the next millennium is to reinterpret our past, to let a new generation of scholars and students understand India for what she really is. We need to free our common heritage from small-minded bureaucrats, self-serving politicians, and employ science as the handmade of the arts so that we can celebrate the diversity of human cultures, and rejoice at the multiplicity of life around us.

All development plans around the temple complex of Khajuraho need to address the health of the natural environment as an essential ingredient of the site. According to a local legend there were once 84 temples that formed the 10th century temple complex. The local people understood the lay of the land and created a wonderful township of 84 temples, 84 lakes and 84 wells. Only 25 out of 84 of the Chandella 10th century temples remain. Most of the lakes are dry and the wells are dysfunctional or filled with garbage. Khajuraho has an airport, five star hotels with hot and cold running water and artificially blue swimming pools but the village tanks are dry and the children have no clean drinking water.

Each year thousands of people, who live around Khajuraho, come to the temples to celebrate *Mahashivratri*. For them

Khajuraho is not a tourist destination, a place to see erotic sculptures. They come to Khajuraho not as aggressive tourists, but with the gentle spirit of pilgrimage. For at Maha-shivratri in Khajuraho, they celebrate the marriage of Shiva and Parvati. On the night of Shivratri they re-enact the wedding of Shiva, the destroyer of Kamadev (desire that causes all suffering) and father of Ganesha (Lord of Wisdom). The erotic sculptures are a metaphor of the union of Shiva and Parvati, the marriage of two cosmic forces, of light and darkness, sky and earth, spirit and matter. Therefore, it is the people who infuse meaning and soul into a historical site, without that pilgrim spirit, buildings are just a heap of stone and human greed is insatiable.

One of the most celebrated manifestations of Indian architecture is to be found in a group of temples at Khajuraho in central India. Situated a hundred miles south-east of the town of Jhansi in the modern-day state of Madhya Pradesh, these temples are over thirty in number. These temples, unlike many others in central or south India, do not illustrate a development over a long period of time, but were erected over a relatively narrow period of hundred years from A.D. 950. The Khajuraho temples represent, one might say, a happy and almost unique coincidence of religious emotion, abundant patronage, artistic genius, and aesthetic sensibility. Fortunately, these temples have weathered the climate for a thousand years and have withstood neglect surprisingly well.

The Khajuraho temples were built during the reign of the Chandelas. While some show marks of a Shaivite sensibility, others clearly manifest the influence of Vaishnaism, Jainism, and tantrism. These temples have an architectural character distinct from that of any other group of temples elsewhere in the country. Instead of being contained within the customary enclosure wall, each temple stands on a high and solid masonry terrace. Though none of the temples are very large, they are still imposing structures because of their elegant proportions and rich surface sculpture.

Unlike the rather plain treatment of other central Indian temple interiors, the Khajuraho temples are richly decorated with sculpture. Other than numerous deities enshrined in wall niches, there are attendants, graceful "maidens" in a variety of provocative postures, dancers, musicians and embracing couples. On one temple alone, the figures thus depicted are over six hundred and fifty in number. Many of these compositions display great sensuality and warmth. There are also scenes of explicit sexual activity which possibly illustrate the tantric rites that accompanied temple worship. It is quite reliably said that some of the sexual postures follow the Kama Sutra, the ancient Indian manual of lovemaking.

Sexual Pose at Khajuraho: The Khajuraho temples now grace the posters of the Indian Tourist office, and numerous films have been shot at the temple grounds. It is with these temples in the background that some of the greatest exponents of Indian classical dance have performed for admiring audiences. But it is in discussions ranging around the cultural construction of sexuality that Khajuraho has featured prominently. The sheer eroticism of the sculptures is often pointed to as evidence of India's libertine past.

Thus, gays and lesbians have found in Khajuraho evidence of the enlightened attitudes of the pre-modern Indian culture, while others point the allegedly baneful influence of the Islamic and British presence in India, which is supposed to have led to repressive sexual mores. But few have asked what Khajuraho tells us about everyday notions of sexuality, or what inferences we are to derive about Indian sexual mores and practices from these temples.

Chaturbhuja Temple: Chaturbhuja temple was built in the declining years of the Chandella dynasty. It is crudely built and lacks the ornamentation and sexual imagery of the other Khajuraho temples. It was constructed by Emperor Lakshavarman primarily to enshrine an image of the four-armed 'Chaturbhuja' Vishnu brought from Tibet. In addition, the temple also enshrines another incarnation of Vishnu known as the 'Narasingha avatar' (an incarnation of Vishnu that is part-man, part-lion). There are also images of the god Shiva, including Shiva's incarnation as the 'Ardhanarishvara', an androgenous deity, as well as his incarnation as the four-armed god of destruction.

Duladeo Temple: Duladeo Temple, constructed in 1130 AD, is among the last to be built at Khajuraho by the Chandella kings. It was sponsored during the reign of King Madanavarman, a devout worshipper of Shiva (in the 'womb' of the temple is a large Shiva lingam). The entire temple is decorated with carvings of Shiva and his consort Parvati, many in erotic poses. On the inside of the temple the roof is supported by 'apsaras' that are carved into the brackets. Legend says that as a wedding procession passed by its gates, the groom died and became a god.

Jagdambi Temple shares the same plinth as Kandariya temple to the south. It is one of most finely decorated temples at Khajuraho, with numerous erotic carvings. In the temple "womb", the griha, is an enormous image of the goddess Devi, though it was probably originally designed as a Vishnu temple.

Kandariya Mahadeva temple sits just to the west of Lakshmana temple. Built in 1025-1050 AD, it is 30 meters tall and the largest in the Khajuraho complex. It is dedicated to Shiva and its name consists of the word "cave" (Kandariya) and Mahadeva, another name by which Shiva is known. The temple is considered to be the most impressive and refined in the Khajuraho complex, with over 900 sculptures carved into sandstone stacked without mortar. The vibrantly carved exterior contrasts with a very plain interior space that houses a Shiva lingam in the womb, or 'griha', of the temple located beneath the main 'shikhara' (spire).

Lakshmana temple, dedicated to Lord Vishnu, was built from 930-950 AD during the reign of King Yasovarman of the Chandella kingdom. It houses a sacred image of Vaikuntha-Vishnu brought from Tibet. Though the temple is one of the oldest in the Khajuraho fields, it is also one of the most exquisitely decorated, covered almost completely with images of over 600 gods in the Hindu Pantheon. The main shrine of the temple, which faces east, is flanked by four freestanding subsidiary shrines at the corners of the temple platform.

The temple is famous for the explicitly sexual carvings on the southern side of the temple, though these make up only a small fraction of the total.

This is the largest of the Jainist temples in the southeastern group of the temples of Khajuraho. It is also one of the finest in the total temple complex. Measuring, it lies within a walled enclosure and is noted for the precision of its construction and its beautifully sculpted figures. The temple has a solid outer wall embellished with three bands of graceful sculptures depicting Hindu Gods (despite its affiliation as a Jain temple). More figures can be found on the outer face of the sanctum, depicting 'apsaras' (heavenly nymphs) in a variety of poses.

The temple was originally dedicated to the deity Adinath, but in the late 19th century an image of Parsvanath was installed there and the temple assumed this new name.

The Parvati temple is a restored shrine just to the south of Vishvanath temple. Parvati is one incarnation of the wife of Shiva

This is one of the finest of the Khajuraho temples and was built by the Chandella king Dhanga in 1002. The temple itself has a most delicate balance. The sculptures are particularly striking in the carving and in some of the subject matter. Dedicated to Shiva, the temple enshrines not only a Shiva lingam but also his "vehicle", the bull Nandi, as well as an image of his consort depicted as Durga. In another subsidiary corner shrine on the temple podium is an image of the Shiva lingam with four faces attached.

The Glory of Khajuraho: The sleepy town of Khajuraho is home to some of the finest examples of Hindu temple construction. Among the many temples that exist, most have been deserted. Hence Khajuraho is not a religious pilgrimage; rather it serves as a magnet for tourists from all over the world.

Khajuraho group of temples in Central India is one of the most illustrious manifestations of Indian architecture. These 10th-11th century temples represent religiosity, patronage, artistic genius and aesthetic sensibility all at once. Built in the typical 'Nagara' style of architecture, over 20 of the original 85 temples have survived the climate for more than a thousand years despite being lost into obscurity and hence, suffering neglect for a long period of time. Believed to have been constructed during the Chandela rule, the temples belong to Shaivism and Vaishnavism sects of Hinduism, Jainism and 'tantrism'. Unlike other temple complexes in the country, there is no enclosure wall surrounding these temples and each of them on a high and solid raised masonry platform. Though not very large, they have elegant proportions and are adorned with sculptures on their exteriors and even interiors.

These walled sculptures include depiction of numerous deities, their attendants, celestial maidens in sensuous positions and provocative postures, embracing couples (some of them in erotic sexual positions), dancers and musicians and couples engaged in various refinements of courtly love.

It is believed that one temple alone sports over six hundred and fifty such figures ranging from sensual and warm depictions to explicit sexual activity (believed to illustrate the tantric rites by some). Some of these much-famed or much-notorious sexual postures are said to follow the Kama Sutra, the ancient Indian manual of art of making love. One of the most preferred destinations after Taj Mahal, Khajuraho has provided a scenic backdrop for many movies as well as many Indian classical dances that have been performed here.

Expectations of Khajuraho Just like people's perception of Taj Mahal changes after seeing it in reality, the feeling one gets at the Khajuraho temples is totally different from one's expectation. The beauty is in the eyes of the beholder and the same object may appear differently to different people. A maiden may appear as a mother to Ramakrishna Paramahamsa, as a sister to Swamy Vivekananda, as a daughter to an elderly person and as a lover to a romantic.

Southern Temple Cities

In our last article, we explained how the typical south Indian city came to be surrounded by a ring of walls because of the need for defense, and then population growth. This led to a number of interesting solutions in city planning and the most visible architectural feature of this expansion was the Gopuram.

Gopuram: The Gopuram (literally Cow-Gate), was erected primarily to emphasis the importance of the temple within the city precincts without in any way altering the form of the temple itself. The formal aspects of the Gopuram were evolved slowly over time. It had to be towering, massive and impressive. But it was not felt necessary to repeat verbatim the square-based form of the temple Vimana. This could be due to the fact that the square was a essentially a static form, signifying calm and rest, while the entrance gateway needed to have some dynamism. Elongating the square and converting into a rectangle with an open entrance in the middle solved this problem. Above this base could be raised tier upon tier of a pyramidal structure comprised of brick and plaster with the topmost tier also a rectangle, albeit much smaller.

The 'Annular' Growth of Cities: Such an increase in importance of the city led to a natural population increase as well as demands for more resources. But growth was also constrained by the huge battlements thrown up around, punctuated by the massive Gopuram. The only viable solution was to erect yet another wall around the existing one. The new wall, too, had its own huge Gopuram. In this way the city grew much like the annular rings of a tree, with successive perimeters being added as population growth dictated. Thus, the great temple of Srirangam at Tiruchirapalli acquired several concentric rings of growth over a period of 500 years. Ultimately, the concentric city and Gopuram, which evolved out of necessity rather than conscious design, came to be accepted as the standard 'form' of temple construction in the south.

Madurai: Meenakshi Temple

So, it came to pass that the Meenakshi temple was designed as a series of concentric courtyards, or parikramas. The spaces around the shrine became hierarchical, diminishing in religious value; the further one went from the main shrine. The outermost ring had buildings of a more practical nature-accounts, dormitories, kitchens, shops selling items for rituals, maintenance areas and 'parking' for the increasing number of chariots.

The inner circles contained parikramas for singing and religious tales, bathing tanks and guest houses. And in the innermost courts were the pavilions for the dancing girls and the treasury-both jealously guarded by the priests! Admittance was restricted to the upper castes only. And finally, the holiest of holies, the Cella containing the idol of the deity was open only to the head pujari and out of bounds for even the king of the land.

One Thousand Pillar Hall: With temple building losing its architectural challenge and becoming more and more a town planning exercise, the craftsman was restricted to working on pavilions, halls and Gopuram, the last of which grew ever larger and imposing. The huge hall in the Meenakshi temple needed 985 pillars to support its roof. This is the famous 'Hall of a Thousand Pillars'. Unfortunately its size cannot compensate for its architectural mediocrity, and according to Satish Grover: ...the hall, surely one of the more arid products of Indian craftsmanship is a museum of drawings and photographs of the entire gamut of the 1200 years of temple architecture of the South.

Rameshwaram Corridors

Rameshwaram, on a tip of land jutting out into the sea, is a maze of huge pillared verandahs. Not only is the temple surrounded by corridors, but it is also linked to the entrances by covered passages. Rameshwaram thus has the distinction of possessing the longest corridors in the world. But, in spite of their huge proportions, the Gopuram and pillared corridors were the last gasp of conceptually revolutionary Hindu architecture in the country. The invasion of Islam had already resulted in the North being a bustling hive of mosque and tomb building. The Hindu stonecutter proved to be equally adept at carving Islamic masterpieces as sculpting nubile forms on the surface of temples. This will form the subject of a later article.

Karnataka Hoysalas

The flourishing temple styles in North India-both the Khajuraho and the Orissi versions-were brought to a rude end with the Muslim invasion. When the Muslims consolidated their hold over North India, temple-building activity virtually stopped. Entire families of skilled craftsmen were now presented with two choices-the first of which was to work for their new masters and abandon the idea of building a temple as an offering to God. This resulted in the fusion of Persian and Indian building styles and was to result in an entirely new idiom.

Second option was to migrate further and further south, in search of work and new patrons, where Muslim influence had not yet made inroads. This was the region around modern Mysore, where the hitherto unknown Hoysala tribe was making its first moves towards glory. Having overthrown their former overlords, the Cholas, the Hoysalas were in no mood to imitate their architectural style and were looking for something with its own distinct identity.

The mixing of the Dravidian and North Indian styles created a temple that is unique, so much so that it is often classified as the Hoysala style. The early experiments were found on the extreme edges of the kingdom, around ancient Dwarasamudra. The profile of the temples at Ittagi, Gadag and Lakhundi reveals that the craftsman's most visible contribution was a subtle merging of the two spire forms-the horizontal tiers of the pyramidal south Indian vimana and the round-shouldered elegance of the northern shikhara.

Gradually this hybrid evolved into an identifiable style, rivaling its predecessors in grace and beauty.

The Star in Plan: To add to its distinctiveness, the Hoysala temple in plan composed of numerous cellas or garbha-grihas served by a common mandapa. The plan of each of these cellas was a star. The departure from the accepted square form of the temple is understandable when we analyze the plan and see that it is made up of a grid of rotating squares. The resulting outline thus emerges as a star. The mandapa remained a square, though it was now distinguished by circular columns, the shafts of which had been lathed and thus acquired a number of parallel knife-edges. Among the examples of the developed

Hoysala style, the Chenna Kesava temple at modern Belur is one of the finest.

This was designed and planned by the architect Janaka Acharya at the behest of King Vishnuvardhan. Though built around a single shrine, the temple has all the distinguishing features of the Hoysala style-a pillared mandapa, bell-shaped towers and above all the star-shaped plan. The gaps between the outer pillars were covered with a *jaali* meant to provide privacy for the Brahmins, and especially the 'highly seductive dancing of the *devdasis*'. The mandapa of this temple has an extremely beautiful circular stone platform, lustrously polished after years and years of dance on it-the ritualistic, devotional Bharata Natyam of the South.

Splendour in Halebid: Not content with this little gem in Belur, the king commissioned an even larger and more magnificent temple in his new capital city of Halebid. The architect proceeded to lay out two identical temples, parallel and connected at their transepts. The Halebid temple is one of the most fitting climaxes to the sculptor's art in India. While architecturally it was not revolutionary, especially after Belur, it is in its rich sensuous sculpture that this example comes into its own.

The high plinth of the temple is a virtual tapestry of sculpture, with bands of dancing figures, animals, vegetation and other objects coming to life on its surface. According to Percy Brown, the 'Halebid Temple and the Parthenon are probably the two extremes of the architectural art of the world'. 'The one revels in the cold purity of its form and the other in the warm complexity of its sculptural architectonics'.

The Hoysala temples were among the last temples of consequence to be built in India. Muslim invasions were fast taking their toll and kings were more concerned about fighting off the invaders than with artistic and architectural endeavors. However, the Vijayanagara empire further south held on a little bit longer. The marvels at Hampi are the last examples of mediaeval Hindu architecture we shall discuss-in the next column.

Death of an Empire

The Ruins of Hampi: The conquest of the North by the marauding forces of Islam had already sounded the death-knell for most of the Hindu empires, with the exception of a few proud Rajput strongholds. The Sultans of Delhi were now in the process of consolidation and administration, and little by little Muslim rule and the Persian-Saracenic way of life began to permeate throughout the land.

The south however was largely ignored, with the rulers of Delhi leaving a governor in Daulatabad who nominally ruled in the name of the Sultan but in reality was a law unto himself. Before long, the inevitable happened with these governors revolting and naming themselves the true rulers. In this melee of changing power, two Hindu princes managed to carve out for themselves a stronghold at Hampi, and established an empire which would be the last great Hindu kingdom before the coming of the British.

A million-strong army ensured that the empire continued to grow in size and importance and numerous military successes resulted in Hampi itself being renamed Vijayanagar-the City of Victory. The site of Vijaynagar is spectacular, a city carved out of low lying hills and massive boulders, the treacherous terrain provided ample defense with only a few well-defended accesses. The Tungabhadra river meanders gently through, and at night the boulder-strewn landscape has an almost magical quality. Fortifications, outlying fields and a fifteen mile long aqueduct were the defence against a siege.

This city has been the subject of many an impassioned travelogue by foreigners-Portuguese and Persians:

> *"The city of Bidjanagar (Vijayanagar) is such that the pupil of the eye has never seen a place like it and the ear of intelligence has never been informed that there existed anything to equal it in the world. It is built in such a manner that seven citadels and the same number of walls enclose each other... The outer citadel has a fortress, of round shape, built on the summit of a mountain and constructed of stone and lime."*

Living Architecture: The site provided ample raw material for building, and the huge massifs of rock were often themselves sculpted to produce a unique architecture that is part organic, part man-made and often is difficult to distinguish from natural features. Hampi shows us a change from the normal centralised temple with outlying ancillaries, in the sense that the religious buildings are scattered around in small units, each with its own importance and function, the planning of the whole obeying the diktat of the terrain. Of the numerous temples and shrines scattered around, we will illustrate two.

The Vithala Temple: It was commissioned by Krishnadeva Raya, the greatest of the Vijaynagar rulers. Its chief peculiarity lies in the extent of its conception (an area of 500 by 300 feet) and the numerous columns, each an orgy of sculpture in itself.

Like a dying gothic monster, the columns rise from massive pedestals and scream upwards into grotesque brackets of enormous proportions. The large space is completely devoured by the forest of columns, and does not have any pretensions to cohesiveness or concept, becoming instead a maze of intricacy, art rather than architecture. The other major feature in the complex of the same temple is a chariot in granite, whose stone wheels lifted off from the ground are actually capable of moving around it.

Hazari Rama Temple : The same suggestion of the grotesque and the fanciful by private chapel of the same ruler. A combination of forms, including the Buddhist barrel vaulted roof, adds to the repertoire of shapes.

The fascination of Vijayanagar continues with its secular architecture. It is a mix of Hindu and Islamic features, as if the rulers were sufficiently impressed to import craftsmen and master-builders from neighbouring Islamic states. Among the most elegant constructions are the so-called 'watch-towers', although in reality most of them may have been built for pleasure, for the nobility to look out over the city. These towers have elements from both Hindu and Islamic vocabulary with typical Islamic arches, an octagonal or square plan, projecting eaves, corbelled brackets under the windows, and a decidedly Hindu finial.

The Elephants' Stable, in consonance with the beast's position as an animal for pomp and war, is mighty in conception and is perhaps one of the most impressive buildings in Vijayanagar. This long, 10-domed structure has mighty arched opening for the animals, very reminiscent of the Lodi tombs in Delhi, and the domes are alternately totally Islamic and with a hint of Hindu influence. The recessed arches in the front elevation as well as the central structure on top (perhaps for drummers and musicians) all combine to make this a must-see.

In the ultimate analysis, the beauty of Vijayanagar-Hampi, lies as much in its architecture as in what it represents. For this was the last stronghold of Hindu architecture and art, which were rapidly disappearing in an increasingly Muslim ruled subcontinent. And here too, the influence of Islam was already visible, slowly subsuming Hindu craft in a Hindu kingdom. For this would be the last Hindu fling at monumental architecture. Hindu craftsmen and traditions would continue, would influence the Islamic style, but would never again be significant.

The sculpture at Hampi, the barren rocky site, the haunting beauty of the landscape by night all contribute to painting for us, as we stand there today, a picture of battles fought, dying elephants and men, charging horses, and finally the eventual sack of the city as it fought vainly to stem the swelling tide of invasion. According to Percy Brown, '..the proud capital was (soon) a forlorn ruin inhabited only by tigers and other wild beasts'.

The Deccan, Gulbarga and Bidar

Beggar turned Prince: The Delhi artists transported to Daulatabad by Muhammad bin-Tughlaq took the Sultanate style with them to the north-western Deccan but trade had long exposed the region to western Asia. The tale of Zafar Khan, the first ruler of Gulbarga, is eminently recitable. According to some accounts, Zafar Khan was a poor laborer who was nominated to the Sultan's service by his master, who was impressed by his zeal and honesty. Later distinguishing himself in battle, Zafar Khan rose through the ranks to become eventual governor of the province of Daulatabad. With the weakening of power at Delhi, he declared the province independent of central authority and assumed the name of Ala-ud-din Bahman.

The Deccan: Golconda and Bijapur

The dynasties which supplanted the enfeebled Bahamanis in the Deccan early in the 16th century continued ardently patronage of architecture. Of these, the Qutb Shahis of Golconda and the Adil Shahis of Bijapur were especially active. Of their military works, the citadels, one each at Golconda and Bijapur, are testimony to the eventual might of these dynasties and cause for their long resistance against the Mughals. The heroic exploits of Chand Bibi, the Sultana of Bijapur, against Murad, son of Aurangzeb, are at least as celebrated as those of Razia Sultana or Rani Lakshmibai.

The Qutb Shahis of Golconda: Golconda fort was built on the remains of a Kakatiya citadel by Sultan Quli about 1544. The main fortress dominates the town 30 metres below. The three successive walls with numerous bastions for artillery and convoluted approaches for better defence testify to a time when wars were common and imminent attack around the corner.

Golconda Fort : On the gates the Hindu motifs show a continued trend of using local craftsmen and decorative vocabulary, and may also be proof of the religious tolerance of the Qutb Shahis. Later architecture of the Qutb Shahis showed a tendency to degenerate into a sort of tired decadence, when the urge to monumentality and impressiveness was muted by the addition of small-scale decorative elements.

This trend is only too visible in the tomb of Sultan Muhammad (c. 1612) at Golconda. Incongruous elements in this otherwise well-proportioned structure, such as the over-thin columns in the gallery on the ground floor, prevent this tomb from attaining the status of a masterpiece.

Similarly, another judgement may be passed on the Char Minar at Hyderabad. Its overwhelming status as the main landmark in Hyderabad, and indeed, as the very symbol of that city, does not add to its architectural effect. The Char Minar is ungainly as a structure and incoherent in its use of decorative features. Be that as it may, its sheer monumentality and visibility have contributed to make it a source of national pride.

Jama Masjid, Bijapur: The chajja on top of the outer arches of the court is supported by numerous brackets, and the central arch in axis with the mihrab stands out by the addition of cusps to its inner curve. The later mosques of the dynasty, like the Anda Masjid of 1608 and the Mihtari Masjid of 1620 show an increasing elaboration of forms.

Of the rauzas (combination of mosque and tomb) the best example is perhaps that of Ibrahim II. Here mosque and tomb are directly facing one another, with the middle space occupied by an ornamental pool, on a rectangular terrace set out along the charbagh concept. The highly elaborate detailing of both structures does not detract in the least from their fine proportions but rather complement them. Muhammad I tried to outdo his successor, and in this he partially succeeded, at least in terms of sheer grandeur.

For it is to him that can be attributed the Gol Gumbaz with its huge dome, the largest in India, and indeed among the largest in the world, along with its famous whispering gallery. It should be said here that the sheer size of the structure is alas, not matched by a corresponding fineness of proportion. For the bulky and squat corner minars, the relatively blank facades of the walls, the out-of-scale detailing of the arcades around the dome, all combine to make the Gumbad magnificently confused. This said, the sheer overwhelming size of the building leaves one wondering at its boldness of conception, surely among the most advanced in late medieval India.

Architecture of Andra

Muhammed Quli Qutub Shah (1580-1612) the son of Ibrahim Quli Qutub Shah ascended the throne at the age of 15. The famous Charminar, Char Kaman, Badshahi Ashur-Khana, Jame-Masjid, and Daru-Shifa were built during his reign.

Nawab Mir Yousuf Ali Khan, Salar Jung III was famous for his collection of antiques and beautiful objects from all over the world. His collection can be seen at the Salar Jung Museum and is regarded as the largest one man collection in the world.

Charminar

Charminar built in 1591 by Sultan Mohammed Quli Qutub Shah, the fifth ruler of the Qutub Shahi dynasty, is a masterpiece of Qutub Shahi architecture. The profuseness of stucco decoration and the design on the balconies are remarkable.

It is a magnificent square edifice of granite, built upon four grand arches facing North, South, East and West. These arches support two floors of rooms and gallery of archways. At each corner of the square structure is a minaret rising to a height of 24 meters, making the building nearly 54 meters tall. It is these four (char) minarets (minar) that give the building, its name 'Charminar'. Each minar stands on a lotus-leaf base, a special recurrent motif in Qutub Shahi buildings.

The first floor was used as a madarasa (college) during the Qutub Shahi period. The second floor has a mosque on the western side, the dome of which is visible from the road, if one stands some distance away. A spectacular view of the city may be had from the roof of the Charminar, although, due to severe overcrowding of the minarets, only visitors with special permission from the Archaeological Survey of India, Hyderabad Circle are allowed to go to the top of the minarets. The clocks above each of the four archways were added in 1889.

Walking around the Charminar area, one is constantly surprised by vestiges of the past intermingling with the present. Towards the Southeast of the Charminar is located imposing edifice of the Nizamia Unani Hospital. About 50m to the West, the line of shops in Lad Bazaar is interupted by an old, crumbling brown wall, which marks the entrance to the old Nizama's Jilau Khana (parade ground). The grounds are now being used for the development of a large commercial complex. Further down, a road to the left leads to the Khilawat Complex (Chowmahalla Palace). The Lad Bazaar road terminates in a square called Mahaboob Chowk where a large 19th century clock-tower looms over a delicate white mosque of the same period.

Badshahi Ashur Khana was built by Muhammed Quli Qutub Shah in 1594. Nearly four centuries later, the Ashur Khana still exudes certain freshness, as the enamel tiles have retained their lustre and vibrant colours.

Gun Foundry located opposite the Mahboobia Girls School was one of the several cannon and cannonball factories set up in 1786 by the French General Monsieur Raymond. This is the only existing gun-foundry today as the rest were dismantled.

Lad Bazar: Is one of the oldest shopping centers of Hyderabad. Noted for the sale of traditional bridal wares such as bangles, textiles, cosmetics, this shopping centre attracts many tourists.

The Mosque on the western side on the roof of Charminar is one of the finest mosques built by the Qutub Shahi artisans.

Mauzam Jahi Market building was inaugurated by Nizam VII in 1935 and the building was named after Mauzam Jah Bahadur, the second son of Mir Osman Ali Khan.

Saroornagar Palace was built by Mir Mahaboob Ali Khan, Nizam VI in 1804.Later he donated the palace for an orphanage—the 'Victoria Memorial Orphanage'.

The tomb of Muhammed Quli Shah, the founder of Hyderabad represents the first attempt at building a tomb of gigantic proportions to impart the monument an imposing stature. Rich ornamental parapets and turrets at the corner are distinctively visible.

A customary practice followed by the nobility and the rich was to offer perfumes called 'itar' to visitors at the time of their departure. The itars were kept in beautiful glass containers called 'itardans'.

Chowmahalla Palace, situated near the Mecca Masjid was built in 1750 by Salabat Jung.

Hyderabad was the only state in India where the ruler was allowed to print the currency notes. This 100 rupee note was introduced in 1918.

The tomb of Michael Raymond, a French Military Commander during the reign of the second Nizam.

Asman Garh Palace—Sir Asman Jah, the Prime Minister of Hyderabad (1887-1894) built this palace at Malakpet as a shikar rest house. At present the Palace houses the Birla Archaeological Museum.

The famous Abids shop belonged to the valet of Nizam VI. Today the whole street is known as Abid Road.

The High court stands on the south bank of the river Musi. This is one of the finest buildings in the city which was completed in 1919 during the reign of the Seventh Nizam.

The construction of the Residency was completed in 1868. Its is now the University College of women.

The legislative assembly was originally a Town Hall. The citizens of Hyderabad raised money to build it to mark the 40th birthday of Nizam VI in 1905.

The beautiful temple is situated near the Nehru Zoological Park. It was built in 1822 by Raja Raghu Ram Brahma Katri.

The Falaknuma Palace was built by Sir Viqar-ul-Umara, a Paigah noble in the late 19th century. In 1897 it was bought by the Nizam VI.

The main entrance of the famous Golconda Fort, situated on the eastern side. The design of peacocks and lions is a blend of Hindu-Muslim architecture.

The palace of Maharaja Kishen Prasad who was the Prime Minister of Hyderabad from 1900 to 1912.

Three granite walls of megalithic construction encircle the Golconda Fort with the outermost wall having a circumference of about 7 kms.

Wearing of waist belts also known as 'Buglus' was compulsory at all official functions during the reign of the Nizams.

Purani Haveli also known as 'Haveli Khadeem', which means old mansion, was constructed for Sikander Jah (1803-1829) by his father Ali Khan Nizam II.

Nizam VII Mir Osman Ali Khan was one of the richest men in the world during the 1940s. He is seen with his daughter-in-law, Princesss Nilofer, who was considered one of the most beautiful women in the world. The Nilofer hospital was named after her.

The Jubilee Pavilion, situated in the Public Garden, was built by the Seventh Nizam in 1937 to commemorate his Silver Jubilee.

Basheer Bagh Palace: Constructed by Sir Asman Jah, a Paigah noble and Prime Minister of Hyderabad (1887-1894). However the Palace was dismantled but the area is still known as Basheerbagh.

In July 1934, Mir Osman Ali Khan, Nizam VII laid the foundation of the Osmania University. An imposing granite structure, it is the example of late Osman Shahi architecture, which combines the Hindu style with that of "Saracenic".

Birla Planetarium, one of the most modern planetariums atop Naubhat Pahad.

Palaces of the Nizam: Asaf Jahi Style (Mainly in and around Hyderabad city)

The Asaf Jahis who succeeded the Qutub Shahis were prolific builders. Several palace complexes of the Nizam, landmarks like the Andhra Pradesh High Court, the Osmania Arts College and the Osmania Medical College building are among their well-known contributions. Asaf Jahi rulers also experimented with European styles and attempted a synthesis of European traditions with Hindu and Islamic forms and motifs.

Chow Mahalla Palace: Among two intervening rulers, Salabat Jung spent a greater part of his time in Hyderabad (Salabat Jung, the officially un-crowned Nizam ruled for a short period during the power struggle between the British and the French, compounded by the interference of the Marathas). By some accounts, he is credited with the building of the first Asaf Jahi Palace in Hyderabad *i.e.* the Chow Mahalla palace. The Asaf Jahis deserted the former Qutub Shahi palace quarter lying North West of Charminar and decided to construct a new palace complex for themselves to the south west of Charminar.

In 'The Unpublished Diary of a French Officer of Bussy's Army', the Officer describes Salabat Jung's palace with its approach from Chowk (later known as Mahboob Chowk) as follows:

> *"the other or second building is the mansion of the Nawab, which is made up of three blocks of residences....... We here see a reservoir, the garden and the reservoir lead up to a large courtyard.... in the midst of this court is the first apartment, which is a large carpeted hall, one storied; its ceiling is supported by a number of small wooden pillars.....the second block of houses is also a great hall of which the ceiling is supported by a number of wooden pillars, each of a single piece, it is carpeted and one-storeyed. In the centre of the hall is the Nawab's throne between four pillars, where he receives the ambassadors.....as for the third block of houses, it lies to the left as you enter the preceding hall. Here are two houses facing each other, between which is a fruit garden with a square medium sized reservoir and a small fountain. In the house on the right is a large screen, and it is here that the Nawab dines and sleeps with his concubines.....such is the apartment of Nawab Salabat Jung."*

The above account is vague and does not clearly correspond to the buildings in Chow Mahalla as they stand now. This however confirms that Salabat Jung selected the site and created the nucleus of perhaps modest structures laid along a series of inter-linked courtyards, the old structures being later replaced by grander ones. The Chow Mahalla Palace complex in fact extends from the Lad Bazaar on the north to the Aspan Chowk road on the south. During different phases of Asaf Jahi rule, portions of Chow Mahalla were built. The durbar was held in the hall or pavilion called the Khilwat. This was built around 1780 during the reign of Nawab Nizam Ali Khan, Asaf Jah II but later extensively renovated in 1911. Khilwat has a composite architectural style with Mughal as well as Qutub Shahi arches, topped by twin octagonal pavilions on the parapet. It is an over decorated building with huge proportions with a curious Asaf Jahi Baroque.

Jilu Khana facing the Lad Bazaar and Daulat Khana e Ali was built during the reign of Asaf Jah I (1724-1748). South of Khilwat one enters the next courtyard around which the main four palaces are located lending the Chow Mahalla name. It is believed that this complex was built during the reign of Nawab Afzal-ud Doula Bahadur, the Nizam or Asaf Jah V (1857-1869). The palaces are named Afzal Mahal, Mahtab Mahal, Tahniyat Mahal and Aftab Mahal. Of these, Afzal Mahal is the most imposing and a two storied building with a European facade of Corinthian columns and a parapet without pediment. Other three buildings are single storied structures with relatively modest scale and facades of Corinthian columns. All the four buildings are laid around a large courtyard garden with a marble cistern at the centre.

There are later additions to the complex in late Mughal style with facades of cusped arches, made between 1912 and 1926 when the older buildings were also renovated.

Chow Mahalla was used even by subsequent Nizams and state banquets were held here. Well known among those is the banquet held in honour of T.R.H the Prince and the Princes of Wales on 10th February 1906. For several decades, the sprawling Chow Mahalla Complex has been lying vacant.

Purani Haveli Palace

Asaf Jah II apparently lived in the Chow Mahalla complex buildings built by his predecessors, since the main palaces were built by Asaf Jah V nearly hundred years later. In 1777, between Chatta Bazaar and Dabirpura Main road, towards north east of Charminar, he started construction of the first buildings of Purani Haveli for his son, Sikandar Jah. But Sikandar Jah, on becoming the third Nizam (1803-1829) went to live in the Khilwat palace in Chow Mahalla. The buildings built by Asaf Jah II therefore came to be known as Purani Haveli. Purani Haveli regained its glory only when the sixth Nizam, Nawab Mir Mahboob Ali Khan made it his official residence.

Purina Haveli Complex is U shaped with a single storied central building in European style flanked by two double storied oblong wings (nearly 1000 feet) of which the western one has the famous wooden wardrobe. Both the wings are wider towards the southern end where these are only single storied and have two extremely well proportioned courtyards surrounded by rooms and deep verandahs with semicircular European arches. Purani Haveli is one of the most important architectural landmarks of Hyderabad combining European facades with traditional Indian courtyards. The complex also includes two annexes attached to the northern ends of the parallel wings. Purani Haveli on the whole is under-used. A training institute runs in parts of the building beside the offices of the Muffakham Jah Trust. Nearby there is another beautiful courtyard house now used as the Princes Esin Women's Education Centre.

King Kothi Palace

Of the three principal buildings of the King Kothi Complex, the main King Kothi building now housing a hospital and the Mubarak Mansion (Nazri Bagh) accommodating the offices of the Nizam's Private Estates (Sarf E Khas) only survive. The third building, Usman Mansion was demolished in the early eighties and in its place a new hospital building is constructed by the State Government. Originally built by one Kamal Khan, the complex was acquired by the Nizam VII. Both the surviving buildings in King Kothi are in European style. Nizam VII, the last ruling Nizam (1911-1948) lived here and passed away in this building on February 24th 1967.

The northern and the main road-facing gateway of Mubarak Mansion is called the Purdah Gate where always a big purdah or curtain hung. When Nizam went out of the Palace, the purdah was lifted up which showed that he was not present. The gate was guarded by Maisaram Regiment, police and Sarf E Khas Army with lances in their hands. To the east of Mubarak Mansion, stands the Ghadial Gate: the gate with a clock. King Kothi complex has various European styles incorporated in it. The canopies over windows, the intricate woodwork, the sloping tiled roofs in octagonal pyramid shapes of the Ghadial Gate complex, and the classical semicircular arches are among the characteristic features of King Kothi. As mentioned earlier, the King Kochi Complex has remained in use for offices and Hospital.

Falaknuma Palace

Falaknuma palace mainly served as a royal guesthouse for the Nizams. The palace was built by Nawab Vikarul Umra Bahadur, a noble from the Paigah family, who later became Prime Minister of Hyderabad (1894-1901). The main buildings were completed in 1884. Nizam VI, Nawab Mir Mahboob Ali Khan Bahadur purchased it in 1897 and later added other structures like the Coronation building. The sixth Nizam occasionally lived here and died in this building in 1911.

Falaknuma palace complex is dramatically located on top of a hill about four km south of the Charminar. The main palace was designed by English architects in 1872. The central building is placed over a large terrace accessed through two levels of basements. The building is in classical style with a two storeyed deep and colonnaded verandah carrying a pediment. Though basically Palladian, the columns are thicker in proportion. The facade has Ionic columns at the ground floor and Corinthian columns at the first floor. A wide staircase leads to the ground floor. On both sides of the main central palace are two identical crescent shaped blocks with classical facade and pediments.

At the rear, there is a long and imposing courtyard, nearly 600 feet long, surrounded on all sides by rooms and corridors. At the southern end, there is a round shaped hall with deep verandas faced by colonnade in Ionic style called Gol Bungla and an interesting glass roofed large verandah overlooking the vast expanse down below. Parts of the side wings are older structures incorporating Islamic features. The Coronation building and a few ancillary structures are in late Mughal or Rajasthani style.

The interior of the main building has a marble entrance hall and fountain, and an Italian marble staircase supporting marble figures, lined with portraits of British Governors General. The reception room is in Louis XIV style. Elsewhere there are French tapestries, beautiful inlaid furniture from Kashmir, and Victorian artefacts.

Dignitaries who stayed at Falaknuma as guests include the future King George V and Queen Mary, Prince of Wales, and

Viceroy Lord Wavell. Falaknuma is one of the largest and most important palaces of India

After years of neglect and non-use Falaknuma Palace is now being given a major face-lift by the Taj Group for a Heritage Hotel.

Mahboob Mansion: This palace, presently in disuse and poor condition, is named after Nawab Mir Mahboob Ali Khan, the VIth Nizam who used to occasionally live here though his permanent residence was the Purani Haveli described earlier. Built in the late nineteenth century, this is a very interesting and large palace in a combination of classical European and Mughal style. It has roofs somewhat similar to the eastern blocks of Mubarak Mansion (Nazri Bagh) in King Kothi.

Anand Buddha Vihara: Located in Mahendra Hills of Secunderabad, this Vihara was established in 1974, and aims to preserve the Buddhist Culture. The trust plans to construct a temple vihara, a cultural centre, a hospital, a school and a meditation centre. Daily prayers, meditation and Dharma discourse take place here.

Andhra Pradesh State Legislative Assembly: Few would believe that this imposing edifice, completed in 1913, was the town hall in the old Hyderabad State. The citizens of Hyderabad raised money to build it to mark the 40th birthday of Nizam Mahboob Ali Khan in 1905. This white gem of Hyderabad's architectural splendour was designed by specially commissioned architects from Rajasthan. This blend of Rajasthan and Persian architecture is now the home of the 295-seat Andhra Pradesh Legislative Assembly.

Ashta Lakshmi Temple: A magnificent temple dedicated to Goddess Lakshmi in eight forms of the deity stands distinctly on the outskirts of the city of Hyderabad in Vasavi Nagar, Dilshukhnagar. Amidst the varied Islamic architectural monuments in Hyderabad, this temple has a different style—a touch of the south-Indian architecture.

The well-known Sculptor, Padmashri Ganapati Sthapathi, conceived the structure and designed the temple. Subbaiah Sthapathi designed the idols of Ashta Lakshmi,

Srimannarayana, Sri Ganapathi and Sri Garuda. About 134 vigrahas (idols) of lesser—known Gods adorn the mahagopuram.

Asman Ghar Palace: The palace was designed and built by Sir Asman Jah, a noble belonging to the Paigah family and one time Prime Minister of Hyderabad State.

The granite turrets and arched windows of Asman Garh stand atop a hill some distance ahead of the Hyderabad TV tower. The palace now houses an archaeological museum.

Birla Archaeological Museum: A lesser known museum but consisting of exquisite excavations from historical sites. The entire collection is housed in Asman Ghad palace.

Birla Mandir: This beautiful white marble temple of Lord Balaji is built on a hillock, the *Kala Pahad*. This exquisite temple has great sculptural excellence and a profusely carved ceiling. It is a beautiful sight at night when illuminated, standing against the dark sky and looking down on Hussain Sagar Lake.

Birla Observatory and Planetarium: The most modern and the first of its kind planetarium in India, it is equipped with the most advance equipment from Japan. This is built on the *Naubat Pahad*, neighbouring the *Kala Pahad* on which stands the Birla Temple.

Mecca Masjid: Southwest of Charminar lies Mecca Masjid, the most impressive mosque in South India. It was started in 1614 A.D. by the sixth Qutub Shahi King Abdullah Qutub Shah and completed in 1687 A.D. by Aurangzeb, when he annexed Golconda. This mosque is said to have bricks from Mecca built into its central arch.

Its lofty colonnades and entrance arches are made of single slabs of granite brought from a stone quarry, 11 Km north of Charminar. Legend says, 1400 bullocks were required to pull these.

Mecca Masjid is poetry in stone, with a hall measuring 67 m and soaring to a height of 54 m. The roof is supported by 15 graceful arches. It can accommodate 10,000 worshippers at a time. The southern end of the mosque has the tombs of all Nizams, from the time of Nizam Ali Khan (who died in 1803) and his successors, except that of Osman Ali Khan Nizam VII.

Hi-Tech City: One of the modern monuments of trade and technology, it embodies the new found attitude of Hyderabad and today finds a place of pride. Situated on the outskirts of the city, it is the nucleus of Cyberabad, the IT destination in these parts of the world.

Kothi—Residency: According to the book "Pictorial Hyderabad: The British Residents", a Madras civilian named Mr. Holland was sent by the Governor and Council of the fort St. George Factory, to the court of the "Subedar "of the Deccan on a purely diplomatic mission. The successors of this envoy, in course of time, when ascendancy of the British over the political affairs of the Nizam gradually asserted itself, came to be known as Residents.

Osmania University: This University is named as "Osmania University" by Nizam the VII. In July 1934, the Nizam laid the foundation stone for the university. The university was started in a rented building near Abid Road and later shifted to its present site. Jasper was the architect. More than 35,000 labourers were employed to construct the university.

The University covers an area of 1400 acres. The main building on the campus is the College of Arts & Commerce. An imposing granite structure, it is the best example of the Osman Shahi architecture. It was completed in 1939 at a cost of Rs.36 lakh and was inaugurated in the same year by its founder, Nizam VII. Other buildings were gradually added to the campus. The Law College, Engineering College, and Science blocks have a similar architectural design. The main post-graduate library building was built later. The Tagore Auditorium was built to commemorate the Golden Jubilee celebrations in 1968.

The University has a large swimming pool. The several hostels on the campus accommodate a large number of students from different parts of the State.

The University campus also houses the American Studies Research Center and the Institute of Public Enterprise. There are ten faculties—Arts, Social Sciences, Commerce, Education, Law, Science, Engineering, Technology, Medicine and Ayurveda, Unani and Homeopathy. There are special facilities for the study of Islamic culture, Russian, German and French languages. Special degree courses are available in modern subjects like Electronics, Astrophysics, Genetics, Astronomy, Journalism, Business Management, Public Enterprise and Public Administration. The university is the first and the only one in India to offer Military Science as a subject of special study. In 1983, a department of Theatre Arts was started which trains students in all aspects of the theatre, from folk forms, classical theatre to the contemporary theatre. There are 167 colleges affiliated to the university.

Raymond's Tomb: Raymond's Tomb is situated in Malakpet near Osmanagar Palace, on the top of a small hill rising to a height of 100 feet from the ground. A gallant French General, Raymond was known as Michel Joachin Marie Raymond. He was employed by the Nizam to completely reorganise his armed forces. He was born in France on 25th September, 1755 AD but died at Hyderabad on March 25, 1798 AD at the young age of 43.

Paigah Tombs: There are many tombs of several generations of the Paigah nobles including Asman Jah, Viqar-ul-Umara and Shams-ul-Umara. The tombs are magnificent structures, decorated in stuccowork, and represent the Asaf Jahi and Rajasthani styles. The geometrical designs in the Paigah Tombs are unique and perforated with screens. This style is unique to the Paigah tombs and is not found elsewhere in the world.

Sanghi Temple

In the nearby industrial town Sanghi Nagar, this temple named after its patron family, Sanghi, is situated on top of a hill. This is a beautiful temple constructed in the South Indian style of temple architecture and hosts all important Hindu god idols. It is a favourite getaway point for the Hyderabadis as well as a popular tourist spot.

Amaravati Museum

The collection includes the antiquities from other Buddhist sites in Andhra Pradesh belonging to the 3rd Century BC to about the 12th Century AD, a gold necklace from Gummadidurru, relic-caskets with bone-relics and gold flowers. The exhibits in the Museum are arranged in different galleries.

Gallery I contents: This gallery displays some of the selected examples of the art-tradition of Amaravati, besides an inscribed relief of Buddha from Gummadidurru. Image of Buddha, Coins, Beads, Terracota, Pottery, and Drum slabs, Dome-slabs, Pillars & Rail fragments and Miscellaneous Sculptures.

Gallery II contents: The exhibits in the gallery comprise a few early relics of the 2nd Century BC, inscribed pillars, drum & dome slabs, Two Buddha images from Alluru and a stone-wheel from Lingarajapalli.

Gandhi Hill: The first Gandhi Memorial with 7 Stupas in the country was constructed on this hill at a height of 500 ft. The 52 ft. Stupa was unveiled on 6th October, 1968 by Dr. Zakir Hussain, the then President of India. Gandhi Memorial Library, the Sound and Light Show on Mahatma Gandhi's life and a planetarium are the other attractions.

Salarjung Museum

SalarJung III, who was interested in collecting rare objects of art resigned from his Prime Ministership at the age of 24 to collect pieces of art from around the world. The Prime Minister of India Shri Jawaharlal Nehru had declared open the entire collection of Salar Jung to the public on December 16, 1951. The collection was shifted to its present building in 1968.

Here one can find art works from Oriental as well as Western countries. The Salar Jung Museum has different sections based on the antique value. The first gallery introduces the visitors to the Salar Jung and their times. The second gallery has major and minor arts of South India, Stone Sculptures, Textiles, Ivory, Metal Ware, Arms and Armour and Indian Miniature Paintings. A separate section for children is on the ground floor.

The textile and costume gallery has some rare exhibits of Mughal Curtains, Kashmiri Shawls and Brocades. The miniature painting gallery abounds with Western, Indian & Mughal miniatures. The painting gallery possesses the works of famous Raja Ravi Varma, Tagore brothers, Chughtai and contemporary artists of Andhra Pradesh and other parts of India. The Veiled Rebecca carved by the well-known Italian sculptor, Benzoni, is an unsurpassed masterpiece & a major attraction of the museum. Another remarkable piece is the two sided wooden statue of Mephistopheles and Margaretta symbolizing good and evil. The same log of wood is used to carve two diametrically opposite characters. The Japanese section exhibits Nikko Furniture, Embroidered Silk Screens, Needlework, Ivory Carvings and Satsuma ware.

Ghantasala: Ghantàsala lies in the Divi taluk of Krishna district 21 km west of Machilipatnam. It is a rare and reputed center for Buddhist sculptures. Here the remains of an important Buddhist stupa and sculptural slabs were found in 1919-20.

Monuments & Antiquities: The main scene here portrays a circular medallion in the style of Amaravati sculptures, which shows the return of Budhistva Siddhartha to Kapilavastu after his renuniciation. There is a museum in this village, which has a collection of Buddhist statues and art. A considerable number of Roman gold coins and Satavahanas coins have been discovered here.

Gummadidurru: Excavations undertaken at the place unearthed a part of the main stupa and a dozen small stupas. The site has also yielded a number of inscriptions dating back from 2nd century AD to late medieval period.

Gunadala Mary Matha Shrine: An annual feast is held every year to commemorate the appearance of Mother Mary at Lourdes on February 11th 1858. A church and a museum of valuable articles offered by the devotees and sacred relics of the past are present. An iron cross is erected atop the hill.

Hazratbal Mosque: A holy relic of the Prophet Mohammed is kept here and displayed once a year. A large number of Muslim population joins the celebrations.

Hinkar Thirtha (Jam Temple), Mangalagiri: A Jain temple being constructed is almost nearing completion. With great artistic work, it is slated to be the biggest Jam temple in the region.

Kanaka Durga Temple: This famous temple is on a hill connected by steps and a ghat road. Inscriptions of different dynasties are found in the temple. The festival of Dussera for Goddess Durga is celebrated here colourfully every year. A large number of pilgrims attend the celebrations and take a holy dip in the river Krishna.

Kondapalli Fort: The fort is located 16 km away towards West from Vijayawada City and is built on a hill. Prolaya Vema Reddy, constructed this fort during 14th Century. The king used to visit this fort for relaxation and recreation. It was the residence of "Bhogamalas" meaning the prostitutes of the kings.

Near the fort, there is a Dargah of a Persian Saint, Gareeb Saheeb. A legend goes that the palace women and the saint were always at loggerheads. Unable to bear the trouble, the queen of the palace ordered the beheading of the Saint. Even after he was beheaded the Saint fought valiantly and dragged the fort soldiers to a distance of 20 km without his head.

Mangalagiri Temple: The unique feature of this temple is that the deity accepts only half the quantity of Panakam (Jaggery dissolved in water) offered by devotees. It has a very tall gopura. The presiding deity is that of Lord Narashimha.

Ovva Temple: Movva is the birthplace of Siddhendra Yogi, the founder of Kuchipudi dance. This ancient town has temples of Vishnu and Shiva.

Prakasam Barrage: Built across the river Krishna, Prakasam Barrage has created a panoramic lake. Its three canals that run through the city give Vijayawada a Venetian look.

Victoria Museum: A place for archaeology lovers, Victoria Museum has a carefully preserved collection of ancient sculptures, paintings, idols, weapons, cutlery and inscriptions.

Sri Bedi Anjaneya Swami: The temple of Sri Anjaneyaswamy facing the Mahadwaram of Sri Venkateswara shrine houses the image of Bedi Hanuman. According to a legend Hanuman attempted to flee from the holy hills in search of his Onte Vahanam (Camel Vehicle).

In order to prevent Anjaneya's flight his mother Anjana Devi residing near Akasa Ganga at Anjanadri of Sapthagiri (7 Hills) prevailed upon her son and tied the celestial bedi (Handcuffs) to his hands with the aid of several monkeys living there, so as to make Anjaneya stay in devotion in front of the Lord's temple to fulfill her desire.

Lord Sri Varaha Swamy: It is customary for the devotees to offer worship at the shrine of Sri Varahaswamy located beside the Pushkarini. Lord Vishnu assumed the form of a boar to rescue Bhudevi from the clutches of the demon Hiranyaksha. According to the legends, Varahaswamy was the Kshetrapala of the hill of Lord Venkateswara and approached him for some space to reside there. Therefore it is ordained that worship should be offered to Varahaswami varu first before proceeding to Lord Venkateswara's shrine. In this temple Sri varahaswamy stands with his leg raised up and holds Bhudevi in his arms.

Akasaganga: The Temple is about 21 km. from Tirupati railway station and 3 km from Tirumala bus stand. There are frequent buses from this place. The place is known as the meditation place of Anjana Devi, mother of Hindu God, Hanuman. The water, which flows here, is to date not known of its origin.

7

Orissan Monuments

The temples at Orissa, or Kalinga which is its ancient name, provide some of the finest examples of the Indo-Aryan style of temple architecture, which is distinct from the south Indian style. The main group of temples is concentrated in the town of Bhubaneshwar where there are over thirty of them. A few miles from this temple town are two of the largest buildings in eastern India, the temple of Jagannath at Puri and the Sun temple at Konark. Other examples of this style of architecture can also be seen further north on the southern borders of Bengal.

The earliest of these temples date from the eighth century A.D and the largest and latest, the Sun temple at Konark, was erected in the middle of the thirteenth century. Thus these temples represent the scene of sustained architectural activity for nearly five hundred years. The earliest temples (about A.D 750 to 900) are all present in Bhubaneshwar. Even in this early phase, the sculptural treatment was elaborate.

The two temples of monumental proportions, the Lingaraja at Bhubaneshwar and the Jagannath at Puri, were constructed around A.D 1000. Both these temples consist of four structures which comprise the fully developed Orissan style of temple architecture. Even today, the great tower of the Lingaraja dominates the entire town of Bhubaneshwar with its height and size; the Jagannath temple at Puri is still larger and of a slightly later date. In colonial times, an elaborate set of representations was built around the Jagannath temple: it became iconic of Hindu fanaticism, as devotees were supposed to hurl themselves in front of the temple's large chariot and get crushed by its gigantic wheels. The word 'Juggernaut' is derived from Jagannath.

The grandest achievement of this school of architecture is the Sun temple at Konark (about A.D. 1250), standing entirely by itself some twenty miles from Puri. The temple is dedicated to *Surya*, the Sun god, who has traditionally been represented as riding his winged chariot drawn by seven horses. The temple is therefore fashioned like a *ratha* (chariot) and the base of the structure has 12 giant wheels, each nearly ten feet high. The entire surface is filled out with sculpted forms, some of outstanding beauty, while the others are of a markedly erotic character. These indicate the emergence of a particular phase of Hinduism, better known as Tantrism. However, it appears that this cult soon lost much of its following, and today the temple lies abandoned, under the care of the Archaeological Survey of India, unlike the Jagannath temple at Puri which is an important pilgrimage site. Though much of this structure is now in ruins, its sheer grandeur and size still inspires awe. The greatest centre of this school is the ancient city of Bhuvanesvara, in which are concentrated almost 100 examples of the style, both great and small, ranging in date from the 7th to the 13th century.

Among the earliest is the Parasuramesvara temple (7th–8th century), with a heavy, stately *latina sikhara*, to which is attached a rectangular *gudhamandapa* with double sloping roofs. The walls are richly carved, but the interiors, as in almost all examples of the style, are left plain. The Muktesvara temple (10th century), which has a hall with a *phamsana* roof, is the product of the most exquisite workmanship. The enclosing wall and the arched entrance, or *torana*, are still present, giving a clear idea of a temple with all its parts fully preserved. The Brahmesvara temple, which is dated on the basis of an inscription to the mid-10th century, is a *panchayatana*, with subsidiary shrines at all of the corners. The most magnificent building, however, is the great Lingaraja temple (11th century), an achievement of Orissan architecture in full flower. The *latina* spire soars to a considerable height (over 125 feet); the wall is divided into two horizontal rows, or registers, replete with statuary; and the attached hall is exquisitely and minutely carved. The most famous of all Orissan temples, however, is the colossal building at Konark, dedicated to Surya, the sun god. The temple and its accompanying hall are conceived in the form of a great chariot drawn by horses. The *sikhara* over the sanctum has entirely collapsed; and all that survives are the ruins of the sanctum and the *gudhamandapa*, or enclosed hall, and also a separate dancing hall.

Of these, the *gudhamandapa* is now the most conspicuous, its gigantic *phamsana sikhara* rising in three stages and adorned with colossal figures of musicians and dancers. Because the Orissan style usually favours a *latina sikhara* over the sanctum, the *sekhari* spire of the Rai Iani temple (11th century) at Bhuvanesvara (Bhubaneshwar) is quite exceptional. Of particular interest as a late survival of early building traditions is the Vaital Deul (8th century), the sanctum of which is rectangular in plan, its *sikhara* imitating a pointed barrel vault. Besides Bhuvanesvara, important groups of temples are to be found at Khiching and Mukhalingam.

Archaeological treasures abounding in Orissa dating from the prehistoric times upto the end of the Muslim rule in the middle of the sixteenth century. The excavations at Sisupalgarh and Jaugada testify to the presence of a highly developed prehistoric civilisation in Orissa. The caves of Khandagiri and Udayagiri represent Orissan cave architecture dating back to the first century BC. The caves were cut out in the solid rock on the orders of King Kharavela for the use of Jain ascetics. There are altogether eighteen caves in Udayagiri and fifteen caves in Khandagiri. The caves are decorated with sculptural motifs. The Ranigumpha cave in Udayagiri is a two-storeyed structure and bears highly artistic sculpture. The caves consist of one or more cells and a few of them are fronted by pillared verandahs. The sculptures of Khandagiri and Udayagiri form a landmark in the history of Indian art.

Buddhism also provided inspiration like Jainism for the development of art and architecture. It was Emperor Ashoka who directed the entire state machinery for the dissemination of Buddhism. We find two versions of his major rock in Orissa one at Dhauli and the other at Jaugada. The archaeological excavations at Ratnagiri have brought to light the remains of a main stupa, two viharas and eight temples containing Buddhist images. A large number of images of the Buddha and Bodhisattvas of great artistic merit have been collected from the hills of Lalitgiri, Olashuni, Landa and Parabhadi hills. A colossal image of Bodhisattva Padmapani has been found at Jajpur it measures 15'8" inches. Buddhist remains have also been discovered at Boudh, Khiching and Solampur. It is seen that the Lalitgiri sculptures contain the living influence of Gupta art tradition

Architecture of Temple: Architecture in Orissa found its supreme expression in the form of temples, some of which are among, finest in the country. Of these, three are most famous the Lingaraja temple at Bhubaneshwar, the Jagannath Temple at Puri and the great Sun Temple at Konark. These mark the culmination of a distinct style of architecture called the Kalinga style remarkable in its plan elevation and details of decoration. In the simplest form, a temple of this style consists of a structural due, the main temple or shrine and the frontal porch. While the main temple, called Vimana or Deula, is the sanctum enshrining the deity the porch or assembly hall called Jagamohana is the place for the congregation of devotees. The former, constructed on a square base, has a soaring curvilinear tower (sikhara) and is known as Rekha Deula.

This two-part structure in the earliest form of temple construction is noticeable in the Parsurameswar temple of Bhubaneshwar (7th century). A modest specimen of the Bhubaneshwar-Lakshmaneswar group of early temples, it has a squattish type of curvilinear sikhara and an oblong pillared jagamohana. The sculptress on the temple walls are also notable for their simplicity and beauty. The Kalinga style reached its perfection during the Genae period when two more structures were added the front of the two-part temple in order to meet the needs of the elaborate rituals; these are the natamandira (dancing hall) and the bhogamandapa (hall of offerings). The four halls of structure as at Lingaraja and Jagannatha, stand in one line with emphasis on the towering sikhara of the main shrine. However, the devotees have to enter through the side doors of the jagamohana leaving the tamandira and bhogamandapa behind.

Temple building activities in Orissa continued uninterrupted between the 7th and 16th centuries. As different religious sects had their successive sway over the land during this period, they provided the necessary fillip for modifications in the architectural designs and sculptural details. The Vaital temple at Bhubaneshwar and the Varahi temple at Chaurasi in the Prachi Valley with their semi cylindrical roofs are examples of a different order of temples described as Eshakhara type in the shilpasastras. The former with its tower resembling a topsy-turvied boat and the later with its barrel-vaulted top are dedicated to the goddess Chamunda and Varahi respectively. The silhouetted interior of the sanctum and the sculptural motifs in the niches of the temples bear the influence of Shakti cult.

There is yet another class of temples which are almost unique in their conception and execution in the whole country; these are the circular shaped, hypaethral or ruffles structures dedicated to the sixty-four yoginis belonging to the Tantric order. Out of all the five shrines of yogini worship existing in the whole country, two are situated in Orissa, the Chausathi Yogini temples one at Hirapur near Bhubaneshwar and the other at Ranipur-Jharial in Titlagarh subdivision of Balangir district. At the centre of these temples is pedestalled the image of Bhairava around which are located the yoginis, each in a niche. The artistic figures of the yoginis, their hair style varying totally in case of each at Hirapur, are superb in execution. However, the Kalinga style of architecture which was the most common order throughout progressed well under the patronage of the Somavamsi Kings of Orissa during the 10th and 11th centuries.

The Mukteswar temple (10th century) of Bhubaneshwar is considered a "gem of Orissan architecture" and is accepted as one of the most beautiful temples of India. Elegantly decorated from top to bottom, it stands within a gracefully laid out compound with an exquisite makara torana in front. The rekha sikhara and rhythmic in treatment, is unrivalled in beauty. The Jagmohana is a harmonious pidha deula crowned with a kalasa at the top. The Rajarani temple (11th century) owing its name to a type of stone known as 'rajarania' is an architectural specimen of the later Somavamsi period.

Picturesquely set amidst a wide expanse of rice fields, this temple in its execution combines grace and elegance, beauty of form and sculptural embellishments The deula, adorned with a cluster of miniature temples is reminiscent of Khajuraho. The Brahmeswar temple (11th. century) characteristic continuation of the Drissan style. The great temple of Lingaraja (11th century) at Bhubaneshwar is the quintessence of Orissan architecture With all the features of temple architecture fully developed and perfectly executed, it is undoubted one of the most finished temples in India. The elaborate temple complex consisting of the lowering sikhara (45 m. in height), jagamohana, natamandira and bhogamandap all in perfect harmony along with the lesser shrines around has a unique grander and majesty.

The earliest Ganga monument of Orissa is the temple of Jagannatha at Puri is the massive edifice standing on a high platform connected with the ground led by a flight of 22 steps is the product of accumulated experience of the past temple architecture. The whole of the main temple was covered by a thick consisting of plaster, which earned for it the name 'White Pagoda'. The plaster has since been removed by the Archaeological Survey of India to reveal the beautiful stone carvings. Finest specimen of Ganga art and the greatest monument of Hindu architect in India is the famous Sun Temple of Konark which is conceived as a chart driven by horses. The chariot had twenty-four wheels and seven horses. The when of the chariot are masterpieces of art. The temple is perfectly proportioned in stupendous size. It is one of the wonders of workmanship in the wood. In the words of Rabindranath Tagore, "Here the language of man is defeated by the language of stone". The temples of Orissa exhibit a majestic grandeur. An Orissan temple (deul) usually consists of a sanctum, one or several front porches (jagamohana) usually with pyramidal roofs, a dancing hall (nata mandir) and a hall of offerings (bhog mandir).

In fact, the Lingaraj temple at Bhubaneshwar boasts of a 150 foot high deul while the Jagannath Temple at Puri is about 200 feet high and it dominates the skyline of the town. Only a portion of the Sun Temple at Konark, the largest of the temples of the Golden triangle exists today, and it is still staggering in size. It stands out as a masterpiece in Orissan architecture. Orissa's history dates back to the days of the Mahabharata. It was under the rule of the Nanda Kings in the pre Christian era and then under the Mauryan rule. Rock edicts of Emperor Ashoka are found in the State. The impact of the invasion of the Guptas is seen in the early temples of Bhubaneshwar. The Matharas ruled Orissa from the later half of the 4th century AD. The Sailodbhavas who followed constructed several shrines the ruins of which can be seen today.

The period between 8th to 11th c. AD was crucial Saivism dominated the religious scene although Budhist, Jain and Vaishnavite monuments also came into being. The Gangas took over after the decline of the Somavamsis. The early Eastern Gangas ruled from Kalinganagara (Mukhalingam near Srikakulam Andhrapradesh). They shifted their capital to Cuttack in the 12th century. Saivism began to decline while Saktism flourished. Further, the religious leader Ramanujacharya had a great influence on the monarch Chodagangadeva who built the great temple at Puri. The Gangas were champions of Vaishnavism. It was during the Ganga rule that Orissan architecture reached its peak. Narasimhadeva of this dynasty built the Sun Temple at Konark.

The Suryavamsi Gajapati rulers succeeded the Gangas, under whom Vaishnavism in the form of Jagannatha worship reached new heights. This period was marked by the influence of Chaitanya Mahaprabhu and by the construction of Jagannatha temples across the length and breadth of the empire. After the decline of the Gajapatis, the kingdom began to disintegrate and was taken over by followed by Muslim rule, the rule of the Mughals, the Marathas and then the British. The Bhoi Gajapatis who ruled Orissa over a small territory built may temples.

Bhubaneshwar and the Great Lingaraja : Meanwhile, the temple city of Bhubaneshwar, which we have discussed in a previous article, was witnessing the construction of its biggest temple – the Great Lingaraja. As is evident from its name, the temple was dedicated to Shiva. Unlike the temples at Khajuraho, the ones in Bhubaneshwar are still active, the most famous example being the temple of Jagannath at Puri. To accommodate the increasing number of pilgrims, a number of additions were made to the Lingaraja in subsequent years. The *Nat Mandir*, or Hall of Dance, and the *Bhog Mandir*, or the Hall of Offering, were the major ones. Unfortunately, these were rather unimaginative and had a detrimental effect on the silhouette of the Jagannath temple as a whole. Thus, though the Lingaraja is unsurpassed in its importance as a centre of pilgrimage in Orissa, many smaller examples can be cited.

The great Lingaraja temple, believed to have been built around 1000 A.D., is a later product of this revivalist movement and has been acclaimed by many as the finest example of a Hindu temple in India. It stands in a cluster of sixty-five smaller shrines in a spacious compound measuring 520 feet by 465 feet and its mighty tower (the vimana, see also: parts of a temple) dominates the landscape for miles around. Constructed without mortar, this tower is 127 feet high and is divided into vertical sections. The angles of the recesses are filled in with miniature vimanas and on the top, are figures representing a lion crushing an elephant. The *vimana* is hollow and consists of several superimposed chambers accessible by a stairway built through the wall, which is seven feet thick.

The temple as originally designed, consisted of the vimana, called Sri Mandir locally, where the image of Tribhubaneswar (the Lord of the three worlds) popularly called Lingaraja is housed, and the jagamohan or the entrance porch to the inner chamber. In the garbha griha (sanctum sanitorium) is enshrined the swayambhu linga, or self-established *Linga*, the symbol of Shiva. The natyamandir or dance hall, and the bhogmandir were probably added a century or so later, although they are in perfect harmony with the architectural scheme as a whole. The interiors of these halls are, generally speaking, devoid of all ornament, but-the outer walls of the building are lavishly carved and embellished with sculptures which are among the best specimens of Orissan decorative art. Although the pilaster decoration presents an effect of exuberance and luxury, particularly in the case of the human figures, there is little of the florid extravagance which characterises some of the southern temples. Among the other notable temples in the neighborhood are those of Bhagavati, Parvati, Ananta, Basudeva, Brahmeshwar, Bhaskareswar, and Kedareswar.

The temple is about a thousand years old and dominates the skyline of Bhubaneshwar from as far as 15 kms. away and exhibits the skill of the Orissan temple architects. This temple is dedicated to Tribhubaneshwar or the Lord of Three Worlds. Interestingly the Lingaraja temple is said to have been built first by the ruler Yayati Kesari in the 7th century who shifted his capital from Jaipur to Bhubaneshwar. Bhubaneshwar remained as the Kesari capital, till Nripati Kesari founded Cuttack in the 10th century. Inscriptions from the period of the Kalinga King Anangabhima III from the 13th century are seen here. Lingaraja temple is an architectural marvel.

The temple is named after the "Linga" or phallic symbol enshrines in it. Built in 617-657 A.D. it soars up to a height of about 54 meters, dominating the skyline for kilometres around. The temple consists of curvilinear walls, a pillared hall, a dancing hall and a hall for serving the offerings. It can be rather called a temple complex as more than a hundred temples of different sizes are situated within its premises. This is one of the famous Shiva Pitha in India. It represents the peak of Kalinga style of architecture spanning over 25 centuries of progressive history.

This temple is one of the best archaeological monuments of the East. This great temple represents the quintessence of the Kalinga type of architecture and the culminating result of the architectural activities at Bhubaneshwar. It sure is a product of the accumulated and crystallised experience of several centuries. In the elegance of its proportions and the richness of its surface-treatment, it is one of the most finished and refined manifestations of the temple-architecture in India. The treatment of its different elements displays the consummate skill of its master-designer; all its constituent parts are effectively integrated into a compact unity of supreme dignity. The crowning achievement of the architect is the design of the graceful contour of its towering 'Gandi'. The Gandi's soaring height and grandeur are almost a marvel. The plastic embellishment of the temple is of equally exquisite workmanship, where all the panoply of Orissan decorative motifs is mustered with a rare aesthetic sense. Every piece of carving serves its appointed role enhancing the majesty of the edifice as a whole. With all the features fully evolved, it is the culmination, in every respect, of the architectural movement at Bhubaneshwar.

The temple is a combination of four structures, all in the same axial alignment-'Deul', 'Gahamohana', 'Nata-Mandira' and 'Bhoga-Mandapa'. The spacious courtyard is full of shrines, big and small, of varying dates, their number exceeding a hundred, of which only a few are of outstanding merit. The complex is enclosed by a massive compound-wall pierced by an imposing portal on the east and two secondary gates on the north and south.

Temple of Parashurameswar: The small temple of Parashurameswar, also at Bhubaneshwar, is believed to be a good specimen of early Orissan architecture of the post-Buddhist period, as is seen from its rudimentary vimana. Although dating as far back as about 750 A.D., it is still in a good state of preservation. It is notable for its intricate stone engraving of the marriage of Shiva and Parvati (Uma) and for the elaborately sculptured medallions on its front facade. The royal lion, Kesari's proud symbol, is conspicuous by its absence. In place of the bold, strapping animals depicted on the walls of other Orissan temples, those at Parashurameswar are almost invariably victims of the huntsman's spear.

The Vaital Deul is another example of the early phase, although it differs fundamentally from the Parashurameswar temple in that it derives from quite another tradition. The tower of its inner sanctuary is reminiscent of the *gopuram* of the Dravidian temples, and many architectural features, such as its elongated vaulted roof in two stories, its ridged finials and its gable-ends, suggest that like those structures, it too developed from the Buddhist chaitya-hall. The Vaital Deul has four replicas of the main shrine in each angle of the jaganmohan, which is also of uncommon design, and is thus representative of a *panchayatana*.

The Raj-Rani Temple: The Raj-Rani temple belongs to a much later period of Orissan architecture (1100-1250 A.D.) and in its pilaster decoration and certain other features, such as the deul suggests a strong kinship with the central Indian type of temple represented at Khajuraho. It is built of a yellowish sandstone, locally called Rajrania, which probably accounts for the somewhat unusual name. The various parts of the temple are not in the same alignment, but follow a diagonal arrangement, which may have been the beginning of the use of the same principle in other regional styles.

Small but elegant, the Mukteshwar temple probably dates back to about 975 A.D. and represents the middle period (approximately 900-1100 A.D.) of the Orissan style in its early prime. It has been called a miniature gem of architecture for its graceful proportions and beautiful finish. The arched gateway or *torana* is the "creation of an artist of superior vision and skill".

The Jagannath Temple: This is a much larger and somewhat later structure than the Lingaraja temple, although both these great structures are built on more or less the same principle. Historical evidence suggests that this temple was originally built as tower of victory by Choda Ganga in 1030 A.D. when he conquered Kalinga, but that it was consecrated many decades later. There are earlier inscriptions which mention Purtishottam Kshetra – of which Puri is an abbreviation. Adi Shankaracharya is believed to have visited this temple in the 9th century.

The temple consists of four edifices in one alignment from east to west, the *bhogmandir*, the *natmandir*, the *jaganmohan* and the *deul* or the inner sanctuary, which is surmounted by a conical tower of immense proportions. The *natmandir*, with its ceiling of iron beams and the *bhogmandir*, however, are believed to have been added in the 14th or 15th century, long after the original structure had been completed. The former, with its 16 pillars, is the only real example of a hypostyle hall in Orissan architecture. A significant feature of the inner enclosure is that, as in the Lingaraja temple, it stands in a large courtyard measuring 440 feet by 350 feet and is surrounded by a high wall.

In the inner sanctuary are the three holy images of Jagannath, his brother Balbhadra, and his sister Subhadra. The entrance to the shrine is decorated with scenes from the life of Krishna, and the gates and walls are heavily ornamented with marble figures of lions and sentries. The profuse decoration on the walls of the nat and bhog-mandirs is, however, stylised and comparatively lifeless. This clearly indicates that when these structures were erected, the Orissan style of architecture had entered a period of decline.

In order to preserve the temple from the corroding effects of the sea breeze, parts of the stone masonry and the elaborate carvings have been covered with thick plaster. Crowned with Vishnu's flag and wheel, the tower, however, retains its commanding appearance in spite of the heavy cement overlay. Distributed around the main building are some thirty to forty shrines of various dimensions and designs, as in the case of the Lingaraja temple, but here these secondary structures are on higher ground, thus adhering closely to the Buddhist *stupa* tradition. The temple of Lord Jagannath ('Lord of the Universe') at Puri is one of the most sacred pilgrimage spots in India, one of the four abodes (dhamas) of the divine that lie on the four directions of the compass. The present temple structure was built in the twelfth century by the Ganga king, Chodagangadeva, replacing an earlier structure which probably dated to the tenth century.

Long before one reaches Puri, the 214 feet (65 meters) spire of the temple can be seen towering over the countryside. This visual dominance is symbolic of the influence which the temple commands over almost every aspect of life in Puri. The huge temple compound, each side of which measures 650 feet (some 200 meters), is surmounted with a 20 foot (6 meters) wall. Within the compound is a city, or, more accurately, a universe unto itself. With 6000 direct temple servitors, a temple kitchen which feeds 10,000 people daily (and some 25,000 on festival days), and a central deity who has become the focus of religious life throughout Orissa, the Jagannath temple is truly an institution unique in the world.

Until recently, almost the entire temple was covered in white plaster, so much so that European sailors in previous centuries used it as a navigation point, referring to it as the 'white pagoda' (in contrast to the 'black pagoda' of Konark, further up the coast). Scholars, however, were long puzzled by the plain facade on this holiest of holy temples, and wondered why it was untouched by Orissa's rich sculptural heritage. The answer was found in 1975, when archaeologists first began removing the plaster, and found that the sculpture underneath indeed rivals that of the other masterpieces of Orissan temple art.

Given the religious importance and hallowed traditions, entrance is forbidden to non-Hindus. To have a good view of the temple and its compound, visitors are welcome to ascend to the roof of the Raghunandan Library which is across the street. In the bazaar area surrounding the temple, dozens of shops display and sell images of the central temple deity, Lord Jagannath, presented in a trinity with his 'brother' Balbhadra and his 'sister' Subhadra. The pervasive quality of the Jagannath cult will be seen when travelling in other parts of Orissa, where the distinctive image of Jagannath appears with great frequency. Even to the non-religious eye, the image is fascinating, perhaps because of the unlikely combination of the endearing, charming form with an undeniable sense of power. Even the non-Hindu visitor to Puri will feel some of the power of this throbbing pilgrimage centre.

The bazaar streets immediately surrounding the temple are filled with activity and bustle, but it is all infused with a palpable sense of gentleness and good spirit. Walk around the bazaar in the early evenings just as the lights are coming on. (Don't worry, your taxi or rickshaw driver will keep an eye on you, and appear like magic when you are ready to leave). Look up to the magnificent tower of Jagannath towering over everything, surmounted by the flag of Vishnu flying in the breeze. Gaze at the faces of the pilgrims entering or leaving the temple, inhale the scents of incense mixed with the tantalising sizzles of frying sweets and snacks, and just let your feet take you where they may. Even the most secular-minded of visitors are bound to feel that they, too, have embarked on a kind of pilgrimage to a uniquely special place.

Yogini Shrines: On the outskirts of Bhubaneshwar, 15 km south-east of the city, is a small, circular temple, the Yogini Temple, dating to the early ninth century. It is hypaethral (open to the sky), and belongs to a genre of architecture completely apart from the major Orissan school. Although it seems that temples of this type existed throughout India at one time, today only four remain. Two of them are in Orissa; the shrine at Hirapur, and one at Ranipur-Jharial, located 104 km from Bolangir.

Growth of Architecture in Orissa

Bhubaneshwar: Popularly called, city of Temples, it is situated on the main railway line that connects Howrah in the north with Chennai in the south. Geographically it is placed at 20 The city is well connected by air as well as land routes with other parts of the country. This place is a bit hot in summer with the mercury occasionally rising to 42 Celsius, sweltering and humid during the monsoon as the onrush of the south-east monsoon wind brings down the gushing rains and is relatively dry in winter, rarely the mercury plunging below 11 Celsius. The Bay of Bengal, barely 100 kms away as the crow flies, exercises a moderating influence over the climate and keeps it temperate. Of course, the seasons have their own charm and the distinctive appeal and Bhubaneshwar can be visited at anytime of the year. The period between mid-September and mid-March is considered as the tourist season when the sun is bright and warm, the sky is blue, the air is cool and the weather is generally pleasant. To the visitor, Bhubaneshwar is a city of contrasts, coexistence and continuity. There is a happy encounter of past and present in this temple town which has a history of about 2500 years. All religions and sects flourished here.

The famous Lingaraj Temple which has been a centre of Shiva-worship is also there is Orissa. Buddhism and Jainism also received royal patronage and general acceptance. Emperor Ashoka won a bloody war in 261 BC but lost his style victory in remorse and repentance and thus he embraced Buddhism. This is also the land of the great Orissan emperor Kharavela whose exploits and achievements have been recorded in the rock-cut inscriptions in the caves of Udayagiri and Khandagiri. The grace and majesty of Orissan art can be seen in the great temples of Lingaraj, Rajarani and Mukteswar.

In the modern part of the city which is only about forty years old, one finds the temples of our time, the major academic and research establishments such as Utkal University, the Orissa University of Agriculture and Technology, the Utkal University of Culture, Regional Research Laboratory, the Institute of Physics, the Indian Council of Medical Research, and so on. Life is quicker here compared to what it is in the ancient section. The city traffic cannot be called heavy even during the peak hours and parts of the city wear a deserted look for the better part of the day. The city is generally safe for travel at all hours. But as a precaution one need not venture out at odd hours at night. One invariably returns from Bhubaneshwar with pleasant memories and a rich haul of memorabilia consisting of exquisite artifacts or beautifully designed hand-woven silk or cotton material or plenty of photographs of temples, caves, landscape and so on, and above all, with a fond desire to come back someday to the land of history and culture, into the folds of affection of the place and the people.

Important places of interest are listed in alphabetical order. Bhubaneshwar has two distinct zones: one belonging to the glorious past that includes the majestic temples, the ruins of ancient shrines and cities, the caves and the historically significant rock-cut inscriptions and royal edicts, and the other belonging to our times with all the signs and symptoms of a modern city, such as the massive complex of the Orissa Secretariat, the nerve centre of state administration, tall buildings that are the veritable beehives of commercial activities, beautiful shopping areas, lovely parks and posh housing localities, the Universities and many other institutions of learning and research, luxurious hotels and restaurants offering comfort and food that would compare favourably with the best anywhere, and so on. This modern city is also the capital of the State.

There is a sense of continuity as one finds the spire of the Lingaraj temple looking over the modern high-rise steel and concrete structures, office complexes and hotels. The city is a living phenomenon expanding and growing with the passing of every day. The visitor to this temple town can reach Bhubaneshwar by air or bus or train. Once in the town he may choose his own mode of travel either by city buses or hired cars and autorickshaws. But to absorb the ambience of the place and have a leisurely pace to his visits, he may prefer the cycle-rickshaw to other modes of fast transport. Figures against each entry indicate the approximate distance between the proposed place of visit and the railway station that is at the centre of the city and the gateway of entry to the majority of visitors to Bhubaneshwar Ananta-Vasudeva Temple 1278 A.D. (4 km) Often considered to be a watered down version of the magnificent Lingaraj temple as far as the architecture is concerned, this 18.29 metre high lone Vaishnav shrine is the most finished temple situated on the east bank of the Bindu Sarovara. It was erected by Chandradevi, the daughter of Anangabhima III during the rule of Bhanudeva in 1278 AD. In support of this date eminent historians offer a fresh reading and interpretation of the text found on the commemorative inscription of the temple. This piece of evidence now is under the custody of the Royal Asiatic Society of Great Britain and Ireland. Other scholars think 1200 AD as a probable date of its construction.

The temple has four component parts; their roofs ascending upward, culminating in the mastaka of the deul. The shrine has a profusely carved exterior and an ornamental platform within the complex. Ananta-Vasudeva temple is an important Vaishnavite place of worship with the images of the Holy Trinity, Krishna, Balarama and Subhadra in the sanctum. The parsva-devatas include at least three incarnations of Vishnu, the Preserver. It is customary for the devout to visit the temple after taking a holy dip in the Bindu-Sarovara, prior to the darshan of Lord Lingaraj. Scores of pilgrims from different parts of the country entering the temple with fresh flowers, sweets, coconuts and bananas as offerings to the deities is a colourful sight. They eagerly await their turn in the rush to partake of mahaprasad or holy food.

Bhaskareshwar Temple: This small temple is remarkable for its 'stepped' design and the unusually high linga in its sanctum. The peculiarity of the temple structure seems to have been dictated by the practical necessity of performing rituals like bathing or garlanding or putting pastes of sandalwood and other perfumery on the tall linga which rises to a height of nearly three metres from the floor level. Some scholars believe that the linga was originally a free standing pillar. Bindu Sarovara (4km) Situated to the north of the Lingaraj temple this large pool. The devotees believe this Sarovara to contain water from every holy stream, pool and river of India and can purify them of all sins.

Hence on its banks, they perform many rituals, or tonsure their heads and take a dip in its water. Once upon a time the tank had all its sides covered with stone. Today only the southern side and parts of the eastern side have the original linings made of blocks of laterite stone. At the centre of the tank there is an island temple to which the icon of Vishnu is customarily taken during the Snana Yatra. The embankment on all sides is dotted with innumerable shrines and temples, some of which are still under active worship. Brahmeshwar Temple 1061 AD. This temple was built by Kolavati, the mother of the Somavansi king Udyotakesari, in the eighteenth regnal year of his reign, in the Siddhatirtha locality at Ekamra. One of the inscriptions, now believed lost, stated that Kolavati presented many beautiful women to the temple. This presentation is interpreted as an early evidence of the devadasi (God's Maids) tradition. This tradition influenced the socio-economic as well as the cultural life of the Odissan people at a later date and formed a dominant and recurrent motif in Orissi music and dance.

The importance of this system can be realised from the fact that this motif had come to be part of the art idiom too. The temple is a fine specimen of innovative and mature Orissan style of temple building. For the first time iron beams have been used to build up the structure. This is the second temple, after the Mukteshwar, to boast of a Jagamohana that has a finely carved interior. The sculptural details and the immaculate iconography show expert workmanship of the Orissan artists of the era. The figures of the musicians and dancers, the lion-head motif, the amusing and erotic figures and others exude a special charm.

One must notice the beautiful figure of a young woman appearing a little bewildered and perhaps a little surprised at her lover's unexpected naughty probe into her body. The floral motifs, the intricately designed creepers, the flying figures, the images of the eight directional guardian deities and so on, are all meticulously executed and the chiselling shows an excellent sense of proportion, harmony and an eye for aesthetic embellishment on the part of the artists. The usual Shaivite door keepers stand above the double vidalas at the bottom of the jambs; the figure of the Gajalakshmi adorns the mid section of the lintel and those of the navagrahas are there on the architrave. This shrine, though dedicated to Lord Shiva, shows a number of images which might have been inspired by the Tantric cult of the time. On the western facade the figure of Chamunda stands on a corpse with a trident and a human head. Elsewhere many other deities, including Shiva, are depicted in their horrific aspects.

B. K. College of Art and Crafts: The college offers higher studies in certain modes of art and craft including wood carving, palm leaf etching, stone sculpture, clay modelling, commercial art, graphic art, line drawing and painting. The college is located in Khandagiri area. It is affiliated to the Utkal University of Culture. Dhauli is a small hillock rising conspicuously on the southern bank of the river Daya, in the midst of green fields that seem to reach out to the horizon.

This is the site where Ashoka waged the final battle against Kalinga in 261 BC. The victory came to him riding over a million corpses bringing him a macabre confirmation of his military prowess that had already earned him the sobriquet, Ashoka the Slayer (Chandasoka). Legend has it that the gory sight of the battle with dead men chocking the flow of the Daya river (literally, the river of compassion) that had turned to be a river of blood, filled the heart of the conqueror with an hitherto unknown feeling of compassion and bouts of remorse. He realised the futility of digvijaya (military conquest) and the nobility of dharmavijaya (spiritual conquest). Thus Ashoka the Slayer changed into Ashoka the compassionate (Dharmasoka). He embraced Buddhism, it is believed, here, at the Dhauli foothill. This is the place where gory deeds were amended by hoary corrections.

At the base of Dhauli, where the approach road to the top begins its incline, one can see on the left the Ashokan rock-edicts, well preserved under a large rock outcropping with a rock-cut elephant head. The edicts are public injunctions, instructions from the emperor to the local administrators to imbibe and adopt the spirit of justice and compassion towards the people in all matters pertaining to the civil administration. Two new edicts, pacifistic in nature, have been added and the 13th edict, that glorified Ashoka's conquest of Kalinga, is conspicuous by its absence. The elephant head over the edicts is a sacred Buddhist motif testifying to the emperor's change of heart. To commemorate the historic events of the past, the Japanese Buddhists have lavishly contributed to erect a peace pagoda on the hilltop.

On a clear day, standing on the steps of the pagoda, the visitor can have a magnificent view of the temple town with the majestic Lingaraj temple rising to the sky or watch at the foothill the silver strip of the river Daya meanderinglazily past its serpentine bends, touching softly the embankments where the glorious past of Orissa has remained hidden. It is a wonderful experience watching the glorious sunset beyond the unending

Ekamrakanan. Spread over a large area, Ekamrakanan is a modern nursery-cum-flower garden. It is a favourite haunt of the plant lovers as well as casual visitors as round the year the well-preserved beds of flowers offer a feast for the eye. The rose-beds present a riot of colours and the air is often thick with sweet smell. Many varieties of cacti can also be seen us.

Harekrishna Mahtab State Library: The building quite close to Rabindra Mandap on Jawaharlal Marg houses the State Library. It is named after late Harekrushna Mahtab, one of the former Chief Ministers of Orissa. There are a large number of books including some old and priceless volumes. It caters to the need of the reading public of the city. It remains open from 8.00 A.M. to 8.00 P.M. on all working days.

Institute of Physics: This is a premier institute of study and research in Physics where scholars from different arts of the country and abroad conduct full time research in different branches of Physics. It has a beautiful campus with hostels for scholars, faculty building and residential quarters for the staff.

Jayadev Orissa State Museum: This is rather a small museum with limited sections of exhibits. But the archaeological wing boasts of some of the rare findings of historical as well as sociological importance. Some of the collections are exquisite specimens of Orissan sculpture. The manuscript section of the museum has a large collection of palm leaf writing locally known as pothi Scholars are engaged in research in this section. The section devoted to the history and culture of Orissa provides a glimpse of the composite character of Orissan culture through carefully arranged exhibits and show windows.

Puri-City of the Lord: A heaven on earth is the common description of Puri. Both the devout and the pleasure-seeker bestow such praise on the place. The world's biggest Vishnu temple dividing the skyline through a host of smaller temples overlooking Puri's wide, sprawling, clean, sunny, buoyant, and vibrant beach, which too is one of world's finest of its kind are its chief attractions. Puri is also famous for the greatest of the temple festivals, the Rath Yatra or the Car Festival which falls in June/July. According to tradition, Puri was originally a densely wooded hill inhabited by Sabaras, a pre-Aryan and pre-Dravidian tribe. Chodaganga Dev, the illustrious ruler of the Ganga dynasty, built the present Jagannath Temple in the twelfth century A.D. Kapilendra Dev, Purusottam Dev and Prataprudra Dev, all rulers of the Surya dynasty, left their distinctive marks on the history, art and culture of Puri.

Jagannath worship flourished even during the Mughal and Maratha periods. The British occupied Puri in 1803 and soon took over the administration of the temple. Modern Puri—its hospitals, its government buildings, its light house, its schools and colleges, its beautiful villas and hotels along the sea front was built during the British rule.

Ai Tota: Ai Tota is the place towards the left side of the Gundicha Temple where Chaitanya used to stay during Car Festivals.

Angira Bata: On the east of the temple of Lord Jagannath can be seen a shady banyan tree known as Angira Bata surrounded by an old boundary wall. The place is associated with the legendary sages Angira.

Annapurna Theatre: Murari Mishra records the first staging of his play at Puri sometime in the 9th century AD. Though the ancient stage is no longer existent, this seventy year old theatre house can still be seen at Puri.

Ardhasani: About 3 km from the Jagannath temple, on the Grand Road, is a small white-washed temple for goddess Ardhasani or Mausi Ma. A Subhadra image is worshipped here. The Puranas describe how the goddess used to drink half of the flood water at the time of deluge, thus saving the creation. On his way back from the Gundicha Temple during the Car Festival, Jagannath is offered here a delicacy known as *podapitha* (fire-baked cake).

Asta Shambhu: A small temple in Tiadi Sahi houses a cluster of eight Shiva *lingas* made of semi-precious stones which appear different in colour when looked at from different directions.

Atharanala: A marvel of medieval Orissan architecture the Atharnala or the bridge with eighteen arches was built by

Bhanu Deba of the Ganga dynasty in the thirteenth century. It is a ferruginous stone structure and is still used as the gateway to the holy city Puri. During the nineteenth century the British Government collected pilgrim taxes here detaining millions of eager devotees enroute for days together.

Aurobindo Dham: This is a newly established institution which popularises the teachings of Sri Aurobindo, a twentieth century philosopher of India. It has a small library. Its impressive complex of buildings can be reached by going to the west from Swargadwar.

Bata Lokanath: The impressive temple on the Swarga Dwar Road is dedicated to Lord Shiva. A beautiful Kali image is also worshipped in the near by place.

Batamangala: At a distance of about three kilometre from Atharnala on the Puri-Bhubaneshwar road is a small temple dedicated to goddess Batamangala. Pilgrims usually pray this goddess for safe journey to Puri.

Bauli Math: The well dug by Guru Nanak popularly known as Dedhasur Bhai Bohu Kua is still to be seen here and this place, the Bauli Math is visited by the devotee round the year.

Bedi Mahavira: A small sea-side temple containing the image of the monkey-god Hanuman, a devotee of Rama. The legend goes that once Hanuman went on a short visit to Ayodhya. In the meantime seawater entered the city, causing considerable damage. The devotees prayed to Jagannath who asked Hanuman to explain his absence. On hearing about Hanuman's unscheduled visit to Ayodhya, Jagannath got his hands and feet tied with rope (bedi) and asked him to be vigilant on the seashore day and night. There is a popular belief that since then, the sea has not ventured into the city.

Bharat Seva Ash Rama: This institution is situated near Swarga Dwar. It is a philanthropic organisation which does commendable work during the Car Festivals.

Bhrugu Ashramaa: Bhrugu Ashramaa or Bhrugu's hermitage is near Atharanala. It is associated with the sage Bhrugu.

Chakhi Khuntia's House : Chakhi Khuntia, a priest of Jagannath, fought the British during India's First War of Independence in 1857. Khuntia was the family priest of Queen Laxmi Bai of Jhansi who led the heroic revolt against the British. His house is situated in Harachandi Sahi. His descendants still live here and a visit to the house can, however, be arranged through the people living there.

Chakra Tirtha: This place on the seashore is believed to be the house of the father of Laxmi, the consort of Jagannath. A small but beautiful temple houses the images of Laxmi and Narsimha. The belief goes that in ancient times a sacred log of wood came floating in the sea out of which the Jagannath triad were carved. To many, this is also the very spot where vishnu saved the elephant from the clutches of a cruel crocodile.

Chaturdham Veda Bhawan: This is a school teaching the Vedas to the young. The students of this school recite the Vedas to the measured movement of hands, fingers and palms. The *Yajna Vedi* or the traditional vedic altar for burning sacrificial fire may also be seen by a visitor here.

Chudanga Sahi: Though the *sanctum sanctorum* of the Jagannath temple was the cradle of Odissi dance and music, the singers, dancers (Maharis) and musicians used to reside in Chudanga Sahi, said to have seen established by Chodaganga Dev in the twelfth century AD.

Dasavatara Math: Dasavatara means the ten incarnations of Vishnu, the significance of which is emphasised in the monastery. The place is dedicated to the memory of Jayadeva (twelfth century A.D.), the famous author of *Gitagovindam*. A quiet place in front of the Gundicha temple, it reverberates with activities during the Rath Yatra.

Dolavedi : An open air museum Dola Vedi is at the northern end of Laxmi Bazar. An exquisitely carved black stone arch atop an equally beautiful altar is the main attraction of Dola Vedi. The miniature images of Jagannath are taken to this place on the fullmoon day of Falguna (March) and are placed in a swing to commemorate Krishna's sports with Radha at Brindaban.

Emar Math : A prosperous monastery near the Lions' Gate dedicated to the sacred memory of the saint-philosopher Ramanuja, an exponent of Vishishtadwaita Vedanta or qualified monism. The monastery has its famous Raghunandan Library containing many palmleaf manuscripts. A non-Hindu visitor can have a clear sight of the Jagannath temple complex by climbing a flight of steps and reaching the third floor. Permission for doing so, is, however, to be obtained from the library on any day of the week except on Sundays and other public holidays.

Gandhi Ghat: A statue of Mahatma Gandhi installed near the Light House at the sea shore commemorates his associations with Puri. Gandhiji's ashes as well as that of Nehru, Indira Gandhi and Rajiv Gandhi were immersed in the sea here. On his visit to Puri in the first half of the century the Mahatma wanted to take a band of his harijan followers to the Jagannath temple. But the orthodox priests objected to such entry. So Gandhi left Puri without entering the temple. His wife Kasturba and his Secretary Madev Desai went inside but had to face Gandhi's displeasure immediately after.

Gangamata Math: Situated on the bank of Sweta Ganga, this monastery is the place of Basudeva Sarvabhouma a famous philosopher who was an associate of Chaitanya.

Ghumusar Math: Situated on the Marichikote Lane, this monastery is the place of Upendra Bhanja, the greatest medieval Oriya poet.

Girnarbant: It is a beautiful place where lived a sadhu named Totapuri. This sadhu is believed to be the guru of Sri Ramakrishna, the great nationalist saint of Bengal who in his turn was also the teacher of Swami Vivekananda.

Gundicha Temple: Gundicha Temple or the garden house of Jagannath is towards northeast direction of the Jagannath Temple. A major part of the present precinct was built during the sixteenth and seventeenth centuries. The compound has two walls, one outer and another inner in the middle of which stands the main shrine. Unlike any other Orissan temple design it is almost a dome with Vishnu's wheel on the top. The inner and parts of the outer walls are full of murals and paintings belonging to the sixteenth century.

A beautiful Garuda idol adorns the eastern most corner of the temple. The images of Jagannath, Balabhadra and Subhadra are annually taken in a chariot procession to the place. The Jagannath triad stay here for seven days. The pious believe that a sight of the Lord here is equal to thousand visits to the main Jagannath temple. Many devotees from North India consider this spot as the birth place of Sita, the consort of Rama. Gundicha temple has two gateway temples-one for Jagannath's entry and the other for his exist. In front of the latter one sees a stretch of land known as Saradhabali or the sand of divine love. It is so named because the devotees flock around Jagannath and his car here out of sheer love and devotion.

Guru Nanak's Places: It is very near the sea on the way to Swargadwar from the Temple. It is believed that when Guru Nanak, the founder of Sikhism, came to Puri he soon sat on the spot and was lost in meditation in which state he remained for days together. The two disciples who accompanied him were starving. When the Guru's mediation came to an end, the disciples were extremely thirsty. But how to get fresh water on the sea shore ? The Guru dug the sand and fresh water gushed out immediately. The well dug by Guru Nanak, popularly known as Dedhasura Bhaibohu Kua, is still to be seen here and this place, the Bauli Math is visited by the devout round the year.

Governor's House: One of the most beautiful specimens of late nineteenth century British architecture, the Governor's House on the seashore is an official bungalow. The President and Prime Minister of the country and other dignitaries normally stay in the building during their visits to Puri.

Holy Lakes: The city of Puri is famous for five holy lakes-Markanda, Shweta Ganga, Narendra, Indradyumna and parvati Sagar. The first one is located in the north. The ancient Markandeshwar Shiva Temple situated on the bank of the lake makes Puri one of the fifty-two sacred Shiva places of the country. A few inscriptions found on the steps to the lake and the Markandeshwar Temple, are of great interest to historians. The second lake Shweta Ganga is towards the south of the Jagannath temple. Shweta Ganga means the White Ganga. It is believed that once in a year the blue water of the lake turns white when Ganga manifests hereself in the lake.

The third lake Narendra is known to North Indians as the Chandan Talab. Here the Chandan Festival of Jagannath is held. Chaitanya, the great exponent of the cult of devotion, used to take his bath thinking the lake to be Krishna's Yamuna. The fourth lake Indradyumna is near Gundicha Temple. Numerous turtles living in the lake entertain the pilgrims. They are believed to be the very people who carried stones on their back for the construction of the Jagannath temple. The fifth lake Parvati Sagar is near the Lokanath Temple. Pilgrims enter the Shiva temple here after sprinkling water on their heads.

Jagannath Ballav Math: Opposite the Municipal Market is situated Jagannath Ballav Math, a monastery which perpetuates the memory of Ray Ramaaananda, the administrator-turned saint of Orissa who lived during the sixteenth century. The garden behind the monastery building has a beautiful temple in the middle dedicated to Hanuman, the monkey-god who is believed to be protector of the trees and plants grown here.

Jagannath Temple Complex: The Jagannath Temple Complex which spreads over an area of about 4,20,000 sq.ft. has four distinct sections-the outer section, the outer compound, the inner compound and the main temple. The outer section has four gateways and each such gateway has four temples. The eastern gate, known as the Lions' Gate, has a black stone pillar in its front having the idol of Arun (Sun) on the top. This tall pillar which is about 12 metres in height is made out of a single block of stone.

On entering the temple through the eastern gate or Lions' Gate the visitor comes across the mural of Patitapabana, literally "Saviour of the Fallen". It is a representation of the Jagannath image.

Baisi Pahacha: On entry the visitor ascends the twenty two steps which have Jain significance. On its left side is situated Jagannath's kitchen which has provision for cooking food for about two lakh people at a time. On its right is the Ananda Bazaar or the Market of Joy where Mahaprasad of various kinds are sold : rice, dal, curry, cakes, sweets, etc.

Cuttak: City of the Fort situated at the apex of a delta formed by the river Mahanadi on the north and its distributary, the Kathajodi on the south, and located at 14.62 metres above sea-level, the city of Cuttack has a history of more than one thousand years. Geographically, it is between 20-55' E longitude. Hot in summer, humid during the monsoon and dry in winter, this densely populated city is spread over an area of 59.57 square kilometres.

Cuttack (or Kataka) was founded by King Nrupa Keshari in 989 A.D. King Marakata Keshari built the stone revetment on the left bank of the Kathajodi in 1006 A.D. to protect the city from the ravages of floods. Due to its strategic location, King Anangabhima Dev III shifted his capital from 'Choudwar Kataka' to the present Cuttack, then known as 'Abhinaba Varanasi Kataka' and built the fort of Barabati in 1229 A.D. Cuttack has witnessed the rule of several dynasties : the Kesharis, the Gangas, the Gajapatis and the Bhois. The Chalukya King, Mukundadev Harichandan, built a nine-storey building in the precincts of Barabati Fort in 1560 A.D.

This last independent Hindu king of Orissa died fighting the Sultan of Bengal, Sulaeman Karni in 1568 A.D. In the fifteenth and sixteenth centuries, Barabati Fort was defended by two rings of forts on either side of the Mahanadi and the Kathajodi. In 1568 A.D., the city passed to the hands of Afghan rulers of Bengal, then to the Moghuls in 1592 and the Marathas in 1751. Cuttack, with the rest of Orissa, came under the British rule in 1803. The Bengal-Nagpur Railways connected Cuttack with Madras (Chennai) and Calcutta (Kolkata) in 1919. It became the capital of the newly formed State of Orissa in 1936 and continued to be so till 1948 when the capital was shifted to Bhubaneshwar. The city completed one thousand years of its existence in 1989. The major places of interest are listed in alphabetical order and distance from the railway station is indicated in respect of each entry. Although town buses ply to certain areas, it is not always possible to reach most places by them because of narrow lanes and by lanes and traffic congestion. A cycle-rickshaw is a better way of getting around. The ruins of the old Barabati Fort lie on the right bank of the Mahanadi, in the western part of the city.

All that remains of the Fort is an arched gateway and the earthen mound of the nine-storeyed palace. Archaeological surveys reveal that the Fort was roughly rectangular in structure having an area of over 102 acres, and it was surrounded on all sides by a wall of laterite and sandstones. To the west of the mound there is a tank. In the north-eastern corner of the mound are remains of what once was a temple. The temple was made of whitish sandstone over foundations of laterite blocks. About four hundred fragments of mouldings and some mutilated pieces of sculptures have been recovered so far. This temple of the Ganga period containing a stone idol of Lord Jagannath was razed to the ground by Feroz Shah Tughlaq in 1361 A.D. The idol of Gadachandi is enshrined in a newly built temple.

It has a seating capacity of nearly thirtyfive thousand. The structure of the Stadium closely resembles that of the Brabourne Stadium of Bombay. Towards the southern part of the Fort area stands the modern Jawaharlal Nehru Air-conditioned Indoor Stadium with a seating capacity for six thousand spectators.

Central Rice Research Institute: The Institute was established in 1946. Its basic aim is to conduct research on crap development in order to increase overall productivity of rice. It has so far produced 42 high-yielding varieties. Chandi Temple the temple of Goddess Chandi, the presiding deity of the city, to the south of the Barabati area is visited by hundreds of devotees everyday. The image of the deity is older than the temple.

Church, Baptist : The present Baptist Church or Jubilee Church at Mission Road was constructed in 1872 to commemorate the golden jubilee of the work of the Baptist Missionary Society at Cuttack. Established in 1822, the Mission conducted church services first in a bungalow before shifting its activities to a Church at Tinkonia Bagicha which was washed away by a flood. A new church was built in its place in 1828.

Church of England: Church of England, later known as the Anglican Church, is presumed to have been established during the days of the East India Company. The Church conducted services in a bungalow at Cantonment Road. The present church building was, however, constructed later.

Church of God : The building of the present Church of God at Cantonment Road was constructed in 1928. But the congregation started its services at Cuttack in 1905 with the visit of John A.D. Khan, the President of the Church of God Association of India. Sunday services were held in the verandah of the Mount House till the construction of the new building.

Church, Roman Catholic : Situated at Cuttack Chandi, to the north of the Mount House, the Catholic Church is one of the oldest in Orissa. It is believed that the first Catholic Church at Cuttack was built on the rank of the Kathajodi by the Portuguese merchants, but there is no trace of it now.

Gadagadeswar Temple: The temple of Lord Shiva on the banks of the Mahanadi towards the northern part of the Barabati area is not very old. The modern temple probably stands in the place of a certain Visvesvara temple of the fifteenth century mentioned in the Oriya by Sarala Das.

Gurudwara Guru Nanak Datan Sahib: Situated on the bank of the Mahanadi to the west of the NH-5, Gurudwara Guru Nanak Datan Sahib is one of the oldest gurudwaras of Orissa. It was built in 1935 in memory of Guru Nanak Dev who visited Orissa in 1506 A.D.

Hanuman Temple: Situated on the bank of the river, Kathajodi, the temple of Panchamukhi Mahavira, a form of Hanuman is visited by the devout. A small temple established in 1914 has been renovated and modernised, There are the shrines of Rama, Sita, Lakshman and Lord Shiva in the temple premises.

Jami Masjid: Built by Nawab Ik Rama Khan in 1689 A.D. on the orders of Aurangzeb Alamgir, the Jami Masjid at Balu Bazar is an Islamic prayer hall. The mosque stretches from east to west to enable the devotees to turn towards Mecca while praying. The present access to it is through the southern gate built much later. There is a 'hauz' (distrain) in the courtyard and a pulpit in the main hall. There are two tall and elegant towers on both sides of the mosque. One can get a view of the city from the top of the towers.

Municipal Office : Cuttack Municipality was constituted in 1876 before which the affairs of the town were looked after by the Town Committee consisting of both native. European members. The area of the Municipality gradually went on increasing to bring the adjoining places under its control. The present office building is, however, a structure raised at a later date.

Orissa High Court : This majestic red-brick structure, with slim decorative columns on the top was constructed in 1948.

Oriya Bazar : The house at Oriya Bazar where Subhas Chandra, the ninth child of Prabhabati and Janaki Nath Bose was born, is visited by many people particularly on 23 January, the birthday of Netaji.

Publishing Houses : Almost all the major Oriya publishing houses are located at Balu Bazar-Binod Behari-Banka Bazar area. Cuttack Students, Stores, Friends Publishers, Grantha Mandir, Vidyapuri are some of the leading publishing houses. Although the first Oriya printing was made in the early nineteenth century in Calcutta soon after a press was set up at Cuttack for missionary purposes. The number of presses have increased manifold since then. The first Oriya newspaper, Utkal Dipika was brought out in Cuttack in 1868.

The Samaja (Buxi Bazar) and The Prajatantra (Chandinichowk), the oldest of the existing Oriya dailies also come out from the city.

Qadam-i-Rasool : Located almost at the centre of the city, Qadam-i-Rasool is enclosed on all sides by high stone walls.

Covering an area of 57 acres and having a tower at each of the four corners, it has three mosques with beautiful domes and a Nawabat Khana (music gallery) inside. The central building with a magnificent dome shelters the footprints of Prophet Mohammed engraved on a circular stone. The main burial ground of Muslims in Cuttack, Qadam-i-Rasool has the graves of some of the nazims who were in charge of the administration of Orissa in the early eighteenth century. It is a good example of Indo-Islamic architecture and a shrine dear to both Hindus and Muslims.

Raghunath Jee Temple : A monument of Maratha period, the temple of Sri Raghunath Jee, also known as 'Sita Rama Thakurbari' is situated at Telenga Bazar in the southern part of the city.

The images of Sri Rama, Sita, Lakshman, Bharata and Shatrughna are enshrined in the temple. In another temple within the precincts and images of Sri Jagannath, Balabhadra, Subhadra and Sudarshan are worshipped. The images of Lord Shiva and other deities are also there in separate temples. Sri Rama in this temple is like Narayan and he holds sankha, chakra, gada and padma in four hands.

Ravenshaw College: The premier educational institution of the State, Ravenshaw College had its origin in a school established by the British Government in January 1841. Intermediate classes started in 1868 and the college was affiliated to Calcutta University. In 1875, largely through the efforts of Mr. T.E. Ravenshaw, the then Commissioner of Orissa, it became a full-fledged first-grade college. At the instance of the Maharaja of Mayurbhanj the college was named after the Commissioner to commemorate his services to the cause of education in Orissa.

The affiliation of the college was transferred to Patna University in 1917 and Utkal University in 1943. It has been upgraded to the status of an autonomous college. The college was shifted to its present location with a large campus spread over 87 acres of land in 1921. The magnificent red building looks very British in its architecture and general layout. The college hall was the venue of Assembly sessions of the newly carved State of Orissa. The Centenary Library, the new open-air pandal and the gymnasium are some of the newly added structures of the college.

Sati Chaura: The historic graveyard on the banks of the Kathajodi can be approached by the ring road. The tombs of poets, writers and greatest social workers remind the visitor of their services and sacrifices.

S.C.B. Medical College : The small dispensary during the days of the Maratha rule in late eighteenth century, set up primarily to attend the sick pilgrims to Puri, was converted to small hospital by the British during the Great famine of 1865-66. In 1875 Dr. Stewart, the then Civil Surgeon of Cuttack, mooted the idea of starting a medical school there. In 1916-17 the Orissa Medical School was affiliated to the Bihar and Orissa Medical Examination Board. Orissa Medical College was established in 1944 and was affiliated to the Utkal University. It was renamed Sri Rama Chandra Bhanj Medical College in 1951 in appreciation of the generous contribution of the Maharaja of Mayurbhanj to the cause of medical education and health care in the State.

Shailabala Women's College : The oldest Women's College in Bihar and Orissa, presently known as Shailabala Women's College, started in Ravenshaw Girl's School in 1913. The institution, then known as Government Women's College was separated from the School in 1946 and was shifted in 1952 to its present Premises which was the residence of late Madhusudan Das, the architect of modern Orissa. The College was named after late Shailabala Das, the daughter of Madhusudan Das.

Sri Rama Chandra Bhavan : Sri Rama Chandra Bhavan near the Municipality Town Hall was built in 1928 with the contributions of the princely states, particularly the state of Mayurbhanj. It has been the centre of social and literary activities of Orissa over the years.

Stewart College: Established in 1944, as a concern of the Baptist Missionary Society, London, the College has developed to a leading institution for higher education in the city. The management of the College has been transferred to the Church of North India.

Stone Revetment: The southern part of the city was protected from the fury off loods of the Kathajodi by a stone revetment, a great engineering feat of the early eleventh century. It is said that Maharaja Marakata Keshari ordered the construction when Baimundi, a commoner from the Bidanasi region made a personal prayer to the King.

Utkal Sahitya Samaj : The oldest among the existing literary associations of the city, Utkal Sahitya Samaj, is located at Sri Rama Chandra Bhavan. The informal meetings convened by the veteran Oriya poet, Madhusudan Rao in 1890s later took the shape of the Samaj and become the forum of many literary meets.

Arun Kumar Mohanty has translated Gopinath Mohanty's novel, Dadi Budha The Ancestor Sahitya Akademi, New Delhi, 1997) and co-translated Manoranjan Das's play August. The Ninth of August Sahitya Akademi, New Delhi, 1998) into English. Martyrs' Memorial at Bhubaneswara decision has been taken to build a Martyrs' Memorial at Bhubaneshwar at a high-level meeting held under the chairmanship of the Hon'ble Chief Minister,

Shri Naveen Patnaik on August 23, 2000. Doordarshan Studio Inaugurated a Doordarshan Studio was inaugurated at Bhawanipatna on September 3, 2000 by the Hon'ble Union Minister of State for Agriculture, Dr. Debendra Pradhan. The meeting arranged on the occasion was presided over by the Honble Member of the Parliament, Shri Bik Rama Keshari Deo. The officials of the Doordarshan and several dignitaries were present.

8

Architectures of Regional Kingdoms

Gujarat: Significance

The Muslim rulers of Gujarat produced architecture on as grand a scale as their Hindu and Jain predecessors. As in Delhi, the first building material for the earliest mosques and tombs came from the demolition of temples in the area. It was with the reign of Ahmed Shah (1411-42), that the city of Ahmedabad was founded. Some of the most spectacular architectural remains at Ahmedabad are the stepped wells or wavs. More than simply a means of bathing, these wavs were associated with stylistic ritual which spanned back to the time of the Rajputs.

Imposing steps lead down to the water table and the vertical exposed walls were treated with rich carving. The mosques at Ahmedabad show a development from the relatively primitive, with an open facade, to the arcaded screen type prevalent in Delhi, with carved pillars visibly produced by Hindu craftsmen discernible through the arcade.

Of the second, arcaded type of mosque, the two most impressive examples are the mosque of Ahmed Shah and the Jami-Masjid. Ahmed Shah's mosque has original Hindu pillars behind a simple arcaded facade, the central arch of which is flanked by two rather bloated minarets rising from the ground, almost like pilasters. The form of the minarets, indeed, brings to mind the battlements of Rajput fort rather than the graceful tapering classical Islamic minaret. In the Jama Masjid, the minarets do not become any more graceful, but their power depends mainly on their massive proportions and the riot of carving on their faces. The base of the minarets is covered by what seems to be almost temple shikharas rising one upon the other, vocabulary extensively used in a classical temple.

Mandu and Pleasure Palaces

In modern Madhya Pradesh, the province of Malwa had as its capital the ancient Hindu city of Dhar, about 24 miles north of Mandu, till it was conquered by the Delhi Sultanate-by Ala-ud-din Khalji in 1305 A.D.-and a governor installed in place. As with all conquests, among the first state buildings to come up were mosques, built with pillars taken from Hindu temples, very similar to the Quwwat-ul-Islam mosque at the Qutb, Delhi.

The decline of the ruling power at Delhi after the sack of the city by Timur prompted the Ghauri governor of Mandu to declare his independence in A.D. 1401, with Sultan Dilawar Khan declaring himself Shah. It was left to his son, Hoshang Shah, to shift the capital from Dhar to the plateau of Mandu. Bounded on three sides by a rift valley, and overlooking the Narmada to the south from a height of 300 metres, the fortress of Mandu was virtually impregnable.

The Plateau of Mandu Chronology detailing main events-Sultan Dilawar Khan Ghauri A.D. 1401, Sultan Hoshang Shah A.D. 1405-1434, Mahmud Shah A.D. 1436 (Contemporary of Rana Kumbha of Chittor), Malwa/Mandu annexed by Akbar A.D. 1569. The fortress enclosed an area of approximately 12 square miles within walls over 25 miles in circumference. The inspirational landscape of Mandu, jutting out from the Vindhyas range, became the site of some of the finest provincial Islamic architecture, with mosques, madrassas and pleasure-palaces dotting the landscape.

The Jama Masjid at Mandu: Near the centre of the Mandu plateau the Jama Masjid was one of the finest achievements of the Ghauri dynasty. A mosque, with its necessarily vast scale to accommodate numerous worshipers, is monumental by its nature, and to endow it with elements of humanism can be counted as a very difficult exercise in design. This problem has been fairly successfully addressed.

Of the elements that make up this mosque, the monumental entrance from the east is a fine exercise in elegance, with a main arched doorway flanked by two smaller openings. A squat yet well-proportioned dome crowns this entrance, with its profile being reflected in smaller domes over the cloisters surrounding the central court, their proportions being 'not unlike in profile to the so-called shoulder shaped contours of the shikharas of Orissan temples. The courtyard is surrounded on three sides by columned cloisters with galleries of majestic arches.

All the construction is faced with red sandstone, with little concession to decoration. Indeed, the only departure from sobriety is in the chattri inside the mosque, next to the mihrab, which shows influences from florid Gujarati architecture. Situated as it was on a plateau, with numerous water bodies through its length, and the home of a prosperous dynasty, Mandu became the site for various pleasure-palaces and resorts for royalty, be they for the women of the harem, the fine arts or hunting.

In Mandu we have architecture dedicated to the pursuit of pleasure on a large scale, in the form of the Jahaz, Lal, Chappan, Baz Bahadur and Rupmati palaces. The Jahaz Mahal, built by Mahmud Khalji, was a departure from the previously stolid and somber style at Mandu. The most striking thing about this monument is its location between two water bodies, the Kaphur Talao and the Munja Talao, which gives the building the appearance of floating on water, hence its name, literally the 'ship palace'.

Architecturally, the building consists of a series of compartments and corridors over the Munja Talao, with terraces, kiosks and numerous open-air baths conforming to the lifestyle at Mandu, which was slowly sliding into decadence. The Jahaz Mahal proved an inspiration for later Khalji sultans to dot the landscape with their own pleasure pavilions and summer retreats. The esoteric character of Mandu later prompted the like-minded Mughal emperor Jahangir to spend a considerable amount on its maintenance.

And so, even though the city of Mandu was eventually absorbed into the Mughal empire, its legend lives on as the city of Joy, and in the forests of the Vindhyas today, if you listen hard enough, echo the strains of the romantic tales of Rupmati and Baz Bahadur to this day.

Tomb of Hoshang Shah: To the south-west of the Jami-Masjid lies Hoshang Shah's tomb, among the earliest Muslim buildings in India to be sheathed entirely in white marble, possibly exerting an influence on buildings to follow elsewhere, and documented fact says that Shah Jahan sent a team of surveyors here for case studies before commencing construction of the Taj Mahal.

Asharfi Mahal vs Hindola Mahal: Although little remains of the Asharfi Mahal, to the east of the Jami-Masjid, it was an extraordinary achievement in its time, serving as a madrassa with open courts surrounded by cells for students on several levels. Here also are the remains of a seven-storey victory tower-which collapsed in the 17th century-echoing Ala-ud-din's megalomaniac flights of fancy near the Qutb. From the remains of Hoshang Shah's palace, it is clear that the whole area was divided into three zones-ceremonials with halls of audience, the king's private chambers and the ubiquitous zenana, or women's chambers.

Bengali Brick and Bamboo

Chronology of events-Muhammad Bakhtiyar Khalji conquers Bengal A.D. 1193, Nasir-ud-Din Bughra Khan appointed Governor A.D. 1282, Shams-ud-Din Ilyas founds Purbiya dynasty A.D. 1352, Sher Shah invades Bengal A.D. 1537, Bengal absorbed into Akbar's empire A.D. 1576. Curved Roof Form at Bengal. It was one of the foremost provincial Islamic outposts, beginning with A.D. 1193, when Muhammad Bakhtiyar Khalji extended Muslim rule right down to the ancient capital of Gaur. It is interesting to note that it was in the same year that Qutb-ud-Din Aibak established the Sultanate in Delhi.

The reason for this rapid conquest, when closer places like Malwa took many years to subdue, was principally that the Ganges provided a great waterway to facilitate the movement, and so hordes of troop transports could navigate the river with ease all the way down to its estuary. The lack of building stone in Bengal meant that most construction was carried out in brick, of which there was an abundant supply, and this meant that no building was possible using the usual column-beam construction so characteristic of early Islamic structures. Instead, right from the beginning, arches were used to span spaces and to support the weight above.

Brick thus lends Bengal architecture a style which is distinct, with its pointed arches and finishes so different from those in stone. Another remarkable feature which predominates is a curved roof form, no doubt derived from its bamboo predecessor.

This curved roof was to prove very popular in north India in general, with later Rajput, Mughal and even Sikh architecture being influenced. The harsh climate of Bengal also means that antiquities decay rapidly; indeed, according to Fergusson: "...the climate of Bengal is...singularly inimical to the preservation of architectural remains. If the roots of a tree of the fig kind once find a resting-place in any crevice of a building, its destruction is inevitable; and even without this, the luxuriant growth of the jungle hides the building so completely, that it is sometimes difficult to discover it-always to explore it."

Of the pre-Islamic architecture, there are traces of Sena and Pala constructions in Gaur, which was long a Hindu capital city. Many fragments of Hindu architecture are still to be found, though not enough to accurately reconstruct the architectural style used. Their chief worth, however, is the influence they had on Islamic architecture in terms of short squat pillars used to support the superstructure above.

The architecture in Bengal can be further divided into two periods-the first from the 13th to 15th century when it was a provincial outpost of the Delhi Sultanate, and the second in the 15th and 16th centuries, when the Bengal Sultanate was established. The first period is marked by construction influenced by Hindu remains, and the major traces of this are to found at Tribeni on the Hoogly river. The mosque and tomb of Jafar Khan Ghazi are adapted from the remains of a Hindu temple but have brick walls, as well as the earliest pointed arches in the province. In the nearby village of Chotta Pandua, the large ruined mosque is a similar mixture of arched and column-beam construction.

The Adina Masjid : Sultan Sikander Shah built the Adina Masjid at Pandua to celebrate his victory over and independence from the Delhi Sultanate, is impressive in size but lacks in architectural significance. Measuring a huge 507 feet by 285 feet, the central court is surrounded by three and five aisled enclosures supported by pillars of basalt. When complete, the mosque had no less than 378 brick dome, as well as a huge central pointed vault over the liwan.

Most of these have collapsed, including the central vault, and so the Adina Masjid today consists of little more than a pile of ruins, marked by arches and crumbling walls, the whole reminiscent of a Greek or Roman city in ruin. Whatever be its architectural merits, the Adina mosque provided a valuable lesson in building in the inimical climate of Bengal, and with brick. In the Eklakhi Tomb we see for the first time an Islamic curved roof inspired from the bamboo version, and the slight slope on the roof is a departure from traditional cubical construction and served to throw off rainwater.

The Eklakhi tomb remains rather tentative in plan as well as in execution. With strange proportions of the dome as well as the structure below, with a rather hesitant curved roof, the tomb nevertheless has stood the ravages of time, attesting to the efficacy of the curved roof as well as its stout construction.

The Bengal Mosque: Once again, after the lessons of the Adina Mosque, the climate of Bengal proved to be a decisive factor in determining the plan. It was evident that a large open courtyard was useless in the long monsoons in Bengal. And so the courtyard was replaced by an enclosed hall. Once this principle had been established, a large number of mosques came up in and around the city of Gaur. Notable among these are the Chotta Sona and Bara Sona masjids. Both apparently had gilt applied to their curved roofs, which gives them their name-literally, 'Golden Mosques'.

Bara Sona Masjid: Situated as it was on a plateau, with numerous water bodies through its length, and the home of a prosperous dynasty, Mandu became the site for various pleasure-palaces and resorts for royalty, be they for the women of the harem, the fine arts or hunting. In Mandu we have architecture dedicated to the pursuit of pleasure on a large scale, in the form of the Jahaz, Lal, Chappan, Baz Bahadur and Rupmati palaces.

The Jahaz Mahal, built by Mahmud Khalji, was a departure from the previously stolid and somber style at Mandu. The most striking thing about this monument is its location between two water bodies, the Kaphur Talao and the Munja Talao, which gives the building the appearance of floating on water, hence its name, literally the 'ship palace'. The building consists of a series of compartments and corridors over the Munja Talao, with terraces, kiosks and numerous open-air baths conforming to the lifestyle at Mandu, which was slowly sliding into decadence.

It proved an inspiration for later Khalji sultans to dot the landscape with their own pleasure pavilions and summer retreats. The esoteric character of Mandu later prompted the like-minded Mughal emperor Jahangir to spend a considerable amount on its maintenance.

And so, even though the city of Mandu was eventually absorbed into the Mughal empire, its legend lives on as the city of Joy, and in the forests of the Vindhyas today, if you listen hard enough, echo the strains of the romantic tales of Rupmati and Baz Bahadur down to the present day.

One of the last of the mosque examples in the Qadam Rasul mosque, a rather smaller example with stocky basalt pillars supporting the arches above. The mosque, according to Satish Grover, is 'flaccid and formless', but possesses nevertheless beauty in its robust proportions, in the aggressive outward thrust of the column bases, and indeed in the columns themselves which are divided into tiers, emphasising their low height and posture. The Dakhil Darwaza, marking the entrance to the remodeled city of Gaur with its broad thoroughfares, as well as the Feroza Minar or 'Blue Tower' marked some of the finest late examples of the Bengal style before the Ilyas Shahi dynasty succumbed to an Abyssinian mercenary in 1489.

Punjab Architecture

Harappan Civilization: The oldest examples of architecture sculpture, and painting in the Punjab belong to the Harappan civilization. The Vedic age, which followed the Harappan age, has not left any artistic relics. The Vedic Aryans lived in villages. They used perishable materials such as wood and bamboo. Some scholars believe that the plan of an Aryan village was based on that of a fortified military camp.

Its layout was rectangular. Its sides oriented to four quarters and it was interacted by two roads or streets, which terminated in four gateways. But no actual remains of a Vedic village have survived. The literature refers to great cities of the age of the Buddha. These cities were well planned, built of bricks and timer.

They had beautiful buildings, royal palaces, broad streets and high gateways. A wall surrounded the entire city. But no example of such and ancient city has survived to this day. The reason is that most of the buildings of wood have perished. In eastern India we have some monuments dating from the Pre-Mauryan times. These are at Rajagriha and at Lauriya Nandangarh in Bihar. No buildings of Pre-Mauryan epoch exist in the Punjab.

Importance of Takshashila: The earliest historical example of art and architecture in the Punjab are those of the Maurya period. The city of Takshashila was the capital of the Uttarapatha province of the Maurya Empire. It was famous city has been excavated in modern times. The ruins of Takshashila consist of three city-cited: Bihar mound, Sirkap, and Dirsukh. These represent three successive phases in the history of the city. At Bihar mouns we have evidence of settlement from sixth to the second century BC Sirkap site represents the second city of Takshashila. Bactrian Greeks built it in the second century A.D. unlike Bihar mound and Sirkap, the site of Sirsukh has not been excavated.

Taxila Jewellery : The city of Sirkap was built on the Greek chessboard pattern, with streets cutting one another at rights angles and regularly aligned blocks of buildings. Besides bricks, coursed rubble-stone was used in building houses. The city had a rempart. But the Parthian and Shaka rules built a defence wall of stone 3, 1/2 miles long. The city had several Buddhist shrines and stupas. There was an upsidal temple also. More important religious establishments lay outside the boundaries of the three city-sites.

The most ancient and the most important sacred building is the Dharmarajika-stupa. Emperor Ashoka originally built it. A stupa is a Buddhist shrine. It is covered from all sided and its shape is semicircular like a cup turned upside down. Inside a stupta are preserved sacred relics either of a Buddha or Buddhist saints. The Buddhists adore the stupa. Emperor Ashoka had the title Dharmaraha or the 'Righterous King'. The Dharmarajika stupa built by him was elaborated and renovated by later kings. It is built on a high platform of stone. It is circular in plan and hemispherical in elevation. From its central hub radiate sixteen thick walls. On the southern portion of Sirkap are a stupa and a monastery of vihara. A vihara is also a sacred Buddhist building. It contains roomed for monks as well as prayer hall and a shrine-room.

Towards the northern gate of Sirkap lie the ruins of a temple at Jandial. It was a Zoroastrian temple. It resembles a Greek temple. It has two pillars at the entrance and two pillars at the front porch, which leads to the sanctuary. Amount the finds at Takshashila are coins of kings of different dynasties, seals, jewellery, sculptures and peltry pieces.

Stupas City-sites : Another important city-cite in the Punjab is Charsdda on the Swat river in Peshawar district. It is the site of Pushkalavati, the capital of Gandhara. Excavations brought to light the existence of Buddha stupas and viharas and other buildings. Traces of stupa architecture have been found at several other places in the Punjab and the northwest. Thus the stupas at Manikyala in Rawalpindi district at Takht-i-Bahai, Sahri-Bahlol and Jamalgarhi near Hoti Mardan, and at Shahji-Ki-Dheri near Peshawar may be mentioned.

Kanishka built the great stupa at Shahji-Ki-Dheri. It is cruciform on plan. Inside it was found a casket containing sacred relics of Buddha. This stupa built by Kanishka was seen by Husan Tsang in the 7th century and by Alberuni in 11th century AD. The stupa at Takht-i-Bahai is famous for its great statue of standing Buddha. The ruins of monasteries were also identified at these places as well as at Sahri-Bahlol. A chatya of Buddhist shrine was also fount at Sahri-Bahlol. Numerous Buddhist monasteries and stupas were built also in Sind and Balochistan; A stupa built of Bricks existed at Mirpurkhas. It had three vaulted cells, which contained images of the Buddha.

This stupa was ruined during the Arab invasions in 712 AD. The stupa may have been built during the early Kushana times. The remains of a stupa also exist at a place called Tor-Dherai in Loralai district of Balochistan. The site of Branmanbad in Sindh had at first Buddhist monasteries and stupas. Later on in the Gupta period, Brahmanical temples were built at this site. Recently Sanghol in Ludhiana District has been excavated. It represents the site of a Buddhist establishment. The very name may be connected with sangha or the Buddhist community. Remains of a Dharma-chakra-stupa have come to light at Sanghol.

Hsuan Tsang's Description : "In the seventh century AD. the Chinese Buddhist scholar and pilgrim visited many places in the northwest. He has described a number of sacred buildings, which existed during his time. We will briefly sum up his account of cities, monasteries, temples and stupas."

The walls of towns and cities of Indians were broad and high. But thoroughfares were narrow. The shops are on the highways and booth line the roads. Butchers, fisherman, public performers, executioners, and scavengers have their habitation marked by a distinguishing sign. They are forced to live outside the city... As to the construction of houses and enclosing walls the country of bricks while walls of houses and enclosures are of wattled bamboo or wood. Their halls and terraced belvederes have wooden flat roofed rooms and are coated with chuna and covered with tiles gurnt of unurnt. They are of extraordinary height, and in style like those of China. The houses thatched with xoarse of common grass are of bricks or boards; their walls are ornamented with chunam; the floor is purified with cow-dung and strewn with flowers of the seadon; in these matters they differ from us. But the Buddhist monasteries are of most remarkable architecture. They have a tower at each of the four corners of the quadrangle and three high halls in a tier.

Hsuan Tsang also mention the viharas or monasteries, stupas and the temple in different cities he visited personally. In Lampaka or Lagman in Afghanistan he saw more than ten Buddhist monasteries and about a score of non-Buddhist temples. In Nagarahara country around Jelalavad district) he was a stupa made of stone and in height 300 feet. There was also a vihara with a smaller stupa. Both these stupas had been built by Ashoka. There were also fine Deva-temples. In Hadda near Jelalavad he saw a two-storeyed shrine in which were preserved some Buddhist relics. In Gandhara there were above 1000 Buddhist monasteries in the country but they were utterly dilapidated and untenanted. Many of the topes also were in ruins. There were above 100 Deva-temples, and the various sects lived pell-mell. This sorry state of Buddhist viharas and stupas was due to the destruction carried together were Branamanical sects such as Shaktism, Shaivism, and Vaishnavism.

He writes: "The treat stupa built by Kanishka was 400 feet high, Near the stupa were large in ages of the Buddha. To the southeast of this great stupa was a stone image of the standing Buddha. It was 18 feet in height. Around this image were more than 100 small stupas."

In the city of Pushkalarvti there was Deva temple with a marvel-working image of the Deve. This was possibly a Shiva temple. Here Deva means Shiva or Mahadeva. To the east of the city was an old stupa built by Ashoka. At a shorty distance from the city was monastery in ruins; close to it stood another stupa erected by Ashoka. At was some hundreds of feet high, the carved wood and engraved stone of which seemed to be the work of strangers. At Palusha in Gandhara he saw Mahesbara's spouse Bhima-devi of dark-blue stone. At the foot of the mountain was a temple to Maheshvara-deva in which ash-smearing Tirthikas performed much workship. According to this passage there was a temple of Shiva at the bottom of the mountain where the devotees worshipped. At the top of the mountain was an in age of goddess called Bhma or Bhishana. She is the same as Durga of Uma.

In Uddiyana on Swat river there had been formerly 1400 monasteries but many of these were now in ruins. Most of these monasteries had been destroyed by the Huna armies. There were ten Deva-temples in the 7th century AD. Buddhist stupas and monasteried were also seen by the Chinese pilgrim in the Mahaban area. Many stupas existed in Mongkil and Darel. The monasteries at Takshashila though numerous were desolate. Stupas built by Ashoka were still in tact. At Simhapura there was an Ashokan stupa 200 feet in height. Several stupas existed in Balochistan some of them were 100 feet in height.

The Gandhara Sculpture: "The Gandhara art represents one of the greatest culture achievements of ancient Punjab. It is called the Ganghara art because it is originated and flourished in the region anciently known as Gandhara. The region in represented by Rawalpindi and Peshawar divisions now in Pakistan. It is also called the Buddhist art of contents. Generally speaking the word Gandhara art is applied to the architecture, sculpture and painting which developed in north-western India form the first to the fifth centuries AD. Formerly some scholars held the opinion that this art was derived from the Greek art. But this opinion is no longer held by anyone. In style and manner of execution some of the Gandhara sculptures resemble between the subject-matte r of the Roman art and the Gandhara art. A few examples of foreing origin have been found in Gandhara region. These include figures in metal of Dionysius and Harpocrates and a bronze figure of Herakles. These articles obviously came from aborad with merchants and soldiers. During the rule of the Bactrian Greeks and Parthians the

Punjab had close contacts with Roman Empire. West Asian Hellenistic and Roman artists may also have come to Gandhara to work for the Kushana Kings. The Kushana emperors, Kanishka I and his successor, were the greatest patrons of Ganhara art."

Scholars holds that the first image of the Buddha in human form was made in the Gandhara school of sculpture. But the Mathura school of sculpture claims equal credit. It seems that the image of the Buddha began to be made in Mathura and Gandhara school at the same time. Before the first century AD. the Buddha was worshipped through sacred symbols such as a stupa, a bodhi, tree a dharma-chakra, and foot-prints. This form of Buddhist worship by employing symbols and emblems is well known form the art of Bodh Gaya, Bharhut, and Sanchi.

The growth of Mahayana form of Buddhism During 200-100 BC. had inspired the production of figures of the Buddhas and Bodhisativas. Image-worship became popular among the Jainas, the Buddhist as well as the Shaivas and Vaishnavas. The creation of a Buddha image was a religious act. The development of Buddhist sculpture was inspire by a religious act. The development of Buddhist sculpture was inspired by a religious emotion. It was considered meritorious to make an image of the Buddha to install it in a shrine, and to adore it. The growth of Buddhist art in Ganghara was goth a cause and consequence of the growth of Buddhist in this area.

The Buddha is depicted standing on one side of the coin. On the other side is a standing figure of King Kanishka wearing a long coat resembling achkan. Another early representation of the Buddha is found in a relic casket of Kanishka's time. The standing Buddha figure from Hoti Mardan near Peshawar shows the influence of the figure of the Greek god Apllo. Cheif features of Gandhara sculpture are wavy hair or curly hair, youthful face like that of Apollo, prominence of physical features and ridged folds on the dress. Some time moustachion are shown on the Buddha's face. This error was due to the artist's ignorance about the details of Buddha's life. The artist, though worked under the guidance of Indian Buddhist scholars, often south to emphasise Greek and Roman features.

Thus even on the Buddha's sanghati or outer garment attempts were made to carve drapes. It is possible hat some text such as the Laita-vistara or the Buddha-charita giving details of the life of the Buddhawas used by the sculptors. The Buddha's human body had 32 marks of a Great Man urna between the two eye-brows, ears-lobes, on the head, etc. The artists have often tried to depicts these marks on the Buddha figures. The figures of Buddha and the events in his life form the main subject-matter of the Gandhara sculpture.

The Buddha is shown either as standing or as seated. The seated Buddha is in a variety of postures. Thus the Buddha seated crossed legged in meditation wit half closed eyes shows the dhyanamudra. This yogic pose is the most common form adopted in seated images. The main events in the life of the Buddha were birth, renunciation of home-life, austerities, struggle with Mara or the forces of ignorance, attainment of Enlightment, first sermon performance of miracles, and the great the passing away.

All these events are carved on stone in a variety of forms. The other series of sculpture depicts scenes form the Jataka stories of Buddha's former births. A large number of figures are those of the Boddhisattvas. The Boddhisattvas are the saviour gods and saints of Mahayana Buddhism. Maitreya and Avalokiteshvara are the two most famous Boddhisattvas depicted in Gandhara sculpture. Interesting also are the figures of Indra and Brahma. Both these Vedic gods are well known devotees of Lord Buddha. They are shown standing with folded hands facing the Buddha.

The Buddha is at the centre flanked by those two gods. The two pieces of sculpture are both on metal. The one called the Reliquary of Kanishaka was found under a stupa at Shahji-Ki-Dheri near Peshawar. The other called the Bimaran Reliquary, was discovered from the ruins of a stupa near Jelalabad in Afghanistan. Areliquary is a casket box containing sacred relics either of the Buddha or of a Buddhist saint. These two pieces are the only surviving important examples of Gandhara sculpture in metal. All the other sculptures are on stone pieces.

There are two fine Muhammedan tombs situated close together outside the Nakodar town. These are maintained as protected monuments by the Archaeological Departments. One of these tombs was built in A.D.1612 in the beginning of the reign of Jahangir(A..D.1605-1627 A.D.) and the other in 1657 A.D towards the close of the reign of Shah Jahan (1627-1658 A.D.).

The Tomb of Mohammed Momin was erected over the mortal remains of Ustad Muhammad Momin also known as Ustad Ustad Muhammad Husseini alias Hafizak, a tambura player in the service of Khan-I-Khanan, one of the Mavaratnas in the court of Emperor Akbar in AD 1021 (AD 1612). Standing on an octagonal platform and approached by a flight of steps on two sides, it is square from inside and octagonal on outside. Surmounted by a pinnacle, the hemispherical dome sits over a low cylindrical drum and is relieved by four cupolas.

Each of the longer face is pierced by deep recesses while the shorter by half octagonal recesses placed one over the other, all covered by pointed arches. The entrances are on the northern and southern recesses while the other recesses are blocked with pierced tracery screens.

The middle portions of the panels on the exterior and the arch spandrels are decorated with geometric design in glazed tile work. The upper and lower panel, arranged in lines of red plastered bricks, contain painted designs showing guldastas. Originally within the burial chamber are two elegant sarcophagi of sienna coloured marble inlaid with white marble inscription, which are now lost.

Tomb of Haji Jamal is close to the tomb of Muhammad Momin. This tomb was raised over the mortal remains of Haji Jamal, a pupil of Ustad Muhammad Husseini, the tambura player, towards the close of Emperor Shah Jahan's region. The two lined inscription engraved on the entrance gate of the tomb refers to its bing the tomb of Haji Jamal and gives a date of AH 1067 (AD 1657). It stands in the middle of the square platform, paneled on all sides with deep recesses concealing two flight of steps on each side.

Each of the four faces have octagonal recesses covered by pointed arches. The southern one gives access to the burial chamber while the remaining ones are closed with pierced tracery screens. Its inner chamber is octagonal where as the outer plan is square having octagonal turrets surmounted with domed cupolas added to the corners. A bulbous dome crowned with pinnacle sits over a high drum and is balanced by the four cupolas crowning the turrets at the cornor. The facade is divided into red stucco covered brick framed panels and painted with white lines.

The larger panels are filled with flower pots and the smaller with geometrical designs. The broad belts between the panels are ornamented with diper designs in tiles of different colours. The octagonal towers and the battlements as well as the pinnacles of the domes are ornamented with glazed tiles. (Notification no. 4687 dated 18-02-1919 Archaeological Survey of India, Chandigarh Circle) On the west of the tombs is a gateway said to have been built in A.D. 1667.

There is another smaller gateway on the east, now in ruins. To the north is a tank, the bricks of which were largely used in the building of Nakodar Cantonment, on one side of it is a summer house, now used as the Sub-Judge-cum-Judicial Magistrate's Court. Beyond the tank is Baradari containing the shrine of Bahadur Khan who died during the reign of Jahangir, and also an old mosque which is now in a dilapidated condition. Dakhni sarai is one of the finest and best preserved specimens of Mughal caravan sarais built along the old highway. It stand in the village Dakhni (31.10' N; 75.25' E) on the Nakodar-Kapurthala road, about 12 km from Nakodar.

The sarai is said to have been built by the well known Mughal noble Ali Mardan Khan during the reign of Mughal emperor Shah Jahan about AD 1640. It comprises of one hundred & twenty four cells around a closed quadrangle with two imposing gateway in the centre of the eastern and western quadrangle. Inside the quadrangle is a mosque and a well. The half dome portal of which is decorated with glazed tiles while its interior contains painted motifs over lime plaster. The wall closing the sarai on the outside at the four corners are strengthened by circular bastion. The three storyed facade of the gateway shows recesses and openings on either side, the smaller one being closed with finely pierced tracery screens in red sandstone.

The gateway projecting out of the wall is strengthened with octagonal towers, crowned with domical cupolas. The arch spandrels and panels framing the central arch and side openings are decorated with glazed tile-work showing geometrical and floral designs. (Notification no. 4687 dated 18-02-1919 Archaeological Survey of India, Chandigarh Circle).

The Mughal Bridge is to the south of the village Mahlian Kalan on Nakodar-Kapurthala road, about 12 km from Nakodar. This is one of the extant Mughal bridge built during the reign of Shah Jahan (AD 1627-1658). The bridge spanned the Dhauli-veni river to the east of the Dakhni Sarai. It is of Lakhauri bricks and has five arched spans, the central begin the highest and other four in receding order. (Notification no. PN, 16721 dated 04-06-1923 Archaeological Survey of India, Chandigarh Circle) Nurmahal is due to the fostering of Nur Jahan (after whom it is named), the consort of Emperor Jahangir (1605-1627 A.D) and who is said to have been brought up here. She had the imperial serai constructed by Nawab Zakariya Khan Governor of the Doab between 1619 and 1621 A.D and settled numerous families in her new town. In 1738-1739 Nadir Shah exacted a ransom of three lakhs of rupees" from Nurmahal, which seriously injured its prosperity. "In 1756-1757 Ahmad Shah demanded a like sum and the people being unable to pay he ordered them to be slaughtered and plundered, and burnt the town".

Almost immediately afterwards the Punjab independent of Delhi and Nurmahal was seized by the Ahluwalia Sikhs and was held for the Kapurthala Chief by Sirdar Kaur Singh and his descendants. It would seem as if before this the Talwan Rujputs had taken possession of the town. They subsequently on the final invasion of Ahmad Shah recovered the serai. The west gateway of this building was restored at public expense during the British rule towards the close of the nineteenth century. The sarai is remarkable specimen of oriental architecture. The serai is maintained as a protected monument by the Archaeological Department.

This closed quadrangle consists of one hundred forty cells on all over the four sides, two gateway placed in the central of the eastern and western wings and double storeyed pavilions in the centre of the northern and southern wings, two storied octagonal tower having three cells on the basement at the corners; a well and a mosque with in the quadrangle of the two gateways, the eastern on is simple while the western one is ornamented.

The gateway comprising guard rooms on either side of a central passage and projecting out has casing of red sandstone. The sliced outer angles are relieved with arch recesses placed one over other. The whole facade is divided in to panels, ornamented with sculptures in bas-relief and foliated scroll work with birds sitting in branches.

The arched opening of the entrance is encased with in a bigger arch and its spandrels being decorated with lotus medallions on either side of the spandrels are placed projecting domed balconies supported on four pillars topped with carved brackets. The space in between the pillars is closed with low stone railings showing fine pierced tracery work. To the corner of the gates are added guldastas which rise above the battlements of the terrace. (Notification no. 4687 dated 18.02.1919 Archaeological Survey of India, Chandigarh Circle) Ancient site (Theh Ghatti), Nagar (Jalandhar).

The village Nagar (31" 05' N, 77" 50'E) is situated about 9 km north-east of phillaur with a threefold sequence of culture. Period 1 is represented by the painted Grey ware with sprinkling of the late Harappa sturdy red ware. Semicircular huts and two ovel structures of burnt earth, probably of religious nature, have been noticed. Copper objects, bone styli, terracota ear-ornaments and animal figures, besides beads and bangles, have been found. Period II has the typical Kushan pottery, terracottas and coins. A terracota seal reads " sri-mahasenapati-Ramaguptasya' in characters of third century is an important discovery.

In period III there was a prosperous medieval occupation. (Notification of 1954 dated 02.01.1954 Archaeological Survey of India, Chandigarh Circle) Ancient site, Katpalon (Jalandhar): The ancient site in the village Katpalon (31' 05' N; 75' 52' E) about 7 km east of phillaur and it was excavated by the survey in 1976-77. In period I the painted Grey ware was found interlocked with the late Harappan pottery. Copper antimony road and terracota beads and wheels are the other main finds. This was followed after a break by period II, kushna. In period III, medieval, the strata are much disturbed by pits.

9

Construction during Raj

British Colonial Architecture

"In the middle of the seventeenth century, Asia still had a far more important place in the world than Europe." So wrote J. Pirenne in his 'History of the Universe', published in Paris in 1950. He added, "The riches of Asia were incomparably greater than those of the European states. Her industrial techniques showed a subtlety and a tradition that the European handicrafts did not possess. And there was nothing in the more modern methods used by the traders of the Western countries that Asian trade had to envy. In matters of credit, transfer of funds, insurance, and cartels, neither India, Persia, nor China had anything to learn from Europe." (Quoted in Auguste Toussaint's 'History of the Indian Ocean')

In the 17th century, the British East India Company made its presence felt in India, during the height of power of the Mughal empire. Instead of selling their own goods, the British eventually found it more profitable to sell Indian goods in Europe. The early days were hard. There was competition from both other Europeans, as well as other trade routes (the Red Sea route through Egypt, the Persian Gulf Route through Iraq, and the Northern Caravan Route through Afghanistan, Persia and Turkey).

Thus the early British Traders were in no position to dictate terms and trade concessions were hard won. However, eventually and with perseverance the Company slowly established trading bases wherever it could along either side of the lengthy Indian coastline. As the East India Company slowly changed in character from a purely trading concern to a political-military-economic machine, it was these trading bases that formed the nucleus of British settlements and it was here that the first British buildings came up. In keeping with the nature of the Company, the first buildings were warehouses, barracks and living quarters, protected by a fort.

The earliest British forts followed Portuguese and French variations of the Italian Renaissance's conception of an ideal city and its defences. In the forts at Madras and Calcutta, the French military engineer Vauban's influence is apparent. Regular polygonal geometry and salient triangular bastions with recessed flanks at each angle maximised all-round cover and minimised vulnerability by offering overlapping fields of fire.

Ditches and earthworks between the main ring of bastions and lower, outlying salients increased defensive capability. The area surrounding the fort was cleared of all obstacles so as to remove any cover for attackers. These first forts at Madras, Bombay and Calcutta were the principal seats from where the Company oversaw its affairs. Features common to them all include doubled walls and angular bastions for artillery to dominate the approach. The fortifications also took advantage of natural features like the sea and rivers for defence.

Around the forts, the first signs of segregation were already apparent-the European and Indian communities lived in separate settlements with very distinct characters. In the case of Fort St. George, Madras, the main fortifications surrounded the warehouses and other military buildings, and the so-called 'white town' had another ring of fortification separating it from the 'black town'.

Madras: Fort St. George: Bombay's Fort St. George was finished in 1715. To place this in context, the Mughal empire was beginning to rapidly come apart with Aurangzeb's death in 1707.

Bombay: Fort St. George: Although Fort St. George Madras was one of the first British outposts, it fell to the

French in 1745, and again in 1758, before it was finally retaken by the British. The French were also weakened by their losses in Europe and were slowly abandoning India to the British.

After the Nawab of Bengal took Calcutta in 1755 and was then defeated by Clive, a new Fort William was begun by the Company's chief engineer in Bengal, Captain John Bohier. On an island site by the river unencumbered by buildings, Fort William's field survives as the maidan, emulated at Bombay.

Calcutta: Fort William: In addition to warehouses within the fort walls, there was also the need for arsenals, barracks and residential accommodation for the British. A church, too, was a necessity. The first English church in India was thus St. Mary's at Madras fort, founded in 1678.

Madras: St. Mary's Church: Early British construction, thus, with the exception of St. Mary's, was restricted to military and utilitarian structures, as the Company was still mostly a trading concern and only interfered in politics where it felt its commercial interests were in danger. Architecture as a symbol of political power was to come later, but the fall of the Mughal empire and infighting amongst the powers that succeeded it was to make it easier for the British to consolidate their tiny footholds into the beginning of a mighty empire that straddled the whole subcontinent. With the defeat of Tipu Sultan of Mysore in 1799, the British became the most powerful political and military force in India. The Military Boards set up by the English contributed the bulk of secular architecture, like barracks, forts, housing for soldiers and other assorted building, but for the purposes of government and the church, something more assertive was needed to proclaim the supremacy of the British.

It is thus that Government Houses and Town Halls, from where the business of governance and justice was carried out, follow closely changing trends in Britain to a great extent, and show also the continued influence of the so-called 'pattern books', from which the bulk of the Company's design was carried out. These pattern books, while conforming more or less to Europe's Greco-Roman heritage, incorporated ideas on the form architecture 'should' take, depending on its function. In essence, a pattern book would show how to put together different elements and combine them into a single whole.

The City of Calcutta

Government House, Calcutta: Calcutta was an early British outpost, like Madras and Bombay its Fort William being the highest point on the Hooghly that ships could reach. Unlike Madras and Bombay, however, principles of urban design were applied here, stemming from its position in the last decades of the 18th century as the Company's main seat. Calcutta was stamped with the hallmark of authority like the era's classic European capitals-indeed contemporaries likened it to St. Petersburg. There were two main axes. The first one led from the civil arm of authority around an expansive square dominated by the barrack-like Writers' Building, to the military arm in the Maidan by Fort William.

The secondary one embraced the Council House, the Courts and the Town Hall. At their perpendicular intersection stood Government House, built for the Governor-General Lord Wellesley from 1798 by Captain Charles Wyatt of the Bengal Engineers-and the architectural family then prominent at home. The model for this imperial work was James Paine's published design for Kedleston Hall, Derbyshire. All four of the satellite blocks projected there were constructed here, linked to the central block by quadrant galleries to full height, unlike in the original, and the rotunda in which the central axis culminated, oddly dissected within, was expressed on the garden front. Wyatt's adaptation was well attuned to the climate: the central-aisled hall on both main levels is flanked by galleries cr vestibules on all sides, maximising ventilation, and the main staircase is outside the north portico.

Wyatt's fellow officers produced the other major buildings of the town. Most distinguished was the 'English Palladian' Town Hall of Colonel John Garstin. Lieutenant James Agg proved himself competent in adapting a particular metropolitan model, Gibb's St. Martin in the Fields, for the stone tower of the church.

However the Company's failure to foresee the inadequacy of brick and plaster in the absence of good cheap local stone, on the one hand, and the soldiers' failure to comprehend the full significance of the Classical motifs reproduced in their pattern books, detract from the authenticity of the work. In these respects, unlike its French equivalent at Pondicherry, Government House Tripilicane (Madras) is typical except for its later Banqueting Hall. The Madras Government Hall was adapted for Lord Clive in the 1790s from an earlier one, after the pattern set at Pondicherry by the residence built for Duplex some fifty years earlier.

There superimposed arcaded verandahs before clerestory-lit major spaces were articulated with Doric and Ionic orders in the Academic classical manner of early 18th century France. At Triplicane, however, much lighter colonnaded verandahs, elegant if not exactly following set 'rules' of spacing, were erected around much of the side as well as the front. The whole complex is dominated by the Doric banqueting hall, which, even in its original form without the lower arcading-but not the least in the application of column to wall-was as remote from its ostensible model, the Parathion, as the main house is from Academic Classical principle.

Town Hall of Bombay: Quite different in its exceptional neoclassical gravitas is the Bombay Town Hall of Colonel Thomas Cowper, Bombay engineers. It is hardly inferior to many of the works of the masters of French neo-classicism. The Greek Doric Order of its powerful temple-fronts doubtless came from the principal source of the English Greek Revival, the work of Stuart and Revet, and the dramatically lit staircase leads to a splendid Corinthian Hall worthy of a mature student of Vitruvius Britannicus. Despite their airy porticoes and slender steeples, the walled and pillared later colonial churches, usually avoid the insubstantiality if not always the coarseness, of detail characteristic of many secular works. St. Martin in the Fields was to be an enduringly popular model.

The most accomplished homage paid to it was certainly in St. George's Cathedral and St. Andrews Kirk, Madras. To the Gibbs formula, Colonel James Caldwell and Major Thomas de

Havilland added side porches for St. George's and study aedicules below the distinguished steeple. St. Andrew's, with an elegant fluted Ionic order and a more purely classical steeple, is adventurous in following Gibb's alternative scheme with circular nave. Contrary to the prevailing fashion, indeed unusual in its centralised plan, is Colonel James Skinner's Greek cross church of St. James, Delhi, the dome of which distantly recalls such High Renaissance works as San Gallo's Santa Maria di Loretto in Rome.

St. James, Delhi: The increase in British influence led to traditional architecture becoming more eclectic in its choice of sources. A projection of British architecture as that associated with power and influence was a first and essential step for its elements to be associated with the architecture of Indian patrons, both Muslim and Hindu. Amongst examples too numerous to count, the Tomb of Mushirzadi (1814) and the Kaiserbagh at Lucknow, the Gopalji Temple, Tipu Sultan's Mosque and the Sitambara Jain Temple, all in Calcutta, can be mentioned.

Tipu Sultan's Mosque, Calcutta: Of course, architecture, is only one facet of the whole picture. The subcontinent was now firmly part of Britain's colonial responsibilities, and one aspect of the structural changes wrought by the British was a change in the education system, and increased intellectual contact between the two countries. It is ironic that these changes, brought about to convince the Indians of the superiority of British civilisation, would partly fuel the nationalist debate in India.

New Delhi-A New Capital: A New Capital-A visible symbol of British supremacy over India was New Delhi-the 'New' being added to distinguish it from the older cities that preceded-the last and most famous being the walled city of the Mughal emperor. One major imperative for the new city, of course, was that it had to surpass in all respects.

New Delhi is thus a strange but wonderful story-of an Empire in its heyday, but also of an Empire that would soon crumble. A search for a monumental and imperial architecture, but also an architectural vocabulary that would be representative of the subcontinent. And Robert Byron, travelling through India in the 1930s, would say:

> *The traveller drives out of Old Delhi, past the Jama Masjid and the Fort. A flat country-brown, scrubby and broken-lies on either side. This country has been compared with the Roman Campagna: at every hand, tombs and mosques Mogul times and earlier, weathered to the colour of the earth bear witness to former Empires. The road describes a curve and embarks imperceptibly on a gradient.*

Suddenly, on the right, a scape of towers and dome is lifted from the horizon, sunlit pink and cream dancing against the blue sky, fresh as a cup of milk, grand as Rome. Close at hand the foreground discloses a white arch. The motor turns off the arterial avenue, and skirting the low red base of the gigantic monument, comes to a stop. The traveller heaves a breath. Before his eyes, sloping gently upwards, runs a gravel way of such infinite perspective as to suggest the intervention of a diminishing glass; at whose end, reared above the green tree tops, glitters the seat of government, the seventh Delhi, four square upon an eminence-dome, tower, dome, tower, dome, red, pink, cream, and white washed gold and flashing in the morning sun. The traveller loses a breath, and with it his apprehensions and preconceptions.

George V used the occasion of his second visit to India, and the great Coronation Durbar that followed, to announce the shifting of the capital from Calcutta to Delhi. This decision was of both strategic and political significance. Delhi was not only more central to the Empire's increasing influence over the subcontinent, but it was also the symbolic head of government for centuries. To shift into an existing city, however, was out of the question-the new power demanded a new city. Planning for the new capital had begun well before the actual shift, and addressed questions of urban planning and an appropriate architectural style.

In Britain, a relatively little-known architect, till now specialising in country houses, managed by dint of enterprise and family connections to become the forerunner for the new capital team. His name was Edwin Lutyens. Together with his friend Herbert Baker, Lutyens appropriated to himself the task of creating an architecture fitted for the Raj, contemptuous of what had passed before as architecture, both by Indian dynasties and by his British colleagues.

Planning inspiration came from other imperial models and new capital cities: the Paris and Champs-Elysees of Baron Haussmann, Wren's unbuilt plan for London, as well as L'Enfant's plan for Washington DC. Other planning ideas came from contemporary British experiments in urbanism: the Circus at Bath for Connaught Place, and Hampstead Garden City for the residential suburbs of New Delhi.

Architecture and Symbology

Elegance of Parliament House: The Montague-Chelmsford reform of 1919 brought a certain legislative responsibility upon Indians, and with it the need for a legislative building as part of the New Delhi complex arose. Parliament House in its final form was Baker's conception, an odd circular form in a predominantly orthogonal planning scheme. In spite of the difficulty of citing a circular building in the urban plan, Baker creation is not without architectural merit, with an imposing exterior colonnade and an interior three-pointed plan with a central, domed space.

Importance of India Gate : Conceived originally as a memorial to fallen Indian soldiers in the service of the British army, India Gate was originally called the War Memorial Arch, and designed after its predecessors, the Arc de Triomphe and Porte St. Denis in Paris. On its walls are inscribed the names of 60,000 men who fell fighting for the British empire. A politically appropriate monument, the archway also completed Kings Way (now Rajpath), the monumental central axis of New Delhi.

Royal House: For the Indian princes, a house ('palace') in the New Delhi scheme was an indicator of their prestige. (That this prestige was mostly on paper was a fact that would be painfully clear soon after 1947). The princely houses in New Delhi-Hyderabad, Baroda and Jaipur among others-were more symbolic than actual representations of power. The biggest of these was Hyderabad House, for the Nizam of Hyderabad, perhaps at the time the richest man in the world. Lutyens' plan was adapted from the 'butterfly' scheme he had already employed as far back as 1902, and took care not to rival in splendour the Viceroy's residence. More clearly classical in origin than the Imperial buildings, Hyderabad House is less ornate and yet more original as a typology.

At Baroda House Luteins chose, with the full approval of his British-educated client, not to indulge in any concessions towards Indian motifs and traditions. Baroda House is Anglo-Saxon in aspect and finishes, and here the butterfly plan is cut in two in the centre.

Many a Church : Although Luteins dreams for a great cathedral were never realised, other churches came up around New Delhi. One of these, the Garrison Church for Delhi Cantonment (Architect: Arthur Shoosmith) would be a forerunner of the modern architectural movement in India). The other, the Church of the Redemption by H.A.N. Medd, was directly next to the Viceroy's House. New Delhi was an enormous political, strategic and also ultimately logistical undertaking. 700 million bricks, 100,000 cubic feet of marble, 3500 stone dressers for the sandstone... all of these under local conditions of heat and dust, irregular power supply and water and finally the numerous and often conflicting directions from various sources of authority. A world war intervened and slowed down construction.

However, after all, 17 years of continuous construction saw New Delhi in a state ready to be inaugurated in 1931. This was a grand gala affair of dances and cocktails, of pomp and grand receptions, all celebrating the British empire's greatest architectural achievement. The impeccable geometry and order imposed by the Delhi plan on the site was emblematic of the order imposed on the world by the British empire.

What irony! In 1931, it was already clear that British rule in India was drawing to a close. Like the Raj, New Delhi was already the symbol of an age that was ending-an age of splendour, an age of Kings.

'rincely States: the Construction

The term 'princely states' applies to those regions of India not under direct control of the British, but which continued to be ruled by their traditional rulers. In that sense the term 'princely' is misleading, since these rulers were kings in their own right. However for the British there was only one King, and he was in London, and so the term 'princely states' came into being.

In the early 19th century, the East India Company had established treaties with many Maharajas who, in return for nominal independence, accepted British rule and Pax Britannica-friendship with their neighbours. However, the Company's policy of war and annexation led to a band of rulers forming a loose confederation against the British, what would be called the Mutiny of 1857. Though the rebellion was crushed, the British Crown became wary of continuing the policy of annexation, and entered into treaties with almost all these states.

After the 1858 transference of power, the British Crown became the guarantor of peace and commerce treaties. From the middle of the 19th century until 1947 the princes ostensibly controlled 40 percent of India. They were, however, watched over by British agents and their powers, though real, were limited to internal matters. The ambiguity of their status led to a substantial concern for the symbols of identity. Many of these symbols were manifested in elaborate patterns of behaviour-parades, durbars, entertainment-but their physical manifestation was in their architecture.

When the British replaced the Mughals as the controlling group, the inspiration for much of Indian architecture became English in origin, closely tied with what was happening in Britain. As for the princes, they were educated along British lines, taken on tours of Europe and introduced to Western manners and norms. This change in lifestyle began to be reflected in their architecture as well. In their palaces, old reception rooms gave way to durbar halls, rooms for European guests were built and ways to entertain guests were provided.

Dining and drawing rooms were introduced; fireplaces, marble fountains and statues, oil paintings and stuffed animals began to be displayed in the halls and drawing rooms. New education, new social functions and new engineering techniques led to a new architecture created by British architects, British army engineers and often the princes themselves. The princes were expected to be both traditional and modern-to retain traditional feudal powers but to create a new India. Some, of course, were more successful than others.

The new princely towns of Jaipur, Bikaner and Mysore showed themselves amongst the most successful in negotiating this divide. Their towns were modelled along British examples-clock towers, railway stations, public offices, assembly halls, water systems and public hospitals were built. Buildings were European classical, or if constructed later, Indo-Saracenic, or again an eclectic mix.

Kapurthala, Jagatjit Palace: In evidence are Mughal antecedents at Bikaner, Beaux-Arts Classicism at Kapurthala, Italian Renaissance at Cooch Bihar, Porbandar, Gwalior and Tripura, and British Classicism at Kashmir. Many palaces mixed styles and out of this mixture emerged two newer sub-styles in addition to the Indo-Saracenic-what Miki Desai has called Renaissance-Oriental and Indian-Eclectic. Some examples of the former are the Falaknuma Palace, Hyderabad built in 1872, the Gwalior Jai Vilas Palace (1872-74) designed by Sir Michael Filose for Maharaja Jayaji Rao Scindia, Lal Bagh, Indore designed as a Palladian Villa by the Calcutta firm of Triggs and Co., Tripura's Vijayanta Palace, and Jagatjit Palace Kapurthala for the Maharaja of Kapurthala, patterned along French Beaux-Arts Classicism. .

The Indian-Eclectic was modelled on royal luxury but its referents were also to Indian myths and folk tales as well as earlier architectural patterns and motifs. Much of it borders on the Indo-Saracenic but it tends to be more eclectic in its selection of ancient referents. The Amba Vilas Palace (1900-1910) in Mysore by Henry Irwin is a mixture of influences: fluted pillars from the Red Fort in Delhi, onion domes from the Taj Mahal, Mughal tracery and European halls.

Bibliography

Addison, K., M.J. Edge, R. Watkins : *The Quaternary of North Wales : Field Guide*, Quaternary Research Association, London, 1990.

Allchin, F.R. : *Journal of Economic and Social History of the Orient*, Oxford, London, 1962.

Annels, A.E. : *The Dolaucothi Gold Mines*, National Trust, New Jersey, 1986.

Bache, J. : *Soil Survey of the Great Orme*, Unpublished B.Sc. thesis, University College of Bangor, North Wales, 1995.

Barker, D. : Great Orme Gardening, *Journal of Great Orme Exploration Society*, London, 1993.

Batchen, G. : *Each Wild Idea*, MIT Press, Cambridge, 2002

Bick, D. : *The Old Metal Mines of Mid Wales*, Oxford, New Jersey, 1977.

Blanco, A. & J.M. Luzon : *Pre Roman Silver Mines at Rio Tinto*, *Antiquity*, McMillan, London, 1969.

Burgess, C. : *The Bronze Age, British Prehistory : A New Outline*, Duckworth, London, 1974.

Burgess, J. : *On the Muhammadan Architecture of Bharoch, Cambay, Dholka, Champanir* and *Mahmudabad*, W.M. Griggs and Sons, London, 1896.

Carlon, C.J. : *The Alderley Edge Mines*, J. Sherratt, Altringham, 1979.

Clough, T.H.M. & W.A. Cummins : *Stone Axe Studies*, McMillan, London, 1988.

Coghlan, H.H. : *Early Metallurgy of Copper in Britain and Ireland*, Proceedings of the Prehistoric Society, 1957.

,les, J.M. & Harding, A.F. : *The Bronze Age in Europe*, Methuen & Co Ltd, New Jersey, 1979.

Cummins, W.A. : *Neolithic Stone Axes : Distribution and Trade in England and Wales*, London Council for British Archaeology, London, 1979.

Cunningham. A. : *The Great Buddhist Temple under the Bodhi Tree at Buddha-Gaya*, W.H. Allen, London, 1892 .

Davies, M. : *Cave Archaeology in North Wales*, BCRA, Limestone Caves of North Wales, London, 1989.

Davies, O. : *Mining Sites in Wales, Section H British Association for the Advancement of Sciences Reports, Nottingham,* Oxford, London, 1937.

Dutton, L.A. & P.J. Fasham. : *Prehistoric Copper Mining on the Great Orme, Llandudno, Gwynedd*, Proceedings of the Prehistoric Society, Ner Jersey, 1994.

Edwards, E. : *Raw Histories: Photographs, Anthropology, Museums,* Oxford, Berg, 2001.

Elphinston. M. : *The History of India*, John Murray, London, 1843.

Evans, T.F. : *On Three Copper Cakes found at Bryndu*, Oxford, Anglesey, 1873.

Falconer, J. : *India: Pioneering Photographers 1850–1900*, The Howard and Jane Ricketts Collection, London, 2001.

Gale, D. & B.Ottaway. : *An Early Mining Site in the Mitterberg Ore Region of Austria*, Early Mining in British Isles, Plas Tan-y-Bwlch Occasional Paper, 1990.

Gale, D. L *Stone Tools Employed in Ancient Mining. Department of Archaeological Sciences*, Unpublished PhD thesis, University of Bradford, 1995.

Gardner, W. : *The Little Orme's Head Hoard of Roman Coins of 1907 and it's Significance*, Archaeologia Cambrensis, 1958.

Hagerty, R. : *The Mineralisation of the Llanrwst Orefield,* North Wales, Berg, 1994.

Harris, C. & Shakya, T. : *Seeing Lhasa: British Depictions of the Tibetan Capital 1936–1947*, Serindia, Chicago, 2003.

Hunt, J. : *A Historical Sketch of British Mining*, Yorkshire, Wakefield, 1887.

James, D. : *Prehistoric Copper Mining on the Great Ormes Head*, Early Mining in British Isles, Plas Tan-y-Bwlch Occasional Paper, 1990.

Jenkins, D.A. & C.A Lewis : *Prehistoric Mining for Copper in the Great Orme, Proceedings of Science in Archaeology,* Bradford, Llandudno, 1989.

King, H. : *Uranium Series Dating of Calcite Flowstones from the Great Orme*, Forthcoming PhD thesis, University of Liverpool, 1996.

Levitan, B. : *The Vertebrate Remains*, Brean Down Excavations 1983-1987, English Heritage, 1990.

Lewis, C.A. : *Underground Survey of Mine Workings at Great Ormes Head,* Llandudno, 1990.

Marshall, J.H. : *Mohenjodaro and the Indus Civilisation*, Probsthain, London, 1931.

Morton, G.H. : *The Carboniferous Limestones of the Country around Llandudno (North Wales),* Quarterly Journal of the Geological Society of London, 1898.

Northover, J.P. : *Alloy Design in the Bronze Age, Aspects of Ancient Mining and Metallurgy*, Acta of the British School at Athens Centenary Conference, Bangor, 1986.

Northover, J.P. : *The Analyses of Welsh Bronze Age Metalwork,* In H.N. Savory, Catalogue of the Welsh Bronze Collections, Cardiff : National Museum of Wales, 1980.

O'Brien, W. : *The Dating of the Mt-Gabriel Type mines of West Cork, Journal of the Cork Historical and Archaeological Society*, 1987.

Parker-Pearson, M. : *Bronze Age Britain*, English Heritage, Batsford Press, 1993.

Penhallurick, R.D. : *Tin in Antiquity*, Institute of Metals, London, 1986.

thenberg, B. : *Timna-Valley of the Biblical Copper Mines*, Thames & Hudson, London, 1972.

Roy, S. : *The Story of Indian Archaeology*, 1784–1947, Archaeological Survey of India, New Delhi, 1961.

Smith, W.D.F. : *The Great Orme Copper Mines*, Creuddyn Publications, Mumbai, 1989.

Sonawane V.H. : *Early Zinc Production in India*, *Mining Magazine*, Oxford, New Delhi, 1985.

Timberlake, S. : Llancynfelin and Nantyrarian mines. *Archaeology in Wales,* Council for British Archaeology, London, 1995.

Tylecote, R.F. : *The Prehistory of Metallurgy in the British Isles*, Institute of Metals London, London, 1986.

Vivian, W. : *Mine Managers Reports 1855 -57*, Unpublished UCNW Archives, Bangor, 1856.

Warren, P.T. : *Geology of the country around Rhyl and Denbigh*, British Geological Survey, HMSO London, 1984.

Williams, C.J. : *Great Orme Mines*, *British Mining No 52,* Northern Mines Research Society, London, 1995.

Yener, K.A. & P.B. Vandiver. : *Tin Processing at Goltepe, an Early Bronze Age site in Anatolia*, American Journal of Archaeology, New York, 1993.

Index

A

B

C

H

I

J

K

L

R

S

❑❑❑